Praise for

'Chris is a powerful force for good in the national debate on criminal justice. You should all go out and buy his book.'

The Secret Barrister

'Extraordinary.'

Krishnan Guru-Murthy

'A passionately written blueprint for resolving some perennial problems with our justice system: dysfunctional prisons, pointless drug laws, unnecessary punishment of children, and more. A powerful case for reform.'

Geoffrey Robertson QC

'A hard hitting, page turning account of the failures of our criminal justice system describing through some of the author's own cases not only how our system evolved but also why it fails to deliver to the public the protection they deserve.'

Cherie Blair QC

'A shocking, disturbing, revealing and enlightening examination of a deeply flawed criminal justice system by someone who's seen at first hand what the problems are – and more importantly, knows how they should be fixed.'

Piers Morgan

'A really shocking portrayal of our criminal justice system as it stands.'

David Lammy MP

'Fast-paced, engaging and littered with fascinating and often shocking real-life cases, Daw portrays a judicial system that's broken from the lowest courts to the toughest prisons in the land, suggesting solutions that are as provocative as they are persuasive.'

Matthew Wright

'Uncomfortable truths told in a compassionate and thoughtful way. Importantly, Chris offers hope and credible solutions.'

Lady Edwina Grosvenor

'Daw is right to call for something different.'

Unherd

'Emotionally searing ... A political homme sérieux with a determination to reform our disintegrating criminal justice system.'

The Tablet

'A great read.'

Adrian Chiles

'Will stand as a blueprint for criminal justice reform for decades to come ... A must read for those in power who genuinely want a system that works.'

Erwin James

'Passionate and pacey ... His reform arguments are persuasive and his storytelling suggests that he could write a gripping crime novel.'

The Times, Law Books of the Year

4/02/23

JUSTICE ON TRIAL

To:
Miss Simm's!!
From
Mrs B and
Blessing!

JUSTICE ON TRIAL

Radical Solutions for a System
at Breaking Point

CHRIS DAW QC

BLOOMSBURY CONTINUUM
LONDON • OXFORD • NEW YORK • NEW DELHI • SYDNEY

BLOOMSBURY CONTINUUM
Bloomsbury Publishing Plc
50 Bedford Square, London, WC1B 3DP, UK
29 Earlsfort Terrace, Dublin 2, Ireland

BLOOMSBURY, BLOOMSBURY CONTINUUM and the Diana logo are
trademarks of Bloomsbury Publishing Plc

First published in Great Britain 2020
Paperback, 2021

ISBN: PB: 978-1-4729-7785-4; ePub: 978-1-4729-7783-0;
ePDF: 978-1-4729-7784-7

2 4 6 8 10 9 7 5 3

Typeset by Deanta Global Publishing Services, Chennai, India
Printed and bound in Great Britain by CPI Group (UK) Ltd, Croydon CR0 4YY

To find out more about our authors and books visit www.bloomsbury.com
and sign up for our newsletters

CONTENTS

To Mum and Dad
Thank you for everything

FOREWORD

I have been a criminal defence lawyer for over twenty-five years.

I have looked into the eyes of murderers, sat down and drunk coffee with rapists, and listened to the tangled tales woven by fraudsters, money launderers and drug barons. I have tried to communicate with children and young people, dead behind the eyes, barely able to comprehend the magnitude of the crimes they are accused of or the wrongs that they have suffered in their short lives.

I have spent many days of my life behind bars, queuing patiently with the wives, children and friends of those locked up by the courts for days, months or a lifetime, waiting for a visit with a prisoner; handing over identification documents and booking reference numbers, passing slowly through each layer of security, bags scanned, clothing and papers searched, with varying degrees of enthusiasm and intensity.

I have waited patiently as keys slid into locks, heavy metallic doors first swung open and then slammed shut, one after the other, into prison visiting rooms, always too hot or too cold, waiting for a client to be brought to see me for an hour or two of escape from the grey monotony of prison life.

Time after time I have seen pupils dilated, faces unnaturally flushed, speech accelerated and thoughts jumbled by mental illness, the ingestion of substances, natural or manmade, minds and behaviour distorted.

I have received the most unexpected courtesy and respect from those guilty of the most base and motiveless crimes; rudeness and arrogance from those from whom – on the strength of appearance – I expected something better.

The guilty may protest the loudest or – just as often – succumb quietly to the inevitability of their fate. The innocent may lose all hope, however encouraged by my words, or rage against the injustice of it all, unable to listen to reason, to assurances that justice will – in the end – be done.

But what is justice? A child locked away by the state after being abused by those who should have cared for him, after being lured by the dazzle of opportunity, shining through the tinted glass of luxury cars, gliding through the neighbourhood, taking care of the timeworn business of supplying drugs? A young man, frightened into carrying a knife, faced with a threat – real or imagined – lashing out, killing or maiming someone just like him, out of allegiance to a different gang? A woman, finally losing control after years of abuse at the hands of a man, all reason lost as she hits out, strikes and – in rare instances – takes a life. Or one of the countless addicted – to booze, drugs or gambling – robbing, cheating, just plain stealing to feed a habit, no more a choice as they see it than for the victims they select.

Does justice mean arrest, charge, trial and years in prison to protect the victims? To deter others from doing the same? To satisfy the cries for vengeance and punishment, spread across the newspapers, splashed across websites and exploding in a million Tweets and Facebook posts?

Over the past twenty-five years, I have seen at first-hand how criminal justice works, not just in Britain but around the world. From the violence of Glasgow to the humanity of Geneva, to the tragedy of the fifth largest 'city' of the most powerful country on earth – the United States prison system.

This book is about what I have witnessed, in my working life in the law and on my travels, but most of all it is about what I have learned. The lesson for me is a simple one: almost everything we do and think about crime and punishment is wrong. I am going to show you why. And what we can do about it.

Chris Daw QC
May 2020

AUTHOR'S NOTE

Some of my clients are now dead. Most are still alive. Many became notorious and were front-page news. For others, even their wives and children never found out that they had become embroiled in the criminal justice system. I have acted for an exotic and eclectic mix of human beings – from international footballers, Russian oligarchs and politicians to some of the poorest and most vulnerable people in our society.

They all have one thing in common, dead or alive – they came to me as their lawyer, expecting and deserving complete confidentiality. Since time began, or certainly for the past few centuries, a core tenet of the legal profession, wherever lawyers carry out their work, has been some variety of legal professional privilege. Like the priest in the confessional, the lawyer in his office, in the prison visiting room, in emails and on the telephone must take his clients' secrets to the grave.

I cannot, then, divulge in these pages what my clients have told me or what I have advised them to do. Or not to do. My notes remain locked away, or shredded after the passage of sufficient time, along with case papers, emails and – the lawyer's stock-in-trade – my written opinions on the law and on the evidence.

But that does not mean that I cannot tell you anything of my work in the criminal courts and beyond, over my long legal career. In some cases my involvement is a matter of public record and the facts and verdict well known to millions. I will make mention of some of these cases, respecting all the while the secrecy of consultations with my clients. In others, it is not the exact details of the evidence, the names of those involved or the location of the crime that matter – it is the core themes that emerge and the lessons to be taken from them.

I must, of course, avoid clients rightly complaining that I have broken the seal of trust between us, and ensure that there is no possibility of disbarment from a career that I intend to continue for many years to come. Save where in the public domain, the names of the innocent – and the most definitely guilty – have been changed, along with locations and certain other details, to avoid any possibility of jigsaw identification of anyone involved.

This inside tour of criminal justice starts, right from the outset, at the heart of our legal system, with a journey towards the most dramatic moment of all – the verdict of the jury in a criminal trial . . .

INTRODUCTION

A study in crime

Stuart Ross was a very successful man.

He owned an international money-transfer business that processed and sent client payments all over the world – from a few pounds sent by a husband in Newcastle to his family in Nairobi, to tens or hundreds of thousands of dollars or euros for the purchase of chemicals, fabrics or IT services – anything at all, anywhere in the world.

Such businesses are not unusual. They are on every high street, some as stand-alone offices, others hidden at the back of a newsagent's shop or, of course, behind the counter of a local bank. Websites abound, offering faster and cheaper ways to convert money from one currency to another and then to transfer it, at the click of a mouse, from one place to another.

Stuart's company had been a roaring success from the moment he opened the doors, launched the website and declared UK Money Services International ready for business. The number of transactions grew exponentially, as did the commissions and charges earned by UKMSI. Stuart soon bought a very large house in Essex, a short drive by Bentley from his London HQ. His three children went to a private day school, very different from the state comprehensive that he himself left at the age of sixteen. He ate in London's best restaurants and the family holidayed in Dubai, Mauritius and Barbados.

When I met Stuart he was housed in the High-Risk Category A wing of Belmarsh prison in South London; home to terrorists, murderers and the leaders of the most notorious Organised Crime Gangs in Britain. Belmarsh, like all high-security establishments, is a bleak place, almost entirely devoid of human spirit. It is a warehouse, not only for the body but for the soul.

Some of the prison officers are polite, and others – very occasionally – might crack a joke to lift the mood in between security checks, as each metal door is opened and shut. Most simply do their job, which seems reasonable given the misery of the environment in which they spend their working lives.

To reach Stuart required, first, a trip to the Visitors' Centre outside the prison walls, to deposit keys, phone, laptop, credit cards and cash – anything at all that might amount to contraband under the detailed and prescriptive Prison Rules. I then had to produce a letter of introduction from my Senior Clerk, together with my driving licence, and undergo a fingerprint scan, to prove my identity. A short walk to the main gate, a long wait there, another fingerprint check, and then an extreme airport-style search and scan of paperwork (no maps allowed!), shoes, body, and inside each of my pens.

More sitting and waiting for an escort to the Main Visits area, in the company of one of the sorriest groups of people on the planet – the mothers and fathers, the wives and girlfriends, the children and infants of the pallid army of the damned that forms our prison population. Eventually an officer arrived and led us all, snaking in an odd semblance of the conga, across gated courtyards and eventually into an anteroom, next to 'Domestic Visits', where most of the visitors would spend the next couple of hours.

I was one of only three people who were told to wait there for yet another escort who would take us, in a small van, from Main Visits to the High-Risk Category A visiting room in the Special Secure Unit (SSU), literally a prison within a prison. Yes; in the incredibly improbable event that someone were to manage to escape from the SSU at Belmarsh, he would find himself in another – only marginally less secure – prison and have to come up with another escape plan to top the first. A Pyrrhic victory indeed.

The other two waiting for the SSU van were a young woman – early twenties – and her baby, no more than a few months old. The mother wore heavy make-up and had big hair; her daughter was awake but very quiet, as if conscious that this was a place where the cries – and certainly the laughter – of a child would be out of place. I flicked through the file of evidence on Stuart's case; time passed, nobody came, the baby grew a little restless and her mother rocked her a little, shushing all the while. In a snatched conversation, just before our driver arrived, I found out that the baby's father had just been sentenced to twenty-eight years for drug trafficking – he was hoping to appeal.

An hour after stepping out of a cab on a grey autumn day, I was shown into a visiting room, deep within the SSU, where Stuart already sat, wearing the 'Cat A' uniform of pristine Nike tracksuit and trainers. The table between us and the steel-framed chairs were bolted solid to the concrete floor. In front of Stuart lay a file of papers, similar in size to my own, clearly well-thumbed, pages marked with slips of paper, where Stuart had found a point of importance during the long hours available to him in the SSU, with nothing to do but read and plan his defence.

We shook hands firmly and I sat down. 'Stupid question I know,' I opened, 'but how's it going?' The answer came back – 'Not too bad, better in the SSU than in the main jail apparently.' Stuart had been in prison for just six weeks and here he was already, giving TripAdvisor-style reviews, weighing up the relative merits of one high-security prison over another.

The facts of Stuart's case were unsurprising to me, given the nature of his business and his current circumstances. It turned out that millions of pounds' worth of transactions had been carried out by international drug traffickers using UKMSI. His was not just a service for hard-working immigrants to send money home to their families. One UKMSI client in particular had transferred over £10 million (around US$12 million at the time) in just three months from Britain to Turkey, the British Virgin Islands, Ghana and Venezuela. That client was now also locked up in the SSU at Belmarsh, charged with six counts of Conspiracy to Import Class A and B Drugs on a massive scale.

Stuart's client was looking at thirty years in prison for the drugs crimes alone; Stuart up to fourteen years, for a dozen counts of money laundering, under the Proceeds of Crime Act. He also faced the confiscation of every brick of his house, every blade of grass on his acre of lawns, and even of the diamond-encrusted Rolex which had graced his wife's wrist until it was seized during a police raid.

The prosecution file was made up of a complex web of surveillance evidence, mobile phone attribution (who was using which phone), call analysis (who called whom, when and for how long), text messages, social media posts, cell siting (showing where a phone was located at any given point in time), fingerprints, ANPR (Automatic Number Plate Recognition) vehicle location tracking, DNA (on drug packaging, banknotes and in vehicles), banking records, cash seizures, and transactions carried out through UKMSI. Naturally there was CCTV footage of the defendants and their associates during the period that the conspiracy had been carried out, at least based on the prosecution case-summary document.

The investigation of this conspiracy had been going on for well over a year, since the cocaine-importation operation had crossed the radar of the police via an informant. Since then the National Crime Agency (Britain's elite crime force) had patiently and persistently built layer upon layer of evidence, said to implicate a total of seven men and two women. Sure of its case, the time came for a coordinated NCA 'strike' – all the defendants' homes were raided at exactly the same time (5 a.m.), and all arrests were made at once, by multiple teams of specialist search officers.

Stuart was arrested, taken to a police station and eventually interviewed by detectives of the NCA. On the advice of his experienced solicitor, he remained silent as the evidence was paraded before his eyes – phone records, stills of meetings captured on CCTV and hidden surveillance cameras, fingerprints here and money transfers there. Stuart said nothing, but he listened very carefully indeed.

Charges followed and, unsurprisingly, the magistrates' court denied Stuart bail at his first appearance, despite his lack of a criminal history. The District Judge decided that there was a real risk that he would 'fail to surrender', 'interfere with witnesses' or even 'commit further offences' if he were to be released before trial. This is how it works in cases of the most serious crime – once the prosecution get you locked up, the system will usually keep you there as long as it can. With a nod to his wife in the public gallery, Stuart was led down the steps of the dock by two security officers and driven away to Belmarsh in a prison van.

A week later, the day before the first preliminary in the Crown Court (where the trial would take place before a jury many months later), there I was, sitting with Stuart, sounding him out – and him me – as we took our first steps on a legal journey together that would end, inevitably, with the verdict of a jury. That verdict would determine whether Stuart would be free to go home or, as with so many, would see him back in the prison van, unable to walk the streets again for a decade or more.

Stuart naturally protested his innocence – they almost all do, at least to start with – and began to bombard me with information. The police were lying about so many pieces of evidence; he could prove that he knew nothing about the activities of his co-accused in the conspiracy – one was his nephew – and he knew nothing about drug trafficking at all.

I listened patiently, nodding in the right places, and waiting until he ran out of steam. For some it can take minutes, others an hour, and a few need to talk for session after session before they finally realise that talking alone is not going to get them out of prison. At some point they are going to have to listen. The more serious the case, the more complicated and difficult the evidence, the more clients like Stuart believe that they have all of the answers and can tell me how things need to be done to win the case.

Rather like patients attending the doctor, armed with snippets of medical information from the Internet, defendants locked up in prison believe that they can self-diagnose and self-prescribe their way out of trouble. They have the dubious benefit of a wealth of advice from those locked up on the same wing, jailhouse lawyers to a man, and at first they do not question how all that wisdom has so spectacularly failed to keep any of their advisers out of prison in the first place.

So they read the prosecution evidence, make spidery notes and comments all over it, and come to that first meeting with their defence barrister (me), armed with a mixture of amateur legal cunning, ingenious and improbable explanations of events, and a complete lack of appreciation for reality. And they talk, quickly and confidently, with superficial credibility and even a tone of injustice. I listen, occasionally making a note when a piece of relevant information shines out from the fog of fantasy and unreality floating across the table. Rarely do I fill more than a page on that first visit; sometimes I write nothing at all.

Eventually, hopefully with some time left before the prison officer bangs on the window to say 'Time's up', the client stops talking long enough for me to speak.

'We're in court tomorrow and the one thing you need to tell me today is whether you are going to plead guilty or not guilty,' I explain, holding up my hand against Stuart's attempts to protest his innocence. 'Just hear me out,' I insist. 'I have to explain how it works. I have to tick a box to confirm that I have told you this. Once we get through this formality we can talk about what happens next.'

Stuart shuffles in his seat, leafs through his paperwork, then finally looks and listens as I explain the system. 'If you plead guilty tomorrow, you will get a discount of about a third on your sentence. But you will definitely go to prison. You will get a minimum of eight years, possibly a bit more, and you will guarantee that the prosecution will take everything you own and everything you will ever own.' He is about to interrupt, but again I make him listen.

'That's Option One for tomorrow,' I say. 'Option Two – you plead not guilty, and from that moment forward the minimum sentence starts to go up, to ten years, twelve years and, if we get to trial and lose, up to fourteen years, and of course you still lose everything . . . but, if we win, you walk out of court by the front door and they get nothing at all.'

Silence, just for a second or two, and then: 'I'm going not guilty.'

'Are you sure?'

'One hundred per cent.'

Now a bridge has been crossed, a fork in the road taken, from damage limitation and mitigation, to a winner-takes-all battle with the prosecution. One that might result in Stuart Ross becoming one of the grey men, imprisoned and institutionalised by the state, losing all touch with the real world, physically and mentally a shadow of himself. Or, just maybe, one day soon he might leave court by the main doors, alongside staff, lawyers, witnesses and interested members of the public, back onto the street and home to his own bed.

In many ways Stuart's case, to which we shall return as the trial reaches its conclusion, poses all of the questions asked in this book. This is why this case and all the others are included, to provide first-hand evidence, accumulated over thousands of days in courts and prisons. Like so many prosecutions, Stuart's case only took place at all because of the prohibition of drugs, our obsession with heavy prison sentences and the influence of ancient moral views of good and evil, lying behind our criminal justice system. There are clearly lessons to be learned from Stuart's case, and the many others in the pages ahead, but this book is not just about my own experiences or those of my clients.

This book is about why we have a criminal justice system at all. What is it for? What works and what is broken? And the only way to decide those questions, at least for a lawyer like me, is by weighing the evidence and coming to a conclusion. In the chapters ahead, that is exactly what I will do, not just offering an opinion based on research, but reaching clear verdicts on everything we believe and everything we do in the criminal justice system. And I will do that, purely and simply, by putting justice on trial.

First, by way of an opening statement in this trial of justice itself, I present a short history of crime and punishment . . .

1

A short history of crime and punishment

Ever since human beings began to form communities, crimes have been committed and punished. It is impossible for a group of people, however small and unsophisticated, to exist in a state of complete anarchy, without standards or rules of any kind. What sets *Homo sapiens* apart from all other species is our formation of groups, tribes, societies and communities, demanding common standards of behaviour between members and, crucially, underpinned by moral values. Or, at the very least, we demand adherence to such values from *most* members of society, *most* of the time.

If I can take my neighbour's oxen, steal his car, kill his dog or abstract electricity from his power cable with impunity, then chaos, violence and destruction will prevail. We do not need to be able to read and write in order to make and enforce rules designed to maintain hierarchies, property rights, public order and the dominance of one group of people over another.

In order to function successfully in groups, we need a set of rules, a means to allow for group enforcement, and consequences of some kind to flow from any infringement. Over the past 5,000 years or so, the human race has experimented with countless different sets of criminal laws, a host of methods to determine guilt. We have also come up with a dazzling array of penalties for the guilty, many at the more extreme end of the spectrum of bloodlust and violence.

The Mayans, from the middle of the third millennium BC, like many civilisations that followed, adopted an absolute monarchy with all power vested in a paramount ruler, who could decide on acceptable standards of behaviour by his subjects and punish any infringements. The noble families of the day provided judges, to enforce the law and to resolve disputes, and those judges passed on their powers to their sons and heirs – a hereditary judicial system.

The ancient Greeks initially treated crimes – even murder – as essentially a private matter, with the right to exact justice left in the hands of the victims or, in the case of the deceased, their surviving families. Before the advent of early forms of democracy, the Greeks too invested all judicial power in the hands of the *basileus:* a tribal leader – later named a king – who could dispense justice as he saw fit.

By the sixth century BC, the free citizens of Athens could be tried in a *geliast* court by something that began to look like a jury, albeit one with a very large number of members indeed. The *geliast* in turn developed, a century later, into the Heliaia, consisting of 6,000 annually elected members – making up ten 500-strong *dicasteries* (juries) plus 1,000 spares – which every citizen could apply to join from the age of thirty onwards (an advanced stage of life in those times). One of the reasons for juries of such size was the belief that it would be difficult to bribe so many people, in order to achieve the desired outcome. The same faith has proven largely well founded to the present day, in respect of our much more modest jury of a dozen (successful cases of 'jury nobbling' remain rare).

And so these massive juries presided over a public trial and delivered their verdicts after a secret ballot, with jurors voting by depositing pebbles in boxes – black for guilty and white for not guilty. Many of the crimes adjudicated upon would be familiar to us today – murder, naturally, together with other crimes of violence, but also treason and various offences against the state. The jury had a wide discretion to decide whether any given action was to be condemned, as the law was not clearly defined in written form.

The trials were serious in their subject matter, but they were also a form of entertainment, with speeches written to a high professional standard by lawyers (logographers), to be delivered by the parties entirely from memory (and without public credit to the speechwriter). Law, evidence, opinion and flights of oratory were all mixed together; a form of advocacy I have witnessed myself, with varying degrees of success, throughout my career in the criminal courts.

The length of speeches was strictly controlled, not by the traffic lights of the modern US Supreme Court, but by a water clock – a pot of water gradually emptied through a small hole in the bottom. When it was empty, it was time to shut up and sit down.

By the fifth century, witnesses gave live evidence and could be cross-examined, and a century later saw the introduction of written statements, to which a witness could attest, much as in an English civil trial in the modern day. Other elements of the process would not meet with contemporary standards – women could not give evidence at all, and the testimony of a slave was only admissible, in theory at least, if he had first been tortured (to ensure that he did not just say what his master told him to).

One of Athens's most prominent citizens, Socrates, was convicted – at the ripe old age of seventy – of corrupting the youth of Athens with his philosophy, by a small majority of the 500 jurors who tried him. He received the death sentence, to be carried out in a rather civilised fashion (as decided by the jury) – he would take a drink of hemlock (a deadly natural poison). Even with the option of fleeing the city for exile, chosen by most prominent citizens of the day who found themselves in the same predicament, Socrates was true to his principles and his lifelong belief in the Rule of Law – he drank the deadly liquid 'as if it were a draught of wine'.

Others were less fortunate when convicted and many met their deaths shackled to a wooden board, where they were left to die.

The Romans at least took the trouble to write down their laws, rather than leave it to the discretion of a jury in each individual case. Those who were convicted faced a creative array of punishments, from whipping, confiscation and fines – for fraud, theft and financial crimes – to crucifixion, fighting in the gladiatorial games, being pushed off a cliff or having molten lead poured down the throat for the most serious offences, including murder.

Naturally, the wealthy and the nobility of Rome tended to avoid punishment, even for the most serious crimes, by choosing instead to go into exile, hoping one day to return to the city. Slaves were almost always crucified, whatever the crime, and sometimes all the slaves in the household were executed at once, based on the unlawful conduct of just one of them.

Deterrence was at the forefront of Roman justice, not only for slaves but for the Roman army, which carried out 'decimation' when a soldier attempted to desert from the legion. The deserter himself was put to death, but one in ten of his comrades met the same fate. On the spectrum of sentencing philosophy, with human decency and rehabilitation at one end, decimation must surely sit close to the opposite end. It was one of the most cruel and unjust punishments ever to be devised by man.

Unlike the Athenian logographers, who hid in the background and scripted speeches and arguments on behalf of their clients, the advocates of Rome were among the greatest entertainers of their time. The modest-sized juries – just seventy-five strong! – were made up entirely from the nobility, and the general public was not only welcome but encouraged to attend the trials. Cicero and the other great legal orators of the day were lauded for their rhetorical displays.

Despite the potential gravity of the consequences for the accused, the entire trial process had a theatrical air. With echoes of the advice I give to my own clients – to dress appropriately, so as to appear both serious and humble – Roman defendants were told to appear in mourning dress, with a haggard look, so as to attract the sympathy of the watching public and the jury alike. Even the families of the accused were brought into the performance, encouraged to engage in ostentatious displays of emotion from the viewing area, such as bursting into tears en masse.

This melodramatic strategy could be surprisingly effective, and at least one defendant was acquitted after his witness – and good friend – turned on the tears and managed to get the whole jury, and even the presiding magistrate, to cry along with him.

The Roman word for 'prosecutor' was the same as that for 'actor', despite the very large difference in the social standing of the two professions (actors were considered low-status individuals). It is said that the methods employed by the protagonists, in theatrical performances and murder trials respectively, were sometimes indistinguishable.

The collapse of the Roman Empire led to a proliferation of different systems of justice, throughout Europe and beyond. In England, the early Middle Ages were marked by the development and authority of the Church and of feudalism, where absolute power in all matters, including criminal trials, was invested in a local lord.

Numerous bizarre forms of trial and punishment were devised, none with even a veneer of rationality, let alone of any aspiration to achieve a standard of fairness as we would recognise it. The most notorious cases involved trial by ordeal, which prevailed as a fact-finding method across much of Europe for centuries.

Ordeals included trial by fire, where the accused walked on superheated ploughshares or gripped a red-hot iron, and trial by water, where the accused had to plunge his hand into a pot of boiling water and retrieve an object from the bottom. The innocent would be saved from harm by divine intervention and the guilty would be abandoned by their creator, to suffer horrific injury or death.

Some suggest that the ordeal actually worked. It was said to cause the guilty to admit guilt – to avoid injury or death – and to offer compensation to the victim; an early form of plea bargaining. The obviously innocent, or those with the money to pay, were handed a lukewarm piece of iron and given plenty of time for wounds to heal, before the verdict was pronounced. Thus the harshest aspects of the ordeal were softened a little in practice.

The most significant development in the trial process in England came about in 1215, as a consequence of two separate but equally momentous events that year. Trial by ordeal was abolished by the Fourth Lateran Council of the Catholic Church, and Magna Carta was signed by King John, enshrining in law the right of an Englishman to be convicted only by the 'lawful judgement of his peers'. Naturally, the right to jury trial was limited to the wealthy at the outset, but the principle was established once and for all.

This was a fork in the road for English criminal procedure, which could so easily have followed the route of most of Europe, in which an inquisitorial system, based on Roman precedent, then prevailed. At the same time, the European system adopted that less than reliable form of torture to extract confessions. It was thought that the innocent would endure, whereas the guilty would confess.

In 1219, when Henry III asked his judges to find a suitable replacement for the ordeal, they settled with minimal delay on the jury system, which quickly became the norm, up and down the land. In 1220 a woman known to history only as 'Alice' was convicted of murder by a jury at Westminster. Those early juries, in direct contrast to the present day, did not come to the case in a state of factual ignorance. On the contrary, they were expected to use their local knowledge, including of the accused and witnesses, to assist in their deliberations; even, to some extent, what we would now call 'the word on the street'.

By placing the verdict in the hands of the jury, rather than of the Church or an official of the state, England established a principle that arguably speaks to the character of the English to this day: the unwillingness of the ordinary citizen to condone injustice and oppression, wherever it may occur. This quality was perhaps most clearly demonstrated, in a very different cause, in the two world wars of the twentieth century, when so many English men and women sacrificed their lives in a stand against tyranny. That our nation, with this proud history and these worthy values, should have allowed its system of justice to become so misguided and, yes, so unjust, is all the more baffling and disappointing.

Trial by jury evolved over the centuries, with a requirement for unanimity in place by the fourteenth century (since abolished in favour of a 10–2 majority), and a distinction between the role of the judge, in making rulings of law, and the jury, in deciding the facts, entering into the process. Despite all this, the superstition of the Elizabethan age saw a return of the ordeal, in the form of the 'swimming of witches' – a somewhat ironic name for the practice of binding the hands and feet of the suspect and throwing (usually) her in a pond. If she floated, she was clearly guilty – the water had rejected her – and she could be safely burned at the stake. If she sank, she was innocent, but it was no doubt important to pull her out quickly, to avoid her being drowned in the conduct of her own defence.

Despite official disapproval, the swimming of witches was exported to the new American colonies and continued in England, at least occasionally, even into the nineteenth century.

In another quirk of procedure, this time due to financial considerations, for almost 600 years a form of torture was retained in England, but only for those who refused to enter a plea at all. Such people were subjected to *peine forte et dure*, in which heavy weights were loaded onto them in prison, until they either entered a plea or died. The reason was a mundane one – only those tried and convicted could have their assets seized and forfeited to the Crown. Those who would not plead could not be tried at all and those untried could not be convicted – their heirs inherited their estates and titles.

What then of punishments, meted out by the English courts down the centuries? As with almost every system of justice, through the ages, the harshest of penalties fell most often on the poorest of men. Death was commonly the sentence, not only for murder but for a host of other crimes.

The notorious and largely self-governing Court of Star Chamber, which exercised wide-ranging powers to try and punish in the name of the Crown, operated until 1640 without even the rudimentary rights and protections available in the courts of common law. There was no right of cross-examination and, with jurors afraid of the consequences of going against the Crown, the conviction rate was so high that the trial process was little more than a formality. The Court had unlimited authority to impose fines, imprisonment and a menu of corporal punishment, of escalating nastiness; pillories and the stocks of course, but then on to branding, nose-slitting and other forms of mutilation. The only small mercy was that the Star Chamber lacked the power to sentence defendants to death.

One defendant, Edward Owen, was found to have assaulted his grandfather, but the old man did not die of his injuries until over a year later. As a result, no murder charge could be brought, due to the 'year and a day' rule, which remained in force until as late as 1996. The Star Chamber ordered that Edward be taken to the scene of his crime, stripped naked before a 'realistic portrait' of his dead grandfather, and 'severely whipped'. In the end this creative – and psychologically telling – form of sentence was not carried out; Edward was pardoned, so as to secure his release from prison, and he avoided a most painful and humiliating fate.

With the abolition of the Star Chamber in 1640, it was to be just thirty years before the supremacy of the English jury, in the matter of the verdict, would be enshrined in law, once and for all. In 1670 an Old Bailey jury returned not guilty verdicts against two Quakers, William Penn and William Mead, for unlawful assembly. The judge then imprisoned the jury without food, water, heat or light and told them: 'I will have a positive [guilty] verdict or you'll starve for it!' They remained locked up for two nights but stood firm in their verdicts.

The case came before the Lord Chief Justice on a writ of habeas corpus ('thou shalt have the body') – a court order to secure the release of a prisoner – after one of the jurors, Edward Bushel, petitioned for the release of Penn and Mead, who remained imprisoned despite their acquittal, for the spurious reason that they had 'not removed their hats in court'. The Lord Chief Justice intervened and laid down the law in a refreshingly unstuffy way: 'The judge may try to open the eyes of jurors, but not to lead them by the nose.' The case is known to lawyers as 'Bushel's

Case' and its significance to the supremacy of the jury is commemorated by a plaque on the wall of the Old Bailey praising the 'courage and endurance of the jury'.

This important feature of the jury system very much endures to this day. I can recall numerous occasions when a client complained to me, during a trial, that the judge was interfering to cut off the defence or to support the prosecution. My reaction is invariably the same. 'Let him,' I tell my clients. 'The more he does it the better – juries hate it when they think that the judge is taking sides.' I recall one judge interrupting my perfectly reasonable cross-examination questions for the tenth time. In front of the jury, I asked if he would mind making a list of the questions I *was* allowed to ask, so that we could save some time. The jury collapsed in laughter and a not guilty verdict for my client was swiftly returned.

The late seventeenth century was significant to the evolution and consolidation of jury trials for another reason. It coincided with the development of the British colonies in North America, which took with them many of the traditions of the common law, developed over centuries in England. Before the American Revolution and independence, the system of justice was operated directly by the British Crown, but often as a tool of repression and control rather than as a beacon of integrity and the Rule of Law.

That same independence of spirit that had emboldened and fortified the London jurors in Bushel's Case was on display in colonial New York in 1734, when a newspaperman, Peter Zenger, was prosecuted by the British Crown for seditious libel. His crime was to have published scornful articles about the unpopular and oppressive royal governor, William Cosby. Despite efforts to rig the jury with Cosby supporters, a number of the jurors were of Dutch stock and had no allegiance to the British.

The judge did his best to ensure a conviction, by excluding evidence from defence witnesses, who were willing to testify to the truth of what Zenger had published about Cosby. In one of the greatest and most important jury speeches in history, Andrew Hamilton of Philadelphia, a lawyer of advancing years and considerable renown, set out the case for the defence: 'It is not the cause of a poor printer, nor of New York alone, which you are now trying. No! It may in its consequence affect every freeman that lives under a British government on the main of America. It is the best cause. It is the cause of liberty.'

The jury returned a not guilty verdict and Zenger was freed from prison. News of the trial fired up the independent spirit of the colonists and caused frayed nerves in the corridors of power in London. Attempts by the British Crown to avoid similar verdicts, such as using non-jury trials in the Admiralty Courts for revenue offences and transferring cases of treason for trial to England, ended up among the catalysts for revolution. The Declaration of Independence cites, as one of the factors in favour of the overthrow of colonial rule, Britain's policy of 'depriving us, in many cases, of Trial by Jury'.

Article III of the US Constitution provides that '[t]he Trial of all Crimes, except in the Cases of Impeachment, shall be by Jury; and such Trial shall be held in the State where the said Crimes shall have been committed'. The Supreme Court took up this theme, with the customary eloquence of American jurists, on matters so central to their system of justice, in a 1968 case, which further embedded the place of the jury in US criminal trials. The justices held that, 'providing an accused with the right to be tried by a jury of his peers [gives] him an inestimable safeguard against the corrupt or overzealous prosecutor and against the compliant, biased, or eccentric judge'.

As we shall discover, when we come to consider the many injustices of the American approach to imprisonment – especially the pursuit of 'mass incarceration' – all those fine words and statements of principle have largely, in modern times, become relics of history. In the twenty-first century, fewer than 3 per cent of US criminal prosecutions ever result in a jury trial, and in those that do the odds are stacked very much in favour of the state.

American jurors do have one duty and obligation not imposed upon their English counterparts: in respect of capital murder cases, the jury must decide whether a convicted defendant should be sentenced to death. Only a few thousand people are charged with capital murder each year in the US, and of those – largely due to the impact of plea bargaining and tactical decisions by the prosecution – only a few hundred are condemned to die by a jury. For an even smaller number is the sentence eventually carried out, almost always following decades of legal wrangling and appeals.

Nevertheless, as we shall consider in the final chapter of this book, the death penalty, and the ideological, ethical and moral forces that it represents, speak to the essence of criminal justice in the modern United States. For its supporters, it is the only appropriate form of deterrence and retribution, for the most serious crime of all. For its detractors, it is wholly ineffective as a deterrent, risks the execution of the innocent, and displays the worst of human nature, legitimised by force of law.

The death penalty itself, whether in ancient or more recent times, is beyond the direct scope of this book. But the values it represents, and the emotions that drive it, also underlie the ethos behind the issues examined in every chapter ahead – from decisions about whether to lock people up in prison, in what conditions and for how long (chapter 2); to the way we treat those who take and supply drugs (chapter 3); to the response of our society to children who commit acts designated as criminal (chapter 4); to our attempts to regulate and control the Internet (Epilogue).

Finally, we will turn to the biggest issue of all: the one that defines who each of us is as a human being, feeds into the decisions we make in our lives, the opinions we express to our friends, families and children, and, in the votes we cast, chooses the politicians we elect and the laws they pass. Are human beings essentially good or evil, and if so, should all criminal justice policy be founded on that binary analysis of our affairs? Or are we all capable, in the right conditions, of committing acts considered criminal and worthy of prosecution and punishment by the state? And, moreover, are we all capable of redemption when we fall? Chapter 5 offers the conclusions I have reached, on the content of the human soul, based on acting for hundreds of criminals, collectively responsible for thousands of crimes.

By analysing the reality of crime and punishment, in practice and on the ground, I will show why personal morality – the separation of our fellow citizens into boxes labelled good and evil – is the worst possible foundation for criminal justice policy. The mantra of 'getting tough on crime', whether through the prison system, in drug enforcement, youth justice or online, leads directly and inexorably to more criminals, more crime and, ironically, more victims. We need to rip up the criminal justice playbook, followed in the UK, the US and around the world, and implement radical reform, starting with the default punishment for most forms of crime – prison.

2

Why we should close all prisons

I met 'Michael' in a stark prison visiting room when he was fifty-four years of age. He was barely over 5 feet tall, wafer-thin, face gnarled as a walnut, fingers stained to the point of brown by nicotine. Out of the previous thirty-six years, Michael had been at liberty for just under three. The remainder of his adult life had been spent behind bars. The only home that Michael had ever really known was in jail.

Given his decades of incarceration, you would be forgiven for assuming that Michael was a murderer, a serial rapist or some other category of dangerous offender. He was not. Michael's crimes largely comprised petty theft, involvement with drugs in one way or another, and persistently breaching the conditions of his parole whenever he was released.

The sentences got longer and longer as he got older, his criminal record grew, and judges – quite understandably – lost faith in his promises to change his ways. At the time I met Michael, we were in the throes of one of the periodic 'get tough' approaches to criminal sentencing so beloved of politicians, especially in the English-speaking world. This particular piece of political grandstanding and electioneering was introduced in the dying days of John Major's Conservative government in 1997, just before Tony Blair swept Labour to power with a landslide.

For a second conviction for one of a number of specified crimes, the 1997 law required judges to impose an automatic life sentence, meaning that the offender would only ever be released if the Parole Board considered that he no longer represented a danger to the public. The facts of the case were to be ignored in the dogmatic pursuit of toughness, a quality invariably measured by politicians solely by reference to the number of years to be spent in prison by the offender.

Released from prison, Michael had nowhere to go, no money and, after so much of his life 'behind the door', neither friends nor family to turn to. Imagine waking up from a coma after five years to find that your home, your car, your career, your money and everyone you knew have all disappeared. You have just the clothes on your back and, if you are lucky, enough money to eat for a few days and possibly a bed in a hostel. You are in poor physical and mental health, have substance-misuse issues, and you have no life skills to survive, take care of your basic needs and live as a functioning member of society.

Welcome to Michael's world and to that of tens of thousands of others in Britain – and countless more around the world – each and every year. Prison, it is often said, provides somewhere to sleep, three meals a day, a roof over your head, heat, light and a basic degree of medical care. Those released, with little or no support, find that one, two or all of those fundamental human needs have suddenly disappeared. Those from the 'tough on crime' lobby argue that prison is 'soft' or even 'like a holiday camp'. They should try spending a few hours there, let alone months or years, and I wonder if they would feel the same way.

The fact remains that prison was all Michael knew. He had no life skills to cope with the more and more confusing world on the outside. And consequently he found himself, days after release, wandering the streets of Manchester city centre alone, anxious and utterly incapable of caring for himself. So he bought a banana. And that was where things started to go wrong.

Michael walked into a scruffy pub, close to the cathedral, shortly after 11 o'clock one Tuesday morning. The landlord had just opened up for the lunchtime trade. Suddenly, there in front of him stood a diminutive figure with what appeared to be a bright orange hood over his head – with makeshift eyeholes – demanding 'the money!'. The landlord looked down to see what appeared to be a gun, concealed in the would-be robber's pocket in the manner of a hundred American films.

'I've only got the float,' said the landlord, with a sigh. 'I've just opened up.'

'Give it here!' shouted Michael, waving the 'gun' from side to side in his pocket for maximum fear factor.

And that is what the landlord did. He handed Michael several bags of coins, each containing a few pounds in value, made up of different denominations. The total came to around £45 in change.

Grabbing the money bags, but dropping one as he made his escape, Michael ran out of the pub and out of sight. The landlord called the police and a firearms team arrived in under five minutes. Their Armed Response Vehicle – a ballistically protected BMW X5 – was manned by two officers in combat gear, each with a 9mm Glock sidearm, an MP5 submachine gun, and various other weapons, intended for deployment in case of terrorist attack or any form of firearms incident.

The armed officers ran into the pub and the landlord pointed them to the right of the exit, where he had last seen Michael's distinctive orange hood as he made his escape. They updated the Force Control Room that they were pursuing a suspect – presumed armed – and asked for all available ARVs to attend.

The officers looked left and right and then, a few feet from the pub doorway, they saw something glinting on the pavement – a brand-new 50p piece, fresh from the mint, catching the sunlight. Then another one, a few feet further along the street. And so it continued, as the two heavily armed policemen followed the trail of coins; first 50p pieces and then various other coins, until the money trail took a sharp right turn into an alleyway, strewn with the wheeled commercial rubbish bins used by restaurants and pubs.

The two officers stopped to take stock of the scene. There was a flicker of a shadow and slight movement near one of the bins. The officers assumed the correct stance for an armed challenge and the senior of the two shouted: 'Armed police! Armed police! Show us your hands! Show us your hands!'

Two slim hands appeared – timidly – above the lid of one of the bins.

'Stand up! Keep your hands raised!' the officer shouted.

Gradually, Michael stood to his full height, arms aloft. His head barely cleared the level of the top of the bin.

'Don't move!' he was instructed, firmly, by the police.

The officers approached, cautiously and with carefully coordinated movements between them, until they rounded the bin and confirmed that Michael was alone and that he was not holding a gun. He was shaking a little but not too afraid. He was placed face down on the ground, handcuffed at the back, and asked: 'Do you have a firearm?' He shook his head, resting his cheek on the ground.

Having secured the suspect, the officers provided an update to the Force Control Room: 'One detained. We need transport to Bootle Street' – a reference to the police station for the city centre, located just a few minutes away. They turned to Michael. 'You are under arrest for robbery with a firearm and possession of a firearm with intent. Do you understand?' Michael nodded. 'You do not have to say anything, but it may harm your defence if you fail to mention when questioned something that you later rely on in court. Do you understand?' Another nod.

Minutes later, a team of uniformed officers from the Tactical Aid Unit, a specialist team for tactical arrests and searches, arrived to take Michael away in a police van, leaving the armed officers to secure the scene and search for weapons. The search was conducted quickly and efficiently, and the results were as follows:

Exhibit 1 - Black waterproof jacket

Exhibit 2 - Banana (from right pocket of Exhibit 1)

Exhibit 3 - Orange Sainsbury's supermarket carrier bag (with several holes)

Exhibit 4 - Loose change (not counted at scene – from Exhibit 3)

Exhibit 5 - Empty bank coin bags (from Exhibit 3)

Exhibit 6 - 1 x £10 note and further loose change (from left pocket of Exhibit 1)

A final radio message was passed to the control room, confirming no firearms present, scene secured and clear, and that the officers were returning to Bootle Street with the seized exhibits.

A few hours later, a different set of officers, this time plain-clothes detectives from the Criminal Investigation Department, sat down in an interview room opposite Michael and his long-time solicitor, Howard Cartwright. Michael's association with Howard went back to his very first case, thirty-six years before, when Howard had not long qualified; they had been together ever since.

The interview did not take long. The officers read from the pub landlord's witness statement, in which he described his fear – although he acknowledged that he did not really think the robber had a gun – and gave a description that matched Michael to a T, right down to the bright orange 'hood' he had been wearing throughout (Exhibit 3). The exhibits were produced one by one, and towards the end of the interview the officers showed the pub's CCTV footage from the external camera angle – Michael removing the plastic bag from his head, throwing the loose change inside, and making off down the street towards the alleyway, a trail of coins forming behind him.

'Anything you want to say, Michael?'

Michael and Howard looked at each other. They both knew the answer.

'I'm going guilty, mate. Not much more to it, is there?'

Shortly after the interview, Michael was brought before the Custody Officer, who charged him with robbery (with an imitation firearm, a crucial detail). He was denied bail, pending a first appearance in the magistrates' court the following morning, from where his case would make its way, inexorably, to the Crown Court, where he would be required to enter his plea.

I saw Michael a few days before that plea hearing, to take his instructions and to tell him something he already knew – the law stated that even a banana, when disguised in a pocket and presented as a gun, was classed as an 'imitation firearm' under the Firearms Act. That meant that Michael was indeed guilty of Robbery *with an Imitation Firearm*, and that offence was on the list of crimes for which a second 'strike' would result in an automatic life sentence. And this was very much a second strike – Michael had used the banana robbery method before. In fact, it was an almost identical crime that led to the five-year stretch from which he had so recently been released.

Sitting with Michael in the visiting room, I chose not to get stuck into the intricacies of the Crime (Sentences) Act – automatic life sentences – or the Firearms Act, with its very wide definition of an imitation firearm. I sat back in my chair, shut my file of papers and put down my pen. Michael looked up at me, with an almost Zen-like expression of calm on his face. He waited for me to speak.

'Michael, I don't get it,' I began. 'You had only been out a week, after five and a half years. You are on a strike already, looking at an automatic life [sentence]. What were you thinking?'

He smiled, looked down at the small stack of documents on the table and then back up at me. 'Truth is, Chris, I am happy in here. This is my life. I know how everything works, everyone knows me, and I can get along fine. Out there, I just can't cope with it.'

I spent two hours with Michael that day, gradually building a picture of his character, his motivation, and the person he had become after spending over 90 per cent of his adult life in prison; now facing a life sentence that would see him remain there into his sixties, when most people are looking to retire after forty or fifty years of work. I saw Michael again in the cells at court before the plea hearing, but there was no magic-wand solution – I told him that he had no option but to plead guilty and that the sentence of life imprisonment was inevitable.

The case was adjourned for various pre-sentence reports, but none of them held out hope for a more lenient outcome. At the sentence hearing, the judge accepted that Michael had walked into the pub with a makeshift hood – manufactured from a plastic bag – and a banana in his pocket, before making his short-lived escape with a few pounds' worth of loose change.

In relatively short order, the judge imposed a sentence of life imprisonment, with a minimum term of eight years before Michael could even apply for parole. In reality it would take much longer than that before he would be released. To Michael, it was a matter of indifference. He would continue with his simple daily routine in prison, which to him represented security and normality, safe from the uncertainties and frightening demands of the outside world.

'Thanks, mate,' Michael said, quite genuinely I think, as I said goodbye to him in the cells of the court basement before he was escorted away by the custody staff.

I never heard from Michael again. He may still be in prison to this day, shuffling from cell to canteen to wherever else he may spend his time, as the clock of his life runs down, locked behind the door.

I do think of him often, though, and his story – by no means uncommon, whether involving mental illness,

addiction or just institutionalisation over decades –
represents everything that I believe is wrong with our use of
incarceration in the criminal justice system. We will return to
the lessons to be learned, and the radical solution I propose,
once we have looked at how we ended up with a society so
mindlessly attached to locking up our citizens, for ever longer
periods, without ever really asking ourselves why we do it.

PRISON IN BRITAIN – HOW WE LOVE TO LOCK 'EM UP

Few would disagree that there are people in our society
from whom we need protection: those intent on rape,
murder, serious violence, child abuse, arson. Put simply,
those who pose a real risk to life and limb. What exact form
that protection should take, even from that group of the
most dangerous offenders, is as much in need of thought –
and, I would suggest, radical reform – as the principle of
imprisonment as a whole. However, fewer than a third of
those in Britain's prisons are there because they committed
an act of criminal violence. Even among inmates locked up
for a crime of violence, most are not so dangerous that they
need to be locked in a prison cell to keep society safe.

In recent decades we have seen a dramatic increase in the
UK prison population, from around 44,000 in 1993 to over
80,000 today. Only the sharp fall in the number of police
officers, and swingeing cuts in the budgets for prosecutions

In England and Wales, we overuse prison for non-violent and persistent crime.
More than

56,000

People were sent to prison to serve
a sentence in the year to June 2019

67%

The majority had committed
a non-violent offence

46%

Almost half were sentenced
to serve six months or less

FIGURE 1

and the courts, briefly halted the seemingly inexorable rise. The British government, under Prime Minister Boris Johnson, has pledged to recruit more police officers, provide additional finance for prosecutions, increase prison sentences, and even build more prisons. Legislation has been introduced that will see many offenders serve ever-longer periods in custody. If this policy is carried out, it is inevitable that we will hit a record number of prisoners over the next few years, possibly reaching 100,000 for the first time.

This ratchet effect, where prison is the default soundbite of politicians standing for election – especially in the English-speaking world – is nothing new. In 1993, the then UK Home Secretary Michael Howard, in charge of criminal justice policy, famously spouted the populist line: 'Prison works!' to loud applause at the Tory Party conference. It didn't work for him and it has never worked for anyone else, before or since.

Almost every year since my career began has seen the introduction of legal and policy changes, with the quite deliberate effects of increasing the number of people in prison and raising the average length of time each will spend there. When I first began to appear in the criminal courts in the mid-1990s, a sentence of ten years' imprisonment was a long one, and relatively rare. Rarer still were periods of twenty years or more, even for murder. Since that time, the maximum sentences for a range of offences have crept ever upwards; new crimes have been created to more seriously criminalise forms of conduct previously viewed as of marginal criminality. Sentencing guidelines have been used to raise ever higher the average level of sentence for almost every category of case. Reducing offenders' automatic release date from two-thirds to half, for some longer sentences, has done nothing to stop the growth of the prison population during this period (a reform that the government intends to reverse in any event).

It really is a relentless march, but one which – surprisingly, given its enormous cost in so many ways – has taken place in the face of all credible evidence as to the impact of prison, whether on levels of crime, rates of recidivism, economic damage, family relationships, employment, housing or, most worryingly and ironically of all, on the protection of victims.

We choose to send people to prison for a long time ... and it's growing.

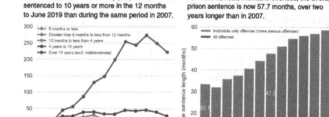

More than three times as many people were sentenced to 10 years or more in the 12 months to June 2019 than during the same period in 2007.

For more serious, indictable offences, the average prison sentence is now 57.7 months, over two years longer than in 2007.

People serving mandatory life sentences for murder are spending more of their sentence in prison. On average they spend 17 years in custody, up from 13 years in 2001.

Judges are also imposing longer tariff periods. The average minimum term imposed for murder rose from 12.5 years in 2003 to 21.3 years in 2016.

FIGURE 2

Anyone leaving custody who has served two days or more is now required to serve a minimum of 12 months under supervision in the community.

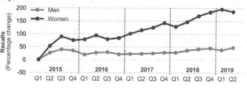

As a result, the number of people recalled back to custody has increased, particularly amongst women. 8,956 people serving a sentence of less than 12 months were recalled to prison in the year to June 2019.

FIGURE 3

Why are our politicians so fixated on using the tired 'lock 'em up' mantra and why do we, as a society, not only accept it but applaud its use and vote for it?

PRISON THROUGH THE AGES

We in Europe have long since abandoned the death penalty and all forms of corporal punishment. And yet, in essence, there is nothing to choose between chastisement of the body and that of the mind. Taking away someone's freedom of movement, their right to live with their family, to have a meaningful sexual and emotional life, and a host of other deprivations, may be far harsher than all but the worst physical punishments. For some, in fact, imprisonment is a prospect worse than death. It is a sad fact that self-harm and suicide rates in prison are many times higher than on the outside.

In the ancient world, where the death penalty was practised very much as a societal norm, extreme forms of torture were considered acceptable and there was no need

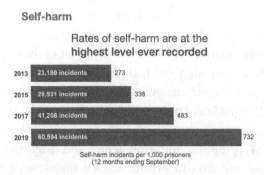

Self-harm

Rates of self-harm are at the
highest level ever recorded

Year	Incidents	
2013	23,180 incidents	273
2015	28,931 incidents	338
2017	41,208 incidents	483
2019	60,594 incidents	732

Self-harm incidents per 1,000 prisoners
(12 months ending September)

FIGURE 4

for fine distinctions between punishment of body and mind. No need, therefore, to justify jailing the citizenry in any way, and certainly not in terms of some purported distinction in principle from any other method of judicial cruelty practised by the state.

In ancient Egypt, prisons were used for a vast range of purposes, some of which we might understand today, others on the face of it obsolete. Some prisoners were confined after the judicial process of the day, including to await execution – in effect on 'death row', although there is no evidence that the condemned were separated from the rest of the inmates. Others were locked away on the order of royal officials, for actual or manufactured offences against the Crown, along with those accused of espionage, deserting slaves, and disgraced members of the king's governing elite.

Ancient Israel also used a form of temporary custody for those awaiting execution, a sentence carried out without the decades of delay for appeal that mark the practice of capital punishment in the modern United States.

As ever, the Greeks were the first to record some philosophical or ethical analysis of punishment generally and imprisonment in particular. Socrates himself, convicted of 'impiety' (disrespect of the sacred values of the day) and 'corrupting the young' (with all that philosophy), carefully mulled over the various potential punishments in his plea in mitigation. He did not see the point of being locked up.

Shall I [propose] imprisonment? And why should I spend my days in prison, and be the slave of the magistrates [elected for just one] year – a slave of the Eleven? Or shall the penalty be a fine, and imprisonment

until the fine is paid? There is the same objection.
I should have to lie in prison, for money I have none,
and cannot pay.

The reference to imprisonment for non-payment of fines
echoes down the ages, even to modern Britain, where fine
defaulters can still be locked away, as a last resort, when
they either cannot or will not pay what they owe. Socrates
rightly identified this as a deep injustice to those upon whom
fines were imposed, when they would never realistically be
able to pay. The same arguments are made today – and I
fully agree with them – that jailing people for failing to pay
fines imposed for crimes of relatively low gravity represents
nothing less than the subjugation of the poor. One thing is
for certain: the rich would never suffer the same fate.

The more interesting analysis is of the concept of
imprisonment as a form of slavery to the state; in Socrates'
case, to the elected magistrates of the day, who used their
office for political ends. The concept of incarceration, not
as punishment for an eternal crime – murder, assault, theft
and the like – but for political purposes, has remained a
feature of prison policy down the ages. The state uses its
power to imprison as a means of removing from society
those who pose a challenge to the established order.

Such an approach, whilst utterly debased in moral
and ethical terms, at least has the benefit of some degree
of logic and pragmatism, judged by the standards and
objectives of unprincipled elites down the ages. If you do
not want someone to 'corrupt' society, what better way
to solve the problem than to lock them away, depriving
them of access to the political process – and the oxygen of
publicity – altogether.

I will certainly never forget my visit to Robben Island, a few shark-infested miles across Table Bay from Cape Town, where Nelson Mandela spent eighteen years in captivity, out of the total of his twenty-seven years behind bars. His modest cell, barely long enough for a man to lie down straight to sleep, and the dusty quarry where he toiled – day after day, year after year – could not fail to make an impression on me. It will remain with me for a lifetime. The imprisonment of Mandela was not really about punishment for a crime at all. It was about the destruction of the human spirit. Wherever it is practised and in whatever form, the removal of liberty – to some degree or another – has much the same effect.

Socrates chose, as he saw it, the intellectual purity of death over all the other potential sentences on the penal menu of the day, including imprisonment by the state.

Plato, describing a mythical city-state named Magnesia, presented a sophisticated analysis of the role of incarceration in the scale of criminal sentencing. He proposed a form of categorisation of custodial institutions, which does not – in hierarchical if not practical terms – differ greatly from the distinctions between different levels in the prison systems of Britain, the US and many other countries in the modern world.

Plato described three classes of institution to which offenders could be sent, according to their 'incorrigibility and reformability'. The lowest level, to be used for the majority – those convicted of petty crimes who would be locked up for a maximum of two years – was to be located 'near the marketplace'. It was clearly important for such offenders to be housed close to their fellow citizens rather than isolated or even exiled from society, never to return.

They were permitted some contact with others and were expected to return to their previous lives – families, work and position – after paying their debts to society.

For more serious offences – committed by those considered 'foolish' rather than 'intrinsically bad' – Plato described a 'Reform Centre', where the minimum period of confinement would be five years and where inmates would have no contact with their fellow citizens whilst serving their sentence. These prisons were located alongside the premises of the 'Nocturnal Council', a form of morality police, whose mission was to improve the prisoners' 'moral character' so that they would be fit to re-enter society at the end of their sentence.

Finally, there was a prison for 'the incorrigibles', those deemed entirely incapable of reform or of reintegration with the good citizens of Magnesia. They would be housed in remote and inhospitable institutions, far from the city – in the 'wildest part of the commonwealth' – guarded and fed by slaves, with no prospect of release. When the prisoners died, their bodies were not even to be buried – they were simply to be left as carrion, beyond the border of the state.

As we will see, the imaginings of Plato, all those millennia ago, are reflected in the unimaginably cruel and wasteful prison–industrial complex of the twenty-first-century United States. In many respects, in Britain we are heading down the same misguided and oppressive path. This is one of the many reasons for the radical reforms I propose in this book. We need to act fast or it may be too late.

The Romans had no use for Plato's fine philosophical approach to imprisonment and no interest in rehabilitation at all. For them, incarceration was a means to an end; a form of coercion to achieve a defined objective. The primary role of deprivation of liberty was the collection of debts from those who had not paid their dues. Recalcitrant debtors could be held in private confinement by their creditors for sixty days to give them the chance to pay up, after which they could be sold into slavery or simply put to death.

At first blush, the Roman approach may sound like a harsh echo of a time long ago, before modern concepts of human rights came to be enshrined in law. However, the use of imprisonment to enforce private debts remained a feature of justice policy in Britain well into the nineteenth century.

One of the reasons why imprisonment for crimes came relatively late in history was the British enthusiasm for putting people to death, whether for 'real' crimes – murder and the like – or for those causing offence to the monarch of the day. By around the tenth century, hanging was the favoured method, while drowning in a pit was a form of execution often favoured by the bloody barons of the Middle Ages. In the reign of Henry VIII (1509–1547) over 70,000 people are estimated to have been put to death at the hands of the king or his loyal lords.

By the early eighteenth century, in further echoes of ancient times, there were over two hundred crimes punishable by death. Acts as diverse as stealing five shillings from a shop or chopping down the wrong tree could lead to the gallows. In the main – and as ever – the death sentence was reserved for the poorest members of society.

The prisons of seventeenth- and eighteenth-century Britain were harsh places. There was no regard for age – yes, children were locked up – or for the crime committed. As in ancient Rome, a significant proportion of inmates were not 'criminals' at all, but those who could not pay their debts. Some were no doubt financially reckless, but many were simply tradesmen or small business owners who had fallen on hard times, either through bad luck or incompetence.

In an early example of the use of private prisons, which have become such a prominent feature of modern criminal justice systems, eighteenth-century jails or 'houses of correction' were funded not by taxes but by charging the inmates themselves for 'board and lodging'. This model of incarceration is making a comeback in the present-day United States and in various other countries around the world.

Overcrowding in prisons was so severe that in 1718 Parliament introduced a form of modern exile. For the first time, rather than facing execution, convicts were 'transported' to the colonies. Many thousands were herded onto ships to make the long journey, at first to the Americas and later to Australia. Over 160,000 people – those convicted of what were considered the more serious of capital crimes, and some as young as nine years old – suffered this form of exile, sometimes as a direct alternative to hanging.

One of the major policy factors in the introduction of transportation was economic; for those who were not to be executed, imprisonment, even in the basic and inhospitable conditions of the day, came at a cost to the state. The only cost of sending criminals to the colonies was the price of the voyage itself. Hundreds were packed onto vessels with limited rations and were left to their own devices as soon as they disembarked, blinking in the sunlight of a distant land. The colonies became an important source of revenue and of worldwide power for the British Crown, which continued well into the twentieth century.

FIGURE 5   Treadmill at Preston Prison, 1902

By 1777, prisons were described by the reformer John Howard as 'filthy, corrupt-ridden and unhealthy'. But not much was done about it. In 1818 the 'penal treadmill' was introduced; an 'everlasting staircase' in which prisoners were forced to climb for hour after hour, going nowhere and achieving nothing; 'grinding the wind'.

By the early nineteenth century, even mass deportation was failing to empty out the prisons quickly enough. The number of incarcerated debtors continued to grow. One John Dickens found himself confined for debt – to a baker – at the Marshalsea Prison in London in 1824, forcing his twelve-year-old son Charles to leave school and find work in a factory. Charles Dickens went on to describe conditions in the debtors' prisons of the era in his novel *Little Dorrit*, whose protagonist was born and raised at the Marshalsea.

Dickens the younger, no doubt deeply influenced by his childhood experiences, spent a lifetime campaigning for prison reform. In 1834, at the age of twenty-four, in 'A Visit to Newgate', he summarised the impact of long-term incarceration:

> Men in full health and vigour, in the flower of youth or the prime of life, with all their faculties and perceptions as acute and perfect as your own; but dying, nevertheless – dying as surely – with the hand of death imprinted upon them as indelibly – as if mortal disease had wasted their frames to shadows, and corruption had already begun!

This short but vivid passage strikes a chord with me. I have often felt that prison is a form of slow death: of body, mind and spirit. Here Dickens encapsulates everything that is – and always has been – wrong with deprivation of liberty, when practised indiscriminately and on a massive scale. Surely, you may think, things have changed? The Victorian age is long in the past. But, tragically and shamefully, as we shall see, Dickens's words describe to a T the lives of many prisoners in Britain, the US and around the world, almost 200 years later.

The nineteenth century saw a succession of Insolvency Acts, designed to offer debtors some relief. The number of prisoners locked up for debt was thereby reduced and the overall prison population came to be dominated by those convicted of criminal offences.

The Gladstone Report of 1895 contained some radical proposals, at least by the standards of the times. Although broadly accepting the concept of the 'irreclaimable' criminal, for whom harsh punishment and very long sentences were in order, the Report set out the 'primary and concurrent objects' of penal policy to be 'deterrence and reformation'. In a phrase that would not be out of place in modern debates on prison reform, the Report admonished the powers that be 'to do better', making a telling observation: 'Prisoners have been treated too much as a hopeless or worthless element of the community, and the moral as well as the legal responsibility of the prison authorities has been held to cease when they pass outside the prison gates.'

It is one of the greater tragedies of human affairs that we find ourselves, well over a century later, surveying a criminal justice system – and a prison estate – which manifests identical failings to those identified by Gladstone's committee in the last years of Queen Victoria's reign.

The reform agenda of the Gladstone Report did find its way into law. The British Prison Act of 1898, for good and for bad, was intended to represent the beginning of a bright new future for the prison system. Hard labour – including the dreaded treadmill – was abolished once and for all. For the first time, the principle was established that prison work should be productive, not least for the prisoners, 'who should be able to earn their livelihood on release'. In theory at least, those locked away, whether due to misconduct or misfortune, were no longer to be disregarded as the mere detritus of a society that no longer had use for them.

Sadly, despite all the good intentions of Herbert Gladstone and the 1898 Act, for prisoners themselves not much changed in the decades that followed. During the First World War, prison conditions were experienced by a novel group of inmates: 'conchies' – conscientious objectors who refused to be conscripted into the armed forces. Hundreds of these men were locked up in prisons all over the country, many from rather different – and occasionally more influential – social backgrounds, compared to most of the prisoners of the day.

Over the century that followed, through to the present day, it cannot be said that nothing has changed at all. However, the stark truth remains that prisons in the 2020s are grossly overcrowded, rife with violence and murder and overrun with drugs of every kind. Inmates are prone to self-harm and suicide at a rate many times higher than for those of us on the outside. Perhaps the bleakest fact of all is that the majority of those leaving custody will be back again, many of them – just like Michael – within a few weeks or months of release. Save for a few shining lights in the darkness of the prison estate, most 'rehabilitation programmes' are proving next to useless in the outcomes they achieve.

PRISON – THE TRUTH

In July 2019, the then British Chief Inspector of Prisons, Peter Clarke, in a scathing report presented to the government, wrote that he would 'never forget' the conditions of squalor he had seen during an inspection at Her Majesty's Prison in Birmingham. 'Rubbish was left lying around in bags and there were problems with fleas, cockroaches and rodents,' he explained. One inmate was housed in a 'filthy flooded cell' and another was forced to endure a floor that was covered in blood following a self-harm incident. It had not been cleaned before the new occupant arrived.

That then is where Britain's prisons stand, in the 2020s – not the 1920s, the 1820s, or some era even more remote.

Why we are here I shall come to shortly, but where our prisons may be heading is of defining and existential concern; not only for those remitted to a prison by the courts, whether on remand before trial or to serve a sentence, but for all of us. Winston Churchill felt that a society's attitude to its prisoners, its 'criminals', was the measure of 'the stored-up strength of a nation'. By those standards, we in the United Kingdom demonstrate a weakness of national character at which Churchill would have been appalled.

As with many practices, much of prison policy is gradually infiltrating Britain from across the Atlantic. By examining the largest and most entrenched prison system in the world, we in Britain can learn and, I deeply hope, apply the brakes before we end up with a system like America's.

The United States does not in fact have a single prison system. It has a nationwide network of local, state and federal facilities, from tiny 'sheriff's' jails' in small towns, housing a handful of short-term inmates, to the 18,000 acres of Louisiana State Penitentiary. Known as Angola, after the former slave plantation that occupied the site, and given some apt nicknames – 'The Farm'/'Alcatraz of the South' – Louisiana's is the largest maximum-security prison in the United States.

Angola houses over 6,000 prisoners, many in solitary confinement or lockdown in their cells for up to twenty-four hours a day. By way of context, that is more than the entire prison population of Sweden, a country of over 10 million people. And Angola is just one of dozens of prisons and jails in the state of Louisiana, which has a total population of under 5 million, of whom well over 40,000 are behind bars; one of the highest rates of incarceration per capita in the world.

But Louisiana's prison population, despite those grim numbers, is as nothing compared with the total locked up across the whole of the United States. One way of putting it into context is to think of those in prison as citizens of a city.

In many ways that is what they are, sharing as much in common in their living conditions as the residents of the sprawling major cities and metropolitan regions of the US. Here then is where the 'City of Incarceration' fits into the table:

1	New York City	8,398,748
2	Los Angeles	3,990,456
3	Chicago	2,705,994
4	Houston	2,325,502
5	**City of Incarceration**	**2,298,300**
6	Phoenix	1,660,272

Yes, the City of Incarceration is the fifth largest population centre in the United States, and well on its way to becoming the fourth. Yet not only is the overall *number* of prisoners many times greater than in any other country on earth, but the *rate* of incarceration per head of population is equally extraordinary, in comparison with other advanced industrialised democratic nations. Only El Salvador – one of the most dangerous and violent countries on earth – comes close, with a figure of 618 per 100,000.

In this table, taking some examples of developed countries, the rate of incarceration is expressed per 100,000 of the population, although the US also heads the list of *all* countries, developed or not.

1	United States of America	655
2	Russian Federation	381
3	Turkey	318
4	Australia	172
5	Mexico	163
6	Scotland	150

The table reveals that the US imprisons almost five times the number of its citizens per capita as the UK (which is the highest in Western Europe), and more than fifteen times the figure for Japan.

A JOURNEY INTO THE DARKNESS

To see at first hand the extreme reach of twenty-first-century prison policy in the US I travelled to Alabama in the Deep South. There I was given remarkably open access to police departments, the judiciary and the custodial facilities used by US society as a permanent dumping ground for those deemed surplus to requirements.

On a bright and hot October day in 2019, I arrived at Mobile County Metro Jail, a short distance from the Gulf of Mexico, in southern Alabama. I was driven there in a police vehicle by the Sheriff Department's Tactical Surgeon, a friend of the family. Dr Tim Hughes is an urgent-care doctor who also supports the Sheriff's officers when they undertake tactical operations, such as dawn raids on suspected drug gangs. His role is to provide medical backup in case one of the officers should come to harm during the 'mission'. He told me that they conducted such raids on a 'military model', with full 'tactical backup', because the risk of armed resistance was high. Thankfully, during his years in the role Tim had not been called upon to treat a life-threatening injury, and no officer had died in the course of a raid.

Tim had arranged for me to interview the warden of the jail, Noah 'Trey' Oliver, his deputy, Sam, and for me to take a tour of the facility. I was welcomed and treated with considerable courtesy and hospitality from the moment I arrived at the jail. A friendly and gracious receptionist welcomed me into the complex.

A sprawling arrangement of redbrick buildings, set behind high barbed-wire fencing between Interstate 10 and the Alabama Shipyards of Pinto Island on the Mobile River, the Metro Jail houses all of those arrested in the Mobile County area. At the time of my visit, the total number of beds was around 1,100, but only 800 or so of those were in the maximum-security units where the majority of inmates were housed. There was a total of 1,550 prisoners behind the walls on the day of my tour, of whom 1,400 were allocated to maximum security; meaning those areas were overcrowded to the tune of around 600 people (an additional 75 per cent). It had reached a 100 per cent overcrowding level not long before. I was soon to see what the numbers looked like in practice.

Unlike Britain, which unified its local jails and national prisons many years ago, the US system retains a clear demarcation between the two forms of institution. 'Jails', like the one in Mobile, are almost all operated by a local County Sheriff's Department. They house those awaiting trial or sentencing, but also, in what seemed to me a particularly unfair twist, those yet to be formally indicted with any crime at all. Some of those in the latter category could be detained for months or even several years after arrest, waiting to find out if they would ever be indicted – and then put on trial – at all. A cruel form of legal limbo.

'Prisons' in the US are reserved for those convicted and sentenced, counting down the days, years or decades until their release, if they are ever to be released at all.

During my trip, one public defender – who represents those too poor to pay for a lawyer (which is nearly everyone) – told me about the most unjust thing she had seen in her two decades of legal practice. Her client had been pulled over by the police, arrested and accused of Possession of Cocaine with Intent to Distribute; a serious felony that could have led to a long prison sentence. The police had searched his car and found a bag of suspicious white powder. The suspect protested that it was not cocaine, but he had a prior record for drugs and nobody believed him.

He was taken to the County Jail, and there he stayed for week after week, month after month and year after year. The small bag of powder remained in its exhibit box, in the police evidence room, the whole time. There was a very long queue at the forensics laboratory and many bigger and higher-priority drug seizures awaited analysis by the single available mass spectrometer (used to isolate and identify substances within seized powders). More drug samples were coming in all the time and this small bag of powder just didn't come to the top of the file . . . for over three years.

Finally, after a sufficient fuss was made by the Public Defender's office, the powder was tested for the presence of controlled substances. The results were clear. The powder tested negative for cocaine, heroin, amphetamine, MDMA ('ecstasy'), and all other drugs prohibited by law. It still took a week for that information to filter through the system and for the District Attorney – the elected public prosecutor – to dismiss the case. The man was released, with just the clothes on his back and not so much as an apology. The life he had left behind three years earlier – home, girlfriend, job – was long gone.

US jails like that in Mobile are packed to the rafters with suspects in the same situation – people against whom no indictment may ever come but who have neither the legal backup to make an effective early challenge to the case, nor the money to pay their bond so that they can get out on bail.

I sat down in the administration block with Robert 'Sam' Houston, the Deputy Warden, who ran the jail from day to day. He was the one that staff called if, as happened during my visit, a cell block flooded or the power went out. Sam fights a relentless battle to keep the place running, despite the levels of overcrowding, the steady influx of drugs, underfunding, understaffing, prevalent mental illness and the constant threat of violence – including murder – that can explode without warning.

Sam was a forty-two-year veteran of law enforcement, having joined the Sheriff's Department as a lowly deputy in 1977. He was not what I expected, which – frankly and to my discredit – was an unsympathetic and cynical prison warden, running down the clock to retirement and with nothing but disdain for those in the cells. He was none of those things and neither was any other law enforcement official I met in my wide travels and many meetings in the South. Every one of them wanted to do the right thing. This makes it all the more mystifying that the US prison system has become one of the most ineffective, damaging, cruel and financially catastrophic public institutions ever overseen by a government of the people.

Against the crackle of radio transmissions from within the main buildings of the jail, I spent several hours with Sam. He gave me an unvarnished account of the US criminal justice system, warts and all. He told me that the entire approach to law and order, crime and punishment, criminal courts and the prison system all came down to one thing – money.

In Sam's early days with the Sheriff's Department, the federal government had made large grants available to support rehabilitation programmes, training and pathways to work for those in custody. A programme of day-release work, even weekend release for the best-behaved and most productive inmates, was introduced, using a fund entirely separate from the tight annual budgets for the running of the jail.

Sam saw those who would previously have been warehoused in confined spaces for up to twenty-four hours a day – perhaps even spending weeks or months in solitary confinement – not only training or getting some form of education, but actually working in a real job and making money. Instead of seeing their fines mounting – inexorably and unaffordably – these men could pay them off completely. They could help out with the rent for their families, keep up with child-support payments and remain – in many important ways – part of society. They had a place and a value and were no longer just worthless criminals, good for nothing but the scrapheap of humanity.

Crime and recidivism rates fell. The jail population began to shrink. But then, just as suddenly as it started, all federal money stopped. Within days, the local authorities made a decision to bring the work-release programme to an immediate halt. Political pressures came to bear on the weekend furloughs, so home release also came to an end. Things went back to normal and, save for a brief burst of funding in 2012, they have remained that way ever since, leading to the level of overcrowding seen when I visited in 2019. It is not how it should be, Sam told me, but it is what it is. He called for a senior officer, a time-served and stocky black lieutenant in his forties, who arrived to take me for a tour.

I have been to many prisons in Britain over the years, and none of them are happy places. But nothing had prepared me for the conditions I saw in Mobile County Jail or, in many ways, the more tragic stories that lay behind it all. We left the administrative building to head into the jail itself. Every door required a separate video check by the central control room before it was unlocked remotely. I followed the lieutenant inside.

Our first stop was the vehicle arrival point, which bore a superficial resemblance to the dropping-off zones at a busy airport. Liveried police vehicles and vans pulled up into a form of airlock, with large rolling doors at each end. Only when the entrance door was fully sealed, so that there was no way out from the arrival bay, were the prisoners unloaded, firmly shackled in handcuffs, and shuffled inside for booking.

And what a sorry sight they were. They all carried themselves with the shamble of the homeless and the deflated spirit of the dispossessed. Most were missing some or all of their teeth. Tattoos were clearly compulsory, many on the neck and face, drawn with varying degrees of skill. There was a pervasive smell of alcohol and cannabis fumes, mixed with the flop sweat of the South. Every arriving inmate had the same look in the eyes – they were all on drugs, booze or both. Not one of the dozen or more being booked when I visited was sober. And this was not a Friday night – it was the middle of a quiet Wednesday afternoon.

Barred cells were set aside for the most affected by drink or drugs to 'sleep it off'. Several new arrivals had taken advantage of the opportunity and were out for the count. It felt like everyone there knew the system – this was a tried and tested routine for arriving prisoners, police officers and guards alike.

One of the few rays of light in all of this was a well-resourced and comprehensively staffed medical suite. Several fully equipped examination rooms lined one hall, including at least two for mental health assessments, and there was even an X-ray scanner for those suspected of having broken a bone (or perhaps of swallowing drugs). The rooms were all spotless, reminiscent of a well-run minor injuries clinic in the UK. Efficient air conditioning kept the temperature – and no doubt tempers, at least for now – under control.

Tim joined us on the tour, after locking away his gun (even police doctors are armed in Alabama). He told me that many of those who were seen by the medical staff had no access to healthcare in the outside world. Some of the new inmates, he explained, had undoubtedly engineered their own arrests in order to see a doctor, which they could not otherwise afford. They would be given help to detox if they needed it, tested for HIV, hepatitis and other common conditions of street life, given medication for the ailments of body and mind. Those who were identified as suffering with serious mental illness would be seen by a psychiatrist and, if needed, prescribed lithium, antipsychotics or other drugs designed to keep the most obvious – and potentially dangerous – symptoms under control.

We left the booking area and walked along a number of corridors winding through the jail, before heading to a cell block. The sight of 1,400 garment bags on a winding storage rail in a hangarlike room, each bag containing the clothing in which a prisoner had arrived, was a poignant spectacle. There the shoddy garments would hang, for the months or years until release, or until the inmate was transferred to prison to serve his or her sentence, in which case the bag of clothes would make its way there too.

Prison uniforms were stacked in their hundreds; toilet rolls, toothbrushes, soap and the other basics of the inmates' kit all handed out on arrival, until money could be sent from outside to allow them to buy their own. One shelf was piled high with uniforms of bright cerise pink, almost like a modern nurse's uniform but in every size up to XXXL. I asked the lieutenant who wore the pink ones. 'Oh, they are for the sex offenders, who have sexually assaulted a prisoner or officer on the inside,' he explained. 'We get a lot of those.' There were browns, blues, orange and several others, each signifying something about the status or predilections of the prisoner to whom they were issued.

We moved on, through the cavernous kitchens. The cooking equipment lay idle as outside private caterers now brought in all the food, pre-prepared. No longer did the prisoners spend time preparing food and cooking for their fellow inmates – this was now a commercial 'heat and serve' operation, managed by one of the largest food-service corporations in the world. The fare on offer consisted mostly of fried and boiled slop, unidentifiable protein slices, white bread, chemicals, sugar, fat and salt – no different from the diets of tens of millions of Americans, whether in prison or not.

We continued to the Administrative Segregation Unit, or Ad Seg, a form of solitary confinement for the most dangerous and those who persistently broke the rules. 'Be prepared for them to shout some stuff at you,' I was warned. As it happened, Ad Seg was quiet that day.

After one more perfectly polished corridor came to an end, the buzzer sounded, the main door to one of the cell blocks opened and we walked inside. Finally, we were in the heart of the American prison system. In blocks exactly like these, and a dozen variations on the theme, the millions of citizens of the US City of Incarceration spend their days; some for the whole of their natural lives.

The closest description that comes to mind, in terms of the physical design, is a massive indoor bird or orang-utan enclosure at a zoo; just with fewer objects for recreation and

FIGURE 6 The view from the observation desk of a 'wedge' at the Mobile County Jail

more overcrowding. We stood next to a raised observation desk, manned by several officers, which provided a direct view into all five 'wedges': separate cell blocks, each identical in size, one next to the other. The thinner ends of the wedges were right in front of us – 12-feet-high reinforced glass panels, perhaps 5 feet wide, with every pane bearing at least one crack or impact point, caused by the application of very heavy force from the inside. The glass was several inches thick.

Behind the glass, each wedge was identically designed. Widening from the central access point, where we stood, towards a rear wall 50 feet or so away, the nearest part of the wedge held steel tables and benches, bolted firmly to the concrete floor. There were six or so of these tables, most occupied by several inmates, all of whom were staring at a point a few feet above the glass through which we observed them. I realised that they were watching a single television, which played constantly, 20 feet above their heads, on the wall above the entrance door.

'That's what we use to keep order,' I was told by the lieutenant. 'They misbehave, we switch it off, so they keep each other in line, especially during the [American] football season!'

At the back of each wedge were two groups of cells, one on top of the other, similar in style to the cell block layout from the Elvis Presley film *Jailhouse Rock*. Two cells per level, each with four over-and-under bunks, making a total of sixteen beds in all. I did not need to do a full head count of the first wedge to work out that there were a lot more than sixteen men inside. I saved myself the trouble and asked how many there were. The duty officer looked down at his desk and told me, 'Thirty-one in the first wedge, then twenty-nine, twenty-nine, thirty, thirty-one, so we have one hundred fifty inmates in the space for eighty.' This is what prison overcrowding looks like up close.

Between each set of double bunks, scattered on the floors of the cells, were plastic beds that looked a little like white canoes. 'Boats,' I was informed. 'We use them for the overflow prisoners – they have to sleep on the floor.'

In each of the wedges, the prisoners wore a different coloured uniform. The sex offenders, of whom there was a wedgeful, occupied the central position in their bright pink outfits. Other more muted colours (dark greens and blues) designated those convicted and awaiting transfer to state prison, some awaiting trial, and another group in the wedge to the left.

I noticed that some of the inmates in that wedge were behaving strangely. One began to jump up and down and hoot like a chimpanzee. Another approached the glass and pressed his face right up against it, like a small child inside a car. Others slumped against the wall and stared into space, mumbling to themselves. Some rocked back and forth, shrieking and shouting. A few just sat silently, barely moving at all.

'That's the psychiatric wedge,' the lieutenant told me. His shrug revealed that this was all wrong but, at the same time, what could he do about it? This is what happens in the wealthiest and most scientifically advanced nation on earth – the mentally ill are left to fester in a glass cage, twenty-four hours a day, controlled by pharmaceuticals and the physical security of a jail cell.

These men, all of them, were locked up in the wedges – at night confined to the tiny cells – every minute of every day. There were exercise yards – I saw them for myself – but they stood empty, weeds poking through the concrete. The Warden was to explain later: 'We should have one hundred sixty staff at the jail, but right now we only have one hundred ten. That means we don't have the manpower to escort the inmates for exercise, or anything else for that matter.'

I was shown the women's section of the prison. It mirrored that of the men's block I had seen – several hundred prisoners in equally crowded conditions; some emaciated from years of crack and crystal meth; others large, aggressive and intimidating. They stared out at us, some shouting to the Lieutenant that they needed to talk to him about something. He smiled, waved politely and we moved on.

So the shifts changed, the lights went on and off, the sun went down and came back up, and the inmates of the County Jail shuffled from one identical day to the next, hoping only that the TV would not be switched off, and that, somehow, some sort of drug would find its way in, so that they could find blessed escape in the only way that most of them knew.

Thinking back to those prisons of nineteenth-century Britain, described with such poignancy and eloquence by Dickens, my sense is that the prison inmates of the twentieth-century United States fail to enjoy much better conditions. Worse still, few Americans seem to know or care enough to try to do anything about it.

Before I left Mobile County Jail, I spoke again with Sam Houston, who told me of the iniquity of the US bail system, which essentially works on the basis of money. No money, no bail. Many were locked up for years because they could not raise a few hundred dollars for their bail bond. 'Had a guy, drugs obviously, stole five hundred dollars, no way to raise the bond so he was here for over two years – costing the County 55 dollars a day all that time,' said Sam. Many of the inmates were locked up for years for the lowest possible forms of non-violent crime, purely because of the bond system.

Sam told me of a fifty-year-old groundskeeper at a university who was arrested for possession of a small amount of marijuana. The judge 'no-bonded' him because he had one prior arrest for the same thing twenty years earlier, meaning he could not get bail at all. He had no other criminal record of any kind. The man spent months in jail and lost his job – for two cannabis charges in a lifetime. 'Who benefits from that?' Sam questioned, ruefully.

More frightening still, Alabama state law dictates that children as young as thirteen, charged with certain crimes, are automatically – with no discretion at all – transferred into the adult criminal justice system; not only the court process but the County Jail itself. It makes no difference what state they are in or the struggles they have. 'What about if they have a learning disability – say a mental age of nine or ten?' I asked. It makes no difference – 'Take 'em to the jail and lock 'em up' is the answer. The only rules are that they should be separated, in sight and sound, from the adult inmates. 'That's the theory – it's not always possible,' I was informed. Not only are children subjected to the same prison conditions as adults, but they face exactly the same draconian sentencing laws.

One police officer told me: 'It's tragic what we do to these kids, but the system is designed this way. It's sad.' The forced incarceration of a child, in the same jail as murderers, rapists and paedophiles, potentially to be locked away for most of his or her young life, surely goes way beyond 'sad'.

I was told by almost everyone I met that federal guidelines have made things worse. A third felony conviction, which might be as trivial as selling an ounce or so of cannabis, could result in a sentence of 'Life Without the Possibility of Parole', known as 'LWOP'. The scourge of many communities, particularly black and Hispanic neighbourhoods all over the United States, the use of LWOP has led to entire generations entering the County Jail, never to be released. In a small mercy, the US Supreme Court has ruled that LWOP cannot be imposed on juveniles for non-violent crimes. It takes a minute to process the fact that, prior to that decision, such sentences, of a whole lifetime in prison, were regularly imposed on young people before they could even vote or legally drink beer.

The US justice system has over 50,000 people serving LWOP. They watch the hands of the clock turn in a prison cell, for ten, thirty, perhaps seventy years or more, many without having harmed another person in any way, let alone killed someone. The cost of it all, human and financial, defies comprehension, but things carry on as they are.

Why would any rational system, particularly in a country that brands itself – with entirely unconscious irony – as 'the land of the free', incarcerate so many people for non-violent crimes for so long?

The answers are simple in many ways. The US prison system is a huge source of revenue for corporate America. Whether directly profiting from running jails, construction contracts, maintenance and prison supplies – including the near-inedible food – or a host of other revenue streams, corporations make huge profits from the estimated $182 billion spent by the US taxpayer on mass incarceration. To place that sum in context, it is more than the entire gross domestic product of Bulgaria, an advanced industrialised nation and a member of the European Union.

Ohio and several other states are even experimenting with a return to the Victorian 'pay-to-stay' approach to imprisonment, where prisoners are presented with a huge bill for 'board and lodging' when they are due for release. Unsurprisingly, given their complete inability to undertake gainful employment during their sentences, the inmates cannot pay the tens of thousands of dollars demanded. And so they either remain in prison, or leave with a millstone of debt around their necks, from which they will never escape.

Corporations in the United States, perhaps more than anywhere in the world, are extremely aggressive in defence of their profit centres, and those making money from this vast prison–industrial complex are no different. The defence they employ, as with so many areas of US political life, comes in the form of political donations and the use of high-priced lobbying firms, at local, state and federal level. In comparison with the well-intentioned – but relatively impoverished – reform lobby, there really is no contest. Money talks, more prisons are opened and it just needs the judges to send enough people to fill them or – more accurately – to overfill them.

But why do the judges play ball? I met several on my travels in the US, and none was willing to go on the record. With the comfort of my assurance that I would leave their names out of it, both state and federal judges told me the same thing: it all came down to politics. Here is how it works, up and down America, in towns and cities, large and small.

Police chiefs in the US are generally appointed by an elected mayor, and sheriffs are directly elected by public vote. In each case, it is for a fixed term, which places them all at the mercy of the electorate every few years. District attorneys, who decide who to prosecute and – almost uniquely for a common law country – what sentence to seek, are also elected every few years. But the real kicker is that federal judges are appointed by an elected politician, including the President himself, and state judges are elected.

Every judge I spoke to told me that not one official, sheriff or judge would *ever* be elected on a platform of *reducing* sentences, no matter what the crimes and despite the mountain of evidence that such an approach might actually work.

US attitudes to criminal sentencing are entrenched, in part as a result of the sophisticated lobbying and PR campaigns of vested interests, to an extent due to the binary nature of media comment on crime and punishment, but mainly because 'Get tough on crime' is a simple message and an easy sell. We hear the same message in the UK, especially in election season. It chimes with the electorate's instincts and prejudices. Very little of the counternarrative receives any coverage, and when it does, it cannot compete with talk of 'cracking down' on criminals.

Even the members of the Grand Jury in Mobile, Alabama – a group of case-hardened citizens, charged with the decision as to whether to indict at the request of the District Attorney (they almost always do) – were surprised to discover that the County Jail sat right by the main highway and so close to the city. Taken on a tour, many were shocked at the human misery behind all those indictments they had returned. 'Out of sight, out of mind' is how it was explained to me.

Unlike the Manhattan skyline, the shores of Lake Michigan or Santa Monica Pier, the City of Incarceration has no instantly recognisable landmark to keep it in the public consciousness. It is a hidden city, a sort of modern-day Atlantis. Only those who have spent time in a US prison truly understand just how inhumane and inhospitable that environment is.

I finished my visit to the County Jail with some final thoughts from Sam and a talk with his boss, the Warden himself, Trey Oliver. They told me that the men and women sent there by the courts often come from communities and families where it is accepted as normal that young people will be taken away and locked up for most or even all of their lives. In those neighbourhoods, up to 80 per cent of crime is committed by a handful of families; generation after generation living the same way and finding themselves, as night follows day, behind bars.

Sam had no doubt that the jail population would increase. Crime was going up. 'The inmates have changed,' he said. 'That age group, from eighteen to twenty-eight, they just don't care about anything – they cannot be controlled and they will end up in jail for a long time.' I asked for his view on the argument that this 'tough' approach to sentencing was there as a deterrent; surely, the logic goes, if your friend, your brother or your father is locked away for twenty years, that will be a lesson to stop you following the same path? 'Not at all,' Sam replied, without hesitation. 'I wouldn't want to spend a single night in jail, but for them, believe it or not, a long sentence is a status symbol.'

I left Alabama with an even greater sense than ever that this approach to criminal justice is a stain on American democracy and the values that the US claims to stand for. In an effort to find some balance, I stopped off at the Ebenezer Baptist Church in Atlanta, en route to the airport for the flight home. Across the street from the modest family church, which was attended by Martin Luther King as a child and lies just a hundred yards away from the small house where he grew up, stands a massive modern megachurch, presided over for more than a decade by the Reverend Raphael G. Warnock Ph.D.

It was the early Sunday service at the new Ebenezer Baptist and the dozens of pews were filling up quickly as I arrived. I was welcomed with a bright smile by one of the ushers and shown to a prime seat, next to the central aisle. By the time the service began, there must have been 500 in the congregation, all impeccably dressed and all black, save for me and possibly five other white people.

This was worship as I have never seen it before, more like a rock concert than a cold English parish church on a dark November morning. Massive video screens sat to each side of the choir of fifty or so choristers, music blasted out from giant speakers and the entire morning's proceedings were streamed live via the church's slick website (www. ebenezeratl.org).

A compère introduced Reverend Warnock with all the enthusiasm and gusto of an announcer at a world title fight. As soon as he appeared and took hold of the microphone, it was clear that this was a man not only of substance and character, but with charisma and charm in abundance. A handsome black man, of indeterminate age and perfectly groomed, he called for quiet. It was, he explained, 'Men's Week' at Ebenezer Baptist – a time to celebrate the men of the congregation and to recognise their value to the church and the community. Looking around, I could tell that men were in a minority, and young men were almost entirely missing from the congregation.

Before his sermon, Reverend Warnock introduced a glossy video presentation which showed some of the campaigning and crusading work undertaken by the church, in Atlanta and beyond. The very first sequence extolled the church's Freedom Day Project, aimed at changing America's approach to imprisonment, which has hit black communities so much harder than any other racial group (black men are more than five times more likely to spend time in prison in the US than whites).

Reverend Warnock himself appeared on screen in a recorded segment, addressing a large rally of criminal justice campaigners. It was as if the film had been made with my visit in mind. His opening line went something like this: 'It is a source of shameful injustice that "the land of the free" is in fact the land of mass incarceration.' These words were delivered in a passionate and powerful timbre, redolent of Martin Luther King himself.

I looked around at the hundreds of women, mostly sitting alone or in groups with other women congregants, nodding and letting out the occasional 'Amen' as the sermon progressed. I wondered how many of them had seen a son, a husband, a brother or father fall into the Venus flytrap of US criminal justice. How many had been forced to make long, expensive and painful journeys to some distant prison, perhaps even out of state, to suffer the indignity of searches and standing in line to spend an hour or two in a visiting room, before an equally arduous trip home.

Statistically speaking I was in no doubt: many if not most of these women, dressed in their Sunday best, must have seen a man in their life spend some time in a correctional facility of one kind or another. For those on the outside, pining for a loved one and the grandchildren they may never have, the sentence is no less real than for the inmate himself.

The guest sermon that day was from Professor Cleophus J. LaRue Junior. He was – if anything – an even greater orator than Reverend Warnock himself. His theme was the need for every one of us to 'take charge of our own lives'; not to wait for God to step in and solve everything for us. He spoke of the independent spirit of all Americans and how that should be reflected in self-reliance, rather than dependence on God or anyone else, to make life better and to live life well.

In a rousing peroration, Professor LaRue quoted William Henley's 'Invictus', a rage against loss of hope in the face of death:

It matters not how strait the gate,
How charged with punishments the scroll,
I am the master of my fate,
I am the captain of my soul.

If only, I thought to myself; if only that were true for that vast hidden army of African Americans and their fellow prisoners of every race and creed, shuffling to the mess hall, waiting in line for medication, sleeping on a plastic canoe on a concrete floor.

After the service, I sought out Reverend Warnock at the free breakfast provided to all those who attended church. Taking my chance, between the many admirers who asked for a moment of his time, I thanked him for the message. I told him of my mission, to understand the US criminal justice system and its prisons, and I asked him straight: 'Your campaign to end mass incarceration, is it ever going to succeed?'

He looked a little surprised at the directness of the question, paused briefly, and replied: 'Well, we certainly hope so, we will keep on trying.' He shook my hand and moved quickly along to the next person in line.

The preacher's answer to my question was the least convincing thing he said all morning.

A DIFFERENT WAY

Looking back at Michael – he of the banana-point robbery – and at so many other clients over the years, and thinking of all the things I saw and heard in the Deep South, it is clear to me that the use of imprisonment, as we practise it today, is an affront to humanity. On top of that, prison achieves the diametrically opposite outcome to that intended – more crime, not less, and more victims, not fewer.

Like so many of those I saw in the Mobile County Jail, in Manchester Michael had been sent to custody for the first time in his teens. He came out after a few months, with greatly reduced life chances, the stain of a criminal record, and a group of friends and associates more criminally experienced than himself. He took drugs and fell into the company of dealers and thieves.

Before long Michael was back inside, this time for a bit longer. And so the pattern grew – sentences increasing, rehabilitation and addiction issues ignored, crimes escalating in gravity and the courts getting 'tougher and tougher' with each appearance. Until he finally received that automatic life sentence that would see many of his remaining days whittled away in a prison cell.

Let me be clear then – prison *does not work*. Every single day of every single prison sentence makes society that little bit poorer. Prison time, whether imposed incrementally or in one go, wipes out the life chances of most of those who go there. It increases the overall level of crime and – the real kick in the teeth for the 'lock 'em up' brigade – prison means more victims of crime. Yes, more victims of theft, burglary, robbery, and even rape and murder.

Prison is a medicine which we as a society keep on taking even when it has grown obvious that, far from helping to make us safer, it is causing harm to all of us, every day.

So what should we be doing instead?

There are a few beacons of light in the darkness of our infatuation with incarceration. The Scandinavian nations have some of the lowest rates of imprisonment in the world and, at the same time, fewer crimes and criminals than almost anywhere else.

Norway, a highly educated and economically advanced society, has one of the smallest prison populations on earth; around 3,000 people out of a total population of 5.3 million. That is a rate of incarceration one-twelfth of that in the US and under half of that in Britain.

Those few Norwegians who do find themselves 'behind bars' will discover that, in some cases, there are not even any bars. Norway's Halden Prison is as far from the British and American model as one could imagine.

Following a philosophy of 'Nordic exceptionalism', the ethos of Halden is that 'everyday life should not be a sentence'. The deprivation of liberty is considered the punishment. As a recent news report explained:

Normalising life behind bars (not that there are any bars on the windows at Halden) is the key philosophy that underpins the Norwegian Correctional service. At Halden, this means not only providing daily routines but ensuring family contact is maintained too. Once every three months, inmates with children can apply to a 'Daddy In Prison' scheme which, if they pass the necessary safeguarding tests, means they can spend a couple of nights with their partner, sons and daughters in a cosy chalet within the prison grounds.

It is easy to imagine the response to such a proposal in Alabama, Atlanta or, for that matter, Milton Keynes. Politicians and the media would be up in arms protesting about going 'soft on crime'. They would trot out the equally clichéd mantra: 'What about the victims?'

Most of us know someone who has been the victim of crime and many of us have experienced it ourselves. It is for victims, even more than for those who commit crime, that I make the arguments set out in these pages. We need to do everything within our power to reduce the number of victims in future.

Back then to Norway and the 'Nordic Way'. Is the 'softness' of the criminal justice system – the small prison population, the shortness of sentences and the benevolent conditions of Halden and the other Norwegian prisons – a recipe for criminals to laugh at society, head out and commit the same crimes all over again?

The answer is a resounding No. For those convicted of a crime and imprisoned in Norway, the rate of recidivism is barely 20 per cent. In the US it reaches a staggering 75 per cent, representing a rate of failure of such huge proportions as to sound like a statistical error. If you do something astronomically expensive and deeply damaging, with specific aims in mind (less crime/fewer victims), *and your strategy fails three times out of four*, do you keep on doing it? Not only keep on doing it but double down and do it even more?

Well, irrational as it sounds, that is exactly what we are doing in Britain. Sentences have been ratcheting ever upwards for decades. The direction of travel for our prison population only briefly paused because of massive cuts in police numbers and funding for the courts, which in turn reduced the numbers coming through the criminal justice system as defendants. As we have seen, Britain's latest Conservative government is intent on seeing prisoner numbers rise. Boris Johnson won the December 2019 election on a rousing 'get tough' platform, without the slightest consideration of the evidence or the consequences.

So what should we do instead? That is a reasonable question to ask of someone who, like me, believes that what we are doing right now is so catastrophically wrong.

I believe that the answer is simple. We should close down all prisons and start again.

For the vast majority of inmates, locked up for non-violent crimes, incarceration in a prison not only lacks any positive purpose but – without question – increases rates of recidivism and a whole host of other harms: loss of employment, financial ruin, relationship breakdown, poor health, homelessness and addiction. Non-violent criminals should never be sent to a prison of the kind that we have now. All of the Victorian and other traditional institutions, designed in a bygone age, should be closed down and turned into entertainment complexes or apartment buildings. Or razed to the ground once and for all.

For those who have harmed nobody, towering walls topped with razor wire, tiny cells with barred windows reminiscent of Alcatraz, guards in quasi-military uniforms, are nothing less than a cruel anachronism. They are there purely because they have been there as long as we can remember. Given a fresh start, without the prejudices and predilections of the past, we would no more build prisons as we know them today than we would decide to make our homes in caves.

What then to do with those prisoners who pose no more risk of harming another human being than anyone else walking the streets among us? The beginning of an answer can be found in Norway and the small number of other nations in which forcible detention in arcane custodial facilities has been largely phased out.

The Norway model is a good experiment but, for me, it does not go far enough. Halden succeeds by taking steps to make life on the inside as 'normal' as possible. The focus of the regime is not punishment – an illusory notion in any event when you consider the likes of Michael (and most other long-term inmates). Nor is it deterrence, which is equally a nonsense, as anyone on the inside of the criminal justice system will attest (nobody commits crime at all if they think they will be caught, whatever the sentence, unless of course they actually *want* to be caught).

The entire ethos of Halden is to focus not on the period of incarceration, relatively short in Norway by UK and US standards, but on the day of the prisoner's release. And the day after that. As we have seen, Norway is extremely effective in releasing inmates back into society, never to see them return to the criminal justice system again.

Bearing in mind that, given the sparing use of custodial sentences in the first place, Norwegian prisons house only the most serious criminals in the system (unlike the UK and the US, with so many petty offenders in custody), Norway's success rate in reducing reconviction is even more remarkable.

Norway has taken several steps towards ending the outdated and perverse practice of exiling our fellow citizens into the otherness of incarceration. The next step is to stop doing it at all, at least in anything like the way we do now.

Setting aside for a moment the tiny group of offenders who present a real and immediate risk of harm to the public – of whom a handful may never be safe to release onto the streets again – every single person entering prison will, sooner or later, come out. If they emerge, as Michael and others did so many times, into an unforgiving and alien landscape in which they are largely excluded from mainstream society and the comforts of life, the evidence – and common sense – suggests that they will offend again. This vicious circle – one of our own creation and perpetuation – will continue.

Many experts, with a deep understanding of imprisonment and a lifetime of experience and research, have come to the same broad conclusions to which I have been driven, both in my professional life and in my wide travels and research for this book.

A 2016 report on the abolition of prisons in their present form concluded that 'prisons are inherently problematic institutions: they are places of interpersonal and institutional violence and legal, social and corporal death, and these terrible outcomes are structured within the very fabric of penal institutions.'

My own conclusion is one of simplicity, pragmatism and logic – leave those convicted of most crimes in their own homes. Let them go to work, to college or to engage in some other productive activity, be it taking their children to school, caring for their elderly parents or the host of other responsibilities that the rest of us have to cope with. Some will need significant support, to cope with addictions, mental and physical health problems, the lifelong scars of trauma that most of those in prison bear, but they will at least have a chance of leaving the custodial merry-go-round once and for all; of having a life without the self-perpetuating psychological destruction that prison represents.

Won't they just go back to a life of crime? Some may do so of course, just as most prisoners do now. But I do not suggest that there should be no attempt to prevent reoffending at all. What more rational means of detention and control, where such measures are absolutely necessary, than the walls of a home? House arrest, home detention, call it what you will; we have the technology to monitor every breath, every heartbeat, and certainly whether a convicted person is staying at home, going to work, or dropping his or her children off at school.

During filming for my recent BBC series on criminal justice, we gained access in London to an exhibition of the latest security and law-enforcement technology, available not in a decade but today, in the 2020s. On display were ultra-high-definition cameras, feeding live video content into an artificial-intelligence engine, aided by facial recognition, biometric monitoring and a host of other technologies. This equipment is already in use in public spaces, to a worrying degree in many ways, but its potential as a substitute for the physical confinement of prison is clear.

A smiling and enthusiastic Chinese saleswoman, whose technology was by far the most sophisticated on display, happily confirmed that the products she was selling could 'monitor everyone in society, wherever they go and whatever they do, twenty-four hours a day'. This was a real selling point for her employer. Indeed, it sounds eerily similar to a rather more ancient form of supervision and control, about which you have been reading – prison, going back to the design intended for total observation and control, known as Bentham's panopticon.

There is no doubt that we have the technology to provide a 'virtual prison' environment for every person who has become embroiled in the criminal justice system, which would allow an unlimited variation of restrictions and permissions so as to cater for each individual. If there is a need to exclude the offender from a particular part of town, or to verify that he is at work or college, attending counselling or a rehabilitation course, all monitoring could be achieved by remote and automated systems, at a tiny fraction of the cost of physical imprisonment for twenty-four hours a day.

Many – if not most – of those currently in prison would not need even this level of monitoring. A large number of non-violent first offenders, provided they were not in the grips of addiction, debt or psychiatric distress, would learn their lesson from the mere fact of being caught. With the right support in the community, they would mostly re-engage with work, home and family, never to enter a police station, let alone a prison, again. And in far greater numbers than if they had been locked away – for weeks, months or years – to 'teach them a lesson'.

With a small fraction of the vast resources freed up through closing down and selling off the whole of the current prison estate, a new era of effective, well-funded rehabilitation courses, drug treatment programmes, family and housing support, psychiatric treatment and care facilities could be established. Furthermore, victims of crime, often now forgotten in the justice system, could be provided with a wealth of practical support, compensation and counselling, currently undreamt of by the hard-pressed volunteers of victim-support services.

Finally, what then of those we fear the most – the killers, the rapists and the paedophiles – who pose a danger of the most serious harm and even death to others? The first thing to realise is just how few such dangerous people there are, relative to the total UK prison population of about 83,000, let alone the millions of the US City of Incarceration. At the time of writing, just sixty-three UK prisoners have committed crimes so heinous, and posing so high a level of risk to the public, that the courts have deemed them unsuitable *ever* to be released. In Britain that means the imposition of a so-called 'Whole Life Order', under which the prisoner will never be eligible for release and will die in prison.

Excluding the tiny number of 'Whole Life' inmates, those deemed 'dangerous offenders', including those serving life and other long sentences for the most violent crimes, are in the order of 10,000. Some of those, and only an expert assessment could best determine how many, certainly do need to be separated from society, at least for some period of time, pending their eventual release. But it is essential to bear in mind that almost all of them will one day be released back into society.

The question is what kind of temporary secure environment will best ensure that the risk they represent now will be minimised or eliminated by the time they next walk the streets, whenever that may be. For me, the answer is clear: we need to make secure environments as close to the real world as possible, taking the Norwegian model one step further and creating secure communities, sharing almost nothing in common with the soulless prison institutions of today.

Naturally, there would need to be a secure perimeter, but modern engineering would permit of a host of solutions to this essential design feature, less psychologically destructive than a redbrick wall and layer upon layer of barbed wire. Within the grounds of these new establishments, what facilities? Again, taking Halden one step further, we should build homes, either apartments or shared houses, as close to their equivalent on the outside as would be consistent with the security required for each prisoner. Those deemed least dangerous, and capable of living without constant observation and control, would occupy living quarters indistinguishable from a basic but comfortable home.

Others might need higher levels of security, but technology would come into play, allowing monitoring and security measures to be as unobtrusive as possible; life would be lived in as natural a fashion as could be achieved. For just a few, to protect others or themselves, direct and constant security, possibly containment for longer periods of time, might be needed, but such conditions would be imposed only in response to a direct and immediate threat to others (or to the prisoners themselves).

Prisoners would have access to medical care, addiction and mental-health services, counselling, and the opportunity to engage in productive work and education, as close in kind to that available to them outside custody. The overriding and guiding principles for the whole regime would be to prepare inmates for release, reduce the risks they represent to others, and to do everything possible to ensure that they could engage, peacefully and fruitfully, with the rest of us.

For most, I have no doubt – and the experiences of Norway, Holland and a few other enlightened nations consistently confirm it – that the risk of harm to others, of further offending and of a return to prison in the future would be dramatically lower than under the system we practise now. Not only would the costs to society be lower, by every conceivable measure, but all of us – as citizens – would be enriched by the disappearance from our national life of our institutions of horror and human degradation.

If we continue down the road of mass incarceration, we face the clear and present danger of ending up like Alabama, where federal investigators found that the state 'routinely violated the constitutional rights of prisoners by failing to protect them from prisoner-on-prisoner attacks and sexual abuse'. An Alabama civil rights group found that 'there are persistent reports of ignoring prisoners' mental health problems, improper use of segregation, and inadequate measures to protect prisoners in segregation at risk of suicide.'

The Justice Department investigated Alabama's Department of Corrections in 2019 and passages of their report were published by the *New York Times*. They included this chilling summary of what the investigators found: 'graphic accounts of prisoners who were tortured, burned, raped, sodomized, stabbed and murdered in largely unsupervised dorms'.

Is that really where we want to end up? Or, when it comes to imprisonment at least, is it time to steer our criminal justice system decisively, once and for all, in a completely new direction?

3

Why we should legalise drugs

'The streets are awash with drugs you can have
for unhappiness and pain, and we took them
all. Fuck it, we would have injected Vitamin C
if only they'd made it illegal.'

– Mark Renton (in Irvine Welsh,
Trainspotting)

In the late afternoon of a dark October day, I parked my
car at the roadside, near a redbrick Victorian mill to the
north of Manchester. I was early for a meeting with junior
counsel and my instructing solicitor. Torrential rain fell,
cold and intimidating as it bounced off the bonnet of my
car; perhaps a northern warning to leave this place and get
on my way.

I flicked through a thick file of evidence – photographs,
plans, video stills, witness statements and police reports.
Some of the photographs depicted the mill now visible
from within my car. Others showed various locations on
the inside of the building and, in particular, its cobbled
courtyard, which is the location we were meeting to examine
in preparation for a trial, due to begin a few weeks later.

Junior counsel arrived, late from a court hearing, and then the solicitor parked up behind me. Like me, they were both case-hardened professionals, veterans of criminal practice, accustomed to processing evidence of the most serious and – on occasion – gruesome crimes.

The rain showed no sign of abating, so we had no choice but to head into the mill, sharing a solitary umbrella, trying unsuccessfully to avoid drenching our black polished shoes and suit trousers in the puddles and the mud. This was a bleak place. Built in a different age, the mill was once a hive of industry, back when Lancashire was home to the most advanced industrial economy on the planet.

Heads down, crime-scene photographs and drawings in hand, we trudged down a short cobbled lane and into the central courtyard of the mill. It was a dark hulk of a building, largely derelict above the ground-floor level. Trees sprouted from the mill's windows and even from the roof several storeys above us. It had been a long time since American cotton arrived at this place or any pristine rolls of fabric emerged.

On the opposite side of the courtyard from the mill itself was a scrapyard, overflowing with the carcasses of cars, vans and trucks. Set behind a high steel fence, topped with barbed wire and overseen by a CCTV camera 20 feet up on a tower, the yard did not look like a business with much profit potential.

The scrapyard's camera pointed downwards, surveying not only skeletal vehicles and car parts but the whole of the courtyard and the lower level of the mill itself. The only commercial activity in evidence at the mill was a small unit where one of the loading bays had been converted into a car-repair workshop. This was presided over by a single mechanic, hammer in hand, oil-stained from head to toe, banging away at a body panel of indeterminate utility. Somewhere between thirty and forty years old, rolled-up cigarette in his mouth, he eyed the three besuited lawyers with suspicion. This was almost certainly the first time that a collar and tie had been worn in this yard in a long time.

We waved politely at the mechanic as we got our bearings from the plans, photos and video stills in the evidence file. Parked up next to the car workshop was a small caravan; the kind usually hitched to the back of a car, no more than 10 feet long and perhaps 7 feet wide. It was filthy on the outside, several of its Perspex windows cracked, and one pane had been replaced altogether with a sheet of polythene, attached with duct tape. Remarkably, there was a glimmer of light from the inside, telling us that a person lived here.

Conscious of intruding not only on a workplace but on someone's home, we walked quickly around the caravan to an area enclosed to our left by the external wall of the car workshop, to the rear by the caravan itself, and to the front by the main wall of the mill building. Each of us turned and looked up, around and behind us, back in the direction of the scrapyard, to confirm what we already knew. This small cobbled space, thick with mud, puddled from the pounding rain, strewn with empty beer cans and weeds, represented the only spot in the whole courtyard that the CCTV camera could not observe.

And that is the only reason why there was any mystery at all about the precise circumstances in which Gary Johnson had suffered the terrible injuries that led to his death, at the age of just forty-three, almost a year earlier.

THE LIFE AND DEATH OF GARY JOHNSON

Gary Johnson was a drug addict.

He was also a father, a son, a friend – a human being.

For much of his adult life, Gary took heroin every day, sometimes crack too, and other drugs if money or supplies were short.

Life for Gary was peppered with a few positive experiences, but mostly it consisted of misery and torment. His days were dominated by one thing – the overwhelming need for drugs and the limited number of ways in which he could get them.

At the time of his death, Gary was already in a terrible state of health, alive but barely living. Physically, he looked at least a decade older than his chronological age. His skin, teeth, hair and nails were in a state of neglect. Things were even worse on the inside – his organs were in poor condition; liver swollen from decades of substance abuse, a terrible diet and a lack of medical care. Mentally he was traumatised from the life on the streets. There was not much right with Gary's life.

Street drugs, especially heroin and crack, are expensive. Users like Gary may need a fix two, three or even more times every day, sometimes alternating between substances. Each hit costs £10 or £20, depending on the state of the local drug market and the purity of the supply. For those with the most entrenched drug habits, the cost of feeding an addiction can reach £100 or more a day, seven days a week, for ever.

That means £30,000 to £40,000 in cash, just to pay for drugs *every single year*. As we shall see, the quantity of heroin or cocaine finding its way into those individual drug deals is actually very small. Over in South America (source of cocaine to make crack) or Afghanistan (heroin), the pure drug needed to sustain the habit of someone like Gary would cost no more than a few pounds for an entire year. This tells you that the drug business, on the streets of Britain, is not about the drugs themselves – which literally grow on trees (and plants) in their countries of origin.

The drug business is about transport, logistics and supply chains. Just as a farmer in Kenya receives only a few pennies for a mango that may sell for twenty or thirty times as much in a British supermarket, so the humble producer of coca leaves or opium poppies receives a tiny fraction of the eventual street price in a developed country. At every stage of the drug supply chain, the pure drug is diluted with cheaper substances, and profit is added each time. Packages travel from farm to processor or producer, to cartel, through countries, across borders, on ships and planes, and on and on, cut and repackaged, until finally reaching a low-level dealer, willing and able to sell people like Gary a bag of smack or a tiny rock of crack.

Along the way, billions of pounds of profit are extracted – tax-free. The human costs associated with the trade are vast beyond imagining. We will consider the overall picture shortly – the human slavery, corruption and unconscionable loss of life in the world drug market – but for now, we can see its terrible impact on the lives of a handful of people in the North of England.

Gary did not have £30,000 or more a year in disposable income to allow him to service his addiction to drugs; at least without resorting to some form of criminal behaviour to raise it. Still less did he have access to some alternative, safer and cheaper source of supply. But he needed those drugs, from the moment he opened his eyes each day until he passed out, somewhere, each night.

Gary tried to avoid harming others, or stealing from his neighbours in the community, and he was not a violent man, capable of robbery or the like. He had, of course, been arrested, locked up a few times, walked the criminal justice treadmill more than once; nobody ever offered him a way out. No help was available to take him away from the daily toil of managing his more and more urgent feelings of withdrawal – the desperate quest for enough money for a first fix, meeting a dealer, shooting up, that brief flash (ecstasy?) as the heroin kicked in, melting the world away for a while, then back to the start of the cycle a few hours later. Day after day until Gary died, following the incident at the mill.

Under the system of drug prohibition, and the criminal supply chains it enables, very few of those who are most addicted to drugs can avoid all involvement in dealing, even if at the very lowest rung of the ladder. By that I mean taking care of the menial tasks that are essential for street dealers and low-level wholesalers to make the business work. Someone needs to store the drugs, cut them, weigh and package them, collect the money and feed it back up the supply chain, link by link, to line the pockets of those higher up.

At the bottom of this drug heap was Gary. There are millions like him around the world. Drug users provide a plentiful supply of cheap labour, abused by the dealers and gangs in the sure and certain knowledge that they will never go to the police, never say no, never cheat their employer, for fear of the consequences. At least, that is how it usually works. Sometimes, despite all the risks, the temptation of some ready cash or a bag of heroin, however dangerous the dealer to whom it belongs, may simply be too much for the Garys of this world. They help themselves to that one extra fix, to a £20 note here and there, and, before they know it, the books do not add up.

Drug dealers, from the bottom up, are nothing if not commercially aware. I once had a client, Steve, who had left school at the age of fourteen, was barely literate, had never passed an exam, but had reached the very top of the drug world. He was an importer of tonnes of cannabis at a time, making millions of pounds a year in profit, running an empire as complex and sophisticated as any international commercial venture.

Given the dangers of writing down details of customer transactions, debts owed, sales made, wages paid and profits earned by drug dealers – although a surprising number do just that – Steve kept it all in his head. He knew exactly where every penny in his business had come from and exactly how much should have been left, provided nobody had his hand in the stock cupboard or was on the take. Those who worked in Steve's business, from the bottom to the top, were painfully aware of the consequences of pocketing even a few pounds or a couple of grams – at best, a harrowing warning, underwritten by extreme menace; at worst, a painful death, as a lesson to others. Rarely was it necessary to give that lesson, such was Steve's grip on his empire.

Gary did not work for Steve, but he did end up working for a dealer of exactly the same ilk. Gary was at the bottom of the ladder; a street runner, expected to collect a few hundred pounds from here and take it to there, maybe hold an ounce or two of stock, waiting for onward supply. For this Gary risked arrest, imprisonment and violence at every turn, both from his own side and from gang rivals for the lucrative local drug market.

Two levels up from Gary was Andy. In his late twenties, Andy had already served a long sentence for drug supply, violent assault and a host of other crimes. Not long out on licence from his most recent period in prison, Andy was soon back in business, running the street-level drug trade in a small part of town. Gary was at first a customer, but before long Andy saw an easy target for exploitation; a disposable human being to be controlled, abused as needed and discarded at will.

It is not clear how long Gary worked for Andy – possibly a week, a month or so at the most. It is also impossible to know the truth of what happened, to set in train the sequence of events that led Gary, Andy and several others to the dismal surroundings of the mill and that blind spot in front of the ramshackle caravan. All we know for sure is that, rightly or wrongly, Andy came to believe that Gary had ripped him off to the tune of about £250. And it was that belief, and that sum of money, which led to Gary's death.

Accompanied by two of his underlings, Andy went on the hunt for Gary in a high-performance BMW. It did not take long to find him, shuffling along a street, somewhere between a high and a low, depending on how long it had been since he last shot up. Gary was forced into the back seat of the car and driven towards the mill. On the way, after a few phone calls, Andy's car stopped next to a Ford Focus, driven by another man, Rick, who had his girlfriend, Sharon (who was also Andy's sister), in the passenger seat and their two young children – aged two and four – in the back.

About all of this there was no doubt. CCTV cameras scattered around the neighbourhood, together with cellphone data from all involved, allowed the police to piece together everyone's movements in the course of the highly efficient murder investigation that followed Gary's death. There were gaps in the footage, however, which could not explain how Rick and Sharon ended up entering the mill, in convoy with Gary's car, around fifteen minutes after the initial rendezvous. By this point, though, the two children were no longer in the back of the second car.

The arrival of the two vehicles at the mill was captured from the lofty perspective of the CCTV camera, perched atop its metal pole, inside the scrapyard. Andy's car pulled to a stop a few yards from the caravan and the vehicle-repair shop. Andy got out of the driver's seat, at the same time as the front-seat passenger and someone from the rear. A few seconds later, Gary was coaxed, possibly cajoled, to get out of the car himself. There was no sound on the recording so it was impossible to know what was said between the men.

What was clear from the body language alone was that Andy was not happy with Gary. With Andy shouting at him, his two sidekicks to the left and right, Gary visibly shrank away, holding up his hands in both protestation and surrender, denying – I have no doubt – that he had stolen the money. 'There must be some mistake', he surely repeated, all the while backing away towards the area of the blind spot created by the caravan and the walls of the mill. Demonstrating a complete lack of surveillance awareness, which quality I have seen in abundance higher up in the drug world, Andy and the other two advanced on him, edging closer all the time with Gary backing slowly away.

At this point, Rick emerged from the second car and walked towards Gary, Andy and the other two. All the men there were dressed in similar clothing – either jeans or tracksuit bottoms, sweatshirts or hooded tops, dark colours, fairly indistinguishable from each other. In fact, one of the men wore his hood up and over his head, hiding his face completely from the view of the camera from the start of the incident to its tragic end. The hooded man has not been identified to this day, at least to the police. As far as can be determined, he continues to walk the streets, whatever role he may have played in what happened next. What others were doing could not be gleaned from the silent footage alone.

Seconds later, an elderly woman emerged from the side door of the caravan, right next to where the altercation was taking place. She said something to the group surrounding Gary and then walked towards Sharon – some form of discussion then took place between the two women. What was said remains a mystery. The caravan lady refused to speak to the police about what she saw and heard that day. There was never an independent eyewitness, any more than there was video footage, as to what happened next.

What we do know is this – Gary backed up further and further, hands raised in front of him in supplication, until he disappeared altogether from the camera's view of events. Andy and his assistants followed, until they too could no longer be seen. Rick, Sharon and caravan lady all entered the blind spot at one stage or another.

Minutes later and it was over, with everyone emerging back into the area captured by the camera, some back to the cars, the lady into her caravan, and away the visitors went. Everyone emerged – that is, except for Gary. He did reappear but, when he did, he was already carrying the injuries from which he would never recover. He staggered across the courtyard, holding his chest; his stomach, clothes and face stained with mud and blood. He hobbled away, slowly, anaesthetised by his last fix of heroin.

Gary somehow managed to get to his girlfriend's house. She was worried about him. He was a mess, even for a drug addict, where injury and a lack of self-care are hardly unusual. She told him to go to hospital, but to start with he refused. Hospitals mean questions and questions mean the police, and the police mean that, next time, he will not be left to walk away. The ticking time bomb of his collapsing organs, already in sub-prime condition, and the haemorrhaging that had begun, had not registered in Gary's mind.

Eventually, it became obvious that something was very wrong; an ambulance was called, which arrived and took Gary to hospital under blue lights and sirens. The medical staff went to work with their customary efficiency and skill, trying to stop the internal bleeding and patch up Gary's numerous wounds and other injuries, which included several broken ribs, one of which had pierced a vital organ. He was stabilised for a time, but for Gary this was the end of the road. His reluctance to call an ambulance and the critical lost hours before he finally got medical help had proved fatal – he died of his injuries within a couple of days.

The greatest tragedy of this story is, of course, the death of a man whose daily life was already filled with suffering, but who left behind a partner, children, family and others who cared for him, no matter how great the impact of his addiction on their own lives.

But that was not the end of things. Gary had been kicked and beaten to death. Before he died, he told his partner who was responsible, where it had happened and some of the miserable details. In the midst of her grief, she told the police what Gary had said and a murder investigation began. The first action of the investigators was to visit the mill where I myself eventually came to stand, many months later, to survey the crime scene.

The sequence of events was revealed by the CCTV in the scrapyard and other cameras in the neighbourhood – on shops, office buildings, operated by the traffic department – and it did not take long for the police to establish the route of the two cars and, from there, the identity of those involved. All, that is, bar the one hooded man whose name nobody ever spoke and who has never been prosecuted for his role in Gary's death.

Andy was arrested; his house searched, which led the police to Sharon and Rick, at the time living under the same roof; then on to one of the other two men from Rick's car, who had not been so wise in his choice of head covering. They were all arrested and taken to the police station; Sharon's two children were left with her mother, Denise, who now found herself in a much emptier house – her son Andy, her daughter Sharon, and Rick, the father of her grandchildren, all detained in police cells, waiting to be interviewed about the circumstances of Gary's death or, more precisely, about his murder.

None of them would be coming home any time soon. Within days, all of them – as well as a teenager identified from the CCTV – were charged with Gary's murder. They each appeared before the courts, were refused bail and remanded to prison to await trial, months later.

Gary's murder typifies so many needless deaths in our world of senseless drug prohibition. Addicts like him live a miserable life, with no compassion or effective medical support. They become embroiled in crime, just to get enough heroin, crack or spice to see them through to the end of each day. Dealers like Andy live between prison sentences, working for someone higher up the chain, using threats, violence, money and drugs to keep the supply chain moving, without interruption, into the veins, noses and lungs of the addicted.

Families, friends and children all become caught up in the trade, directly or indirectly, whether they like it or not. Nobody – absolutely nobody – benefits from the whole sorry mess. Not even the dealers and suppliers at the very top – they too have low life expectancies, and most will eventually be identified, investigated and locked up, for decades or even for the rest of their lives. Someone else will then at once take their place – drugs never, ever, stop reaching those who seek them out, for pleasure or addiction. The incidental human cost of the drug trade is on a scale only otherwise seen in times of war and pestilence. All of it – as we shall see – is a direct consequence of the irrational policy of prohibition, characterised for decades as a 'War on Drugs', but which is in truth a war of politicians against some of the most vulnerable people in our society.

I do not for a minute excuse Andy, nor those he took with him to visit upon Gary a ruthless and sustained punishment beating. They knew what they were doing, and they chose to do it. But they, just as much as Gary, were only there because the law has surrendered the supply of drugs to those labelled criminals, because society has absolved itself of all responsibility for ensuring the safety of drugs supplied, for the health of those addicted to them, and for the security of communities in which gang crime and lethal violence are out of control.

The painful irony is that there is barely a foodstuff or consumer product that does not have a host of regulations to ensure its safety for the public, and yet drugs enter the human body with no official quality control at all, sold on an unlicensed black market where the deadliest and most sinister of commercial practices prevail.

A few weeks after the defendants were charged, I received a call from my clerks to ask if I would be interested in acting for one of them. For twenty years my practice consisted almost entirely of serious and organised crime cases, including murder, as well as numerous forms of financial crime. Since my appointment as Queen's Counsel in 2013, however, I have undertaken fewer and fewer cases of what lawyers call 'general crime', meaning everything from robbery and rape to murder and serious assault. This is, in part, because of drastic cuts in legal aid funding for such cases (up to 70 per cent in real terms) for QCs defending in murder trials, but also because such cases eventually blur into one.

My diary for the year ahead was full of commitments in an exotic array of hearings, from illegal fishing off the coast of West Africa (a very big business) to police officers accused of serious misconduct, billionaires attacking their staff and financial wrongdoing of every possible kind. Not only would defending in a murder case mean a vast amount of work – and rightly so – but it would represent a net financial loss for every hour spent working on it. Fees for criminal legal aid cases have reached such low levels that they are no longer covered by the Bar's longstanding 'Cab Rank Rule', which obliges barristers to take cases offered to us, at a proper professional fee, provided they are within our experience and expertise. This rule, designed to ensure representation even for the morally reprehensible, no longer protects the poorest of defendants, who are wholly reliant on legal aid.

All of those very sensible, practical and commercial considerations went out of the window when my Senior Clerk – ever the salesman in his quest to fill diaries – told me what the case was about. I was not being asked to defend Andy, Rick or the young man directly implicated in kicking and beating Gary to death. The solicitors involved wanted me to act for Sharon, Rick's girlfriend and Andy's sister, who found herself accused of murder on the basis of a much-maligned concept of English Criminal Law: 'joint enterprise'.

By going to the mill with Rick and by approaching the exact location where Gary was attacked, out of view of the camera, it was alleged that Sharon was jointly responsible for the murder. The prosecution case was that, either by words of incitement or by making up the numbers, Sharon had encouraged her brother and the others to assault Gary, with every intention that he would be killed or caused to suffer serious bodily injury. If she had offered such encouragement with that intent in mind, even without laying a finger on the victim, the law would deem her as guilty of murder as the others. And in English law there is only one sentence for murder – life imprisonment. In practice, as we saw in chapter 2, that means an average minimum of over twenty years behind bars. For Sharon's young children, at the time shuttling between the care of their grandmothers, whilst their mother was on remand, this would mean that, for the entirety of their precious childhoods and beyond, their only contact with their parents would be in prison visiting rooms.

As soon as I understood that I was being asked to defend a 25-year-old woman, with two young children, who had never been arrested for anything in her life, now charged with murder, I knew that this was a case I had to accept. I would make room for it in my diary. This was exactly the sort of trial that I had in mind, back in my late teens, when I realised that becoming a criminal defence lawyer, specifically a jury advocate, was the only career I could ever imagine would satisfy my ambitions and match such skills and attributes as I possessed. It was also a case that arose from the world of drug dealing, about which I knew a lot, having acted in some of the largest heroin- and cocaine-trafficking cases for over twenty years. I accepted the brief.

In every murder case, in fact in every case where the events have taken place in a single location, it is my invariable habit to visit the scene of the crime – ostentatiously given the Latin title *'locus in quo'*, which translates as 'the place in which [it happened]'. Due to the same savage cuts previously described, such visits have become less common in criminal defence in England than they once were. In twenty-six years of practice, I have never yet visited a crime scene and failed to discover something that enhanced my understanding of the case and improved my client's chances of acquittal.

Which is why we suited lawyers were there, trudging through the mud and puddles, taking photos and videos on our phones, matching up the real location with the partial and distorted pictures we had seen on the CCTV footage. I often tell juries, in my closing speeches, that none of us are robots when we deal with cases of serious crime, especially the more tragic and horrific amongst them. As a law student of twenty years old, I worked for a summer in the office of the Crown Prosecution Service, part of a placement scheme operated at the time. I recall seeing a file of evidence, in a case involving the death of a child of around three years of age. She had been burnt by her parents, or one of them at least, with lit cigarettes. The post-mortem photographs are seared in my memory and will never leave – dozens and dozens of individual burn marks, at various stages of healing, the accumulation of which, in the end, had caused the child's death, writhing in pain.

Almost thirty years after seeing those photographs – with hundreds of cases of homicide, rape and serious violence under my belt – I found myself contemplating Gary's death: the sheer waste of human life, the senseless brutality and futility of it all. Imagine suffering injuries that would soon end your life, in a place like this, I thought to myself, bowing my head for a moment in the rain that had already soaked through my trousers and was running down the back of my neck. This was a truly sorry way for a life to end.

Why on earth did it have to happen at all? The answer is a simple one, but its origins go back a long way. Gary died for one reason – because he had no way to get drugs *without* becoming embroiled with those who eventually killed him in this dark and miserable place. He died because of our drug laws, pure and simple; he and thousands of others, in Britain and all over the world. How on earth did we get here? Why are we addicted as a society to laws that do no good, cost so much to enforce and destroy so many lives?

The suffering is not inflicted just on those, like Gary, whose lives are spent in misery, ending in a violent death. The lives of the dealers, the killers, their families, their children, whole communities besieged by drugs, crime and violence – all could be saved, if only some reason could be brought to bear on the laws and politics of the drug business.

We will return to the murder at the mill and the trial that took place. First, though, we will look at how we ended up with the madness of drug prohibition and, before long, will come to understand how we can finally escape from it, once and for all.

WHY PEOPLE WILL ALWAYS TAKE DRUGS

It is difficult to think of an example of human behaviour, other than those evolved directly to facilitate the creation and sustenance of life itself, more ingrained and universal than the ingestion of substances that alter our perception of reality.

There are countless research papers on the subject of the use of intoxicants by prehistoric mankind. They tell us something that we all know deep down – whether we like it or disapprove of it, people love to get high.

The earliest date for which I could find a credible reference to drug use by hominids was around 200 million years ago, from which period archaeological remains are said to provide evidence of the ingestion of psychoactive plants. Palaeogenetic research – not a form of evidence I have ever come across in day-to-day criminal practice – suggests the evolution in early humans of a capacity to metabolise ethanol (the form of alcohol found in beer, wine and spirits these days) around 10 million years ago.

The science simply confirms what is obvious: humans have always taken and will always take drugs. A highly regarded Spanish professor, Dr Elisa Guerra-Doce, wrote in 2015 of the evidence of drug use 10,000 or so years ago, including all of the drugs in common use today.

South and Central America are blessed (some may say cursed) with a cornucopia of natural hallucinogens, which the aboriginal inhabitants discovered – and became fond of – a very long time ago. Fossil records from a Peruvian cave suggest the ingestion by humans of the hallucinogenic San Pedro cactus between 8,600 and 5,600 BC. Intoxicating mescal seeds, in modern Texas and northern Mexico, appear to have been used in religious rituals for as long as 9,000 years. Stone sculptures in Guatemala, Mexico, Honduras and El Salvador point to the use of 'magic mushrooms' in 'sacred cults' between 500 BC and AD 900.

The evidence shows that coca leaves – the raw ingredient of cocaine and crack – have been chewed by humans in South America since around 8,000 BC.

Opium poppies – the source of morphine and heroin – have been harvested and prepared for human consumption since at least the mid-sixth millennium BC, based on archaeological findings from a dig site close to Rome.

What then of cannabis, marijuana, weed? The plant itself evolved some 28 million years ago on the eastern Tibetan Plateau and is closely related to the common hop, used all over the world in the brewing of beer. The cannabis plant still grows wild – just like any other weed – over much of Central Asia, and has been cultivated and harvested by Chinese farmers for use in oil, rope, clothing and paper for over 4,000 years.

Cannabis is the most popular of the widely prohibited drugs, with an estimated worldwide user base in the hundreds of millions. The earliest clear evidence of using weed to get high comes from the unlikely location of a cemetery in the far west of China, 3,000 metres up in the Pamir Mountains. Remains of wooden braziers, 'concentrated in the more elite tombs', tested positive for high levels of THC – the active and psychotropic ingredient of cannabis. The theory is that cannabis leaves and stones were placed in the brazier and set alight in the enclosed space of the tomb, allowing mourners to inhale the intoxicating fumes.

In the millennia that followed, right up to the present day, there has been no reduction in the use of these substances by our species. On the contrary, as our ancestors moved around and adapted to new environments and territories, agricultural techniques improved yield and increased potency in every category of drug. Shipping routes opened up to allow growers, particularly of opioids, cocaine and cannabis, to export their products to every corner of the planet.

The number of users has expanded rapidly, and the only obstacle to equilibrium in supply and demand has been the imposition of prohibition, taxation and other forms of control on the manufacture, supply and use of these popular substances.

There are many reasons why we as a species have become hooked on so many drugs – mixed, processed and imbibed in an infinite variety of ways – without pause, for tens of millennia. Some perhaps are obvious – opium seeds and opium itself are an excellent form of pain relief and must have seemed like something magical to those who first discovered them (presumably by chance or trial and error).

Coca leaves and cannabis, as we have seen, date back beyond history in their use and abuse, though 'drug abuse' is a term with which I would take issue; the use of a substance surely cannot be said to have an inherent moral quality, whether good or bad.

The mundane and timeless truth is that people take drugs – both of the 'legal' and the prohibited varieties – and that they always will. Set aside those, like Gary, held in the grip of a lifelong struggle with the most physically and psychologically addictive substances our species has ever seen; most drug users are, thankfully, not afflicted to that degree, to the extent that their every thought and action is underwritten by their last fix or dominated by their next one.

Most of those who take drugs are not addicted in the medical sense of the word. They are largely able to function 'normally' (whatever that means), even if impaired – at least some of the time – by their choice or impulsion to drink, smoke, snort, chew, swallow or inject. They work, study, raise children, live, love and die, sometimes harmed in numerous ways, large or small, but often finding that their habit actually enhances their achievements – creative, educational, social – or simply that it helps them get through hard times.

How then did we move from ancient tribal, cultural and religious use of hallucinogens and other intoxicants, fully accepted by all and with no element of moral impropriety, to a bizarre and inconsistent patchwork of restrictions, including – in the most extreme cases – laws imposing the death sentence for even low-level 'drug offending'?

HOW PROHIBITION HAPPENED (OR WHY WE ARE IN THIS MESS)

> 'Queen Victoria, I think by any standards, she loved her drugs.'
> – Tony McMahon, author and historian

The adjective 'Victorian' has become synonymous with a morally judgemental and repressive approach to many things in life, and in particular to personal conduct in the social and sexual spheres. From the length of skirts, to preserve the modesty of a young woman's calves and ankles, to bowdlerising Shakespeare's works to make them family-friendly, nineteenth-century Britain was marked – in public at least – by demonstrations of prudishness never seen before. As one historian put it: 'Between 1780 and 1850 the English ceased to be one of the most aggressive, brutal, rowdy, outspoken, riotous, cruel and bloodthirsty nations in the world and became one of the most inhibited, polite, orderly, tender-minded, prudish and hypocritical.'

The last of those qualities – hypocrisy – has come to define the approach of successive generations of politicians to the issue of drugs, as each has taken the reins of power. Until the nineteenth century, the use of intoxicants, whatever their chemical composition, was not considered a matter of moral failure, in and of itself. Naturally, drunken brawling in the streets after consuming far too much ale was a matter of concern for the local residents of many communities, but it was not the alcohol itself that caused moral opprobrium to be visited upon those – largely 'working-class' men – responsible for such behaviour. It was unseemly conduct in a public place – what we would now call 'antisocial behaviour' – that met with social disapproval.

When it came to the use of drugs, of whatever description, what went on behind closed doors, particularly in the homes of the upper classes, attracted little reprehension at all. That is not surprising, given the lead from the top. For, as many historians have noted, Queen Victoria herself – surely the very embodiment of proper behaviour and etiquette – really liked taking drugs.

The monarch enjoyed the full set of drugs derived from nature and available at the time. One of the first women to be given chloroform to ease the pain of childbirth, Her Majesty described the effects as 'soothing, quieting and delightful beyond measure'. This – I presume – was not an experience of childbirth that could have been achieved without the benefit of some pharmaceutical assistance.

Victoria would start the day with a tincture of opium – the drug was contained in a liquid of 90 per cent alcohol, so as to provide efficient delivery to the bloodstream – ensuring no doubt a pleasant segue from sleep to wakefulness and then into the many daily responsibilities of her rule. Visited by a young Winston Churchill, long before his role in saving the world from the Nazis, it is said that the Queen was always happy to accept a piece of the chewing gum of which the future Prime Minister was fond.

Rather than mint, however, the young Churchill's gum was laced with cocaine, which again rapidly made its effects known, entering the body through the mouth and gums.

More controversially in historical terms, it is said that Queen Victoria's personal physician, Sir J. Russell Reynolds, prescribed cannabis preparations to ease the monarch's 'menstrual cramps'. Whether or not Her Majesty was actually among those for whom Sir Russell provided this service, as a doctor he was certainly a big fan of the drug, writing in 1890: 'when pure and administered carefully, [cannabis] is one of the most valuable medicines we possess'.

It was only after the invention of the syringe, with its superior mechanism for delivering pain relief and, later, anaesthetic, that the use of cannabis for medical purposes began to diminish, given that the drug could not be prepared in injectable form.

In the nineteenth-century United States, Britain and many other countries, cannabis, cocaine, and opium preparations such as tincture of laudanum were available, with little difficulty and minimal sanctimony, to those who could pay for them; either from general stores, pharmacists or from doctors, and in a multitude of forms.

There were drug wars in the Victorian era but, unlike 'the War on Drugs' of modern times, they were provoked by the British, not with the aim of keeping drugs out of Britain and stopping their use, but to secure access to the lucrative Chinese market by force. The British fought the two Opium Wars of the nineteenth century in order to prevent the Chinese emperor from passing laws to prohibit trade in the drug, in the same hopeless manner as drug prohibition in modern times, by attempting to stop his subjects from taking opium at all. Unsurprisingly, with demand and addiction rising in the Chinese population, smugglers filled the gap in the supply chain, ensuring continuity of supply and ever-increasing profits for the British East India Company.

Given the profits to be made, and despite Chinese attempts at prohibition, it did not take long for the newly independent Americans to get in on the act. The grandfather of President Franklin Roosevelt, and the ancestors of former US Secretary of State John Kerry, were heavily involved in the illicit opium trade to China, which, at its peak, saw thousands of tonnes of the drug entering the country every year from British India.

Eventually, in a foretaste of contemporary news reports of 'massive drug seizures' by the US Drug Enforcement

Agency and the British National Crime Agency, the Chinese authorities decided to 'get tough'. Thousands of tonnes of opium were seized from the ports, but before long the British Royal Navy intervened to protect this valuable source of revenue, both for traders and for the Crown. Eventually, the Chinese were forced not only to fully legalise the opium trade but to grant access to even greater numbers of local ports and to permit freedom of movement for foreign traders throughout China.

Through pleasure for some and addiction for many, opium was entrenched in the lives of many Chinese men and women by the late nineteenth century, and the most powerful nations of the day controlled the trade and made the biggest profits from it.

This pattern characterises drug trafficking, trading and use to the present day. Millions of individuals want to take drugs, and are willing to pay a price for them high enough to handsomely reward everyone in the supply chain, from top to bottom, together with the political or military powers that permit the trade to operate in the first place.

There are at least 10,000 years of history and prehistory to demonstrate the irresistible and persistent attractions the use of intoxicants offers to mankind. Still, just a decade after Queen Victoria's death, the world began to move towards the system of moralistic and entirely unenforceable prohibition that continues to guide drug laws, in almost every country on earth, to this day.

'The War on Drugs' did not start with Richard Nixon's infamous declaration of 1969, nor his description of drug use as 'public enemy number one' two years later; although we will return to those. As in so many aspects of our lives in the past century or more, the United States was the driving force, leading us into the modern era of prohibition, law enforcement, mass incarceration, alienation, violence and death.

Despite its own decades-long role in the trafficking of opium to China, the United States took a sharp turn away from condoning the drug trade by convening an International Opium Commission in Shanghai in 1909. This was at the same time that the US prohibited the importation, sale, possession and use of opium for smoking, marking the first federal law to ban the non-medical use of a substance. It was followed by the First International Opium Conference in The Hague a little over two years later. Amid growing unease at the opium trade, in part due to a wave of domestic moralising over intoxicants in the US itself, thirteen nations, including the UK, France and China, eventually agreed the text of an International Opium Convention, which was signed at The Hague on 23 January 1912. This was the first international treaty designed to dramatically restrict the drug business. Its mission was clear, and applied not only to opium and its derivatives but to cocaine as well: 'The contracting Powers shall use their best endeavours to control, or to cause to be controlled, all persons manufacturing, importing, selling, distributing, and exporting morphine, cocaine, and their respective salts, as well as the buildings in which these persons carry such an industry or trade.'

Initially the Americans saw this as a regulatory provision, not an attempt to ban drugs altogether. In 1914, Congress passed the Harrison Act, which introduced rules and taxes affecting the production, importation and distribution of opiates and cocaine. This marks the last even vaguely sensible piece of drug legislation passed by the US Congress, and its effects were quickly whittled away to almost nothing by successive prohibitions of the substances to which the Act applies. A requirement to include understated words of caution on any licensed product containing opioids and other drugs is the only vestige of the Act that remains: 'Warning: May be habit forming'. You can say that again.

The Hague Convention entered fully into international law when it was incorporated into the Treaty of Versailles in 1919, following the end of the First World War. However, it was never intended to lead to the prohibition of drug trafficking or drug use. For that reason it was not long before the United States withdrew support for the Convention. Given the imminent introduction of the Volstead Act, which prohibited the sale of alcohol anywhere in the US, the Americans could no longer condone the supply of other intoxicating substances. Continuing a tradition of moralising around intoxication, grounded in the puritanism of the first settlers, the United States was set on the prohibition of all substances having the effect of interfering with man's 'God-given gifts' of intellect and reason.

In a ruling of brazen ignorance and moral hypocrisy, the US Supreme Court stated, in the landmark 1919 case of *Webb v United States*, that the maintenance of drug addicts by prescriptions from doctors was not a legitimate form of medical treatment. Thus, a court of politically appointed judges, with no experience at all of the treatment of addictions, saw fit to interfere in the exercise of professional discretion in the practice of medicine, based entirely on the court's *moral* view of those who had grown dependent on drugs. Having spent time in Switzerland with some of the most compassionate doctors I have ever met, with decades of experience of dependency and addiction treatment, I have no doubt at all of the idiocy of the position taken in *Webb* and of its pernicious impact on US drug policy ever since.

It was the perceived moral culpability of the user, rather than any inherent immorality of the substance, that so offended religious sensibilities and led to the prohibition of alcohol and so much of US drug policy at the time. As one historian put it, 'Drink itself was not looked upon as culpable, any more than food deserved blame for the sin of gluttony. Excess was a personal indiscretion.'

Despite the eventual repeal in 1933 of alcohol prohibition, widely considered one of the most catastrophic and damaging periods of public policy in history, the United States remained resolute in its opposition to the manufacture, supply and use of other intoxicants.

The Second World War marked a temporary respite from the accelerating march of drug criminalisation, but it was not long before even tighter legal controls were to be mandated throughout most of the world, driven largely by the values and policy priorities of the United States.

In Britain, in the meantime, it took much longer for the tub-thumping about 'cracking down' on drugs, and other language attributing moral opprobrium to both the substances and their users, to begin to influence public policy and to restrict society's access to drugs. Although opiates and cocaine-based products were restricted to prescription by doctors in the early 1920s, relatively few people were entirely dependent and addicted. Those who were addicts – and they were generally not from the poorest socio-economic groups, for whom alcohol remained the drug of choice – could access reliable supplies of drugs from a doctor.

From the 1920s right through to the 1960s, the number of 'therapeutic addicts' prescribed opiates to treat addiction ranged in the hundreds. Separate official committees, in 1926 and 1961, confirmed that the so-called 'British system' of medical prescriptions of opiates to addicts was the most sensible approach to the issue. The sad irony, that the British for so long adopted a rational, humane and medically sound approach to those addicted to drugs, will soon become apparent when we look at the results of the US-led prohibition agenda following its importation, first into British law and then onto the streets of our country.

As the *Journal of the Royal Society of Medicine* put it, by the 1980s 'heroin use had moved from a small, mainly metropolitan phenomenon supplied chiefly by doctors and the overspill from their prescriptions, to a habit affecting all parts of the country met by a labyrinthine international black market.'

What then was the catalyst, in Britain, the US and so many other places, for such a sudden increase in the use of drugs such as heroin and cocaine? In Britain, those drugs had largely been confined to a small number of addicts, supplied under prescription by a sympathetic medical practitioner.

The answer is surprisingly simple, given the apocalyptic impact of drug policy in the past fifty years. In 1961, the United Nations, heavily influenced by US demands, passed the Single Convention on Narcotic Drugs, aimed at prohibiting the production and supply of all drugs, save under licence for medical and research purposes. Less than a century after the Queen of England sat down with one of the greatest leaders in history to share some cocaine, the world was set firmly on a path of universal prohibition of almost every form of intoxicant known to man, other than alcohol, nicotine and caffeine.

This single document was the catalyst for the system of drug prohibition that prevails to this day in almost every country on the planet. It did not take long for its impact to be felt in Britain, where in 1965 a new wave of controls on drug prescription and use, including the establishment of a 'Home Office Addicts Index', was proposed by a government committee.

Following the Brain Committee's recommendations, the Dangerous Drugs Act 1967 prohibited physicians from prescribing heroin or cocaine to drug takers without a special government licence, save for the relief of pain resulting from a physical illness or injury. In practice such licences were granted only to a small number of newly established clinics, with limited capacity, meaning that most of the – still relatively tiny – number of drug users could not access prescriptions, let alone other forms of medical support for addiction. For most users, the British system of pragmatic and humane drug supply by doctors was effectively at an end.

If the 1967 Act represented a coffin for the formerly humane British system, and its historically more rational approach to drugs, the Misuse of Drugs Act 1971 (MoDA) hammered in the nails. In part introduced to meet British obligations under the 1961 Convention, MoDA finally outlawed drugs by means of harsh prison sentences, including in some cases for those convicted of 'simple possession' of small quantities of drugs for personal use. The concept of different 'classes' of controlled drugs, A, B and C, was introduced for the first time. Class A drugs attract the harshest penalties, but many experts have observed that there is no rhyme or reason to the categories.

Ecstasy, widely regarded as one of the least inherently damaging and addictive drugs provided it is taken at safe dosage levels, is in Class A; whereas amphetamine, whose effects are arguably far worse, is in Class B. Cannabis was originally in Class B, then moved to Class C in 2004 on the advice of an independent panel of experts and then moved back to Class B in 2009, for entirely political reasons, under the then British Prime Minister Gordon Brown. This pattern of ignoring – or even sacking – experts when they put forward a rational scientific approach to drug policy has been repeated, time and again, in Britain and elsewhere.

MoDA remains largely in force to this day, and has been used to prosecute nearly every case of drug trafficking and supply in which I have been involved over the past twenty-six years. Put simply, it has been, and remains, a death warrant for thousands of users, dealers, runners, even police officers, and of course innocents, whether literally caught in the crossfire of gang wars or falling victim to drug-related crime in its infinite variety.

The Americans were slightly ahead of us, bringing in the Controlled Substances Act (CSA) in 1970. It was signed into law by President Richard Nixon, who, probably more than any other, was responsible for intensifying the prohibition and law-enforcement model of drug policy that continues to cause so much harm to the present day. The CSA mirrored MoDA in Britain in introducing drug classifications, this time in five numbered schedules, with Schedule 1 listing those said to be the most dangerous, to pose the highest risk of addiction and to offer the least medical benefit. Cannabis or marijuana, LSD, heroin, MDMA and various other drugs are listed in

Schedule 1. The CSA goes right down to Schedule 5, where cough medicines with small amounts of codeine can be found.

What stood US policy apart, even from the implementation of MoDA in Britain and similar legislation elsewhere, was the unashamed political grandstanding, without even a veneer of evidence-based policy, which underpinned everything that Nixon and his willing accomplices in Congress did about drugs. The irony and hypocrisy reached levels that would be laughable, but for the death and destruction that continues to flow from the decisions of that era to this day.

On 17 June 1971, exactly a year to the day before burglars entered the Watergate Building in Washington, DC, Nixon was beginning to look ahead to his campaign for re-election in 1972. The CSA had accomplished what every attempt to get tough on drugs has ever done – increased the risks and the rewards to be had for every link in the supply chain. Business was booming for the cartels, organised crime groups, national and local dealer networks, which were not only expanding their customer bases but engaging in increasingly deadly gang warfare to win territory and market share. The number of addicts, supplied with potent varieties of every form of drug, was going up and up, as were overdoses and all forms of drug-related crime.

As the Vietnam War continued to rage, growing more and more unpopular and heading slowly but surely to a humiliating US defeat, Nixon chose to begin a new war, this time mainly on his own population. This is how 'the War on Drugs' was declared by Nixon at the White House:

I [begin] by making this statement, which I think needs to be made to the Nation: America's public enemy number

one in the United States is drug abuse. In order to fight
and defeat this enemy, it is necessary to wage a new, all-out
offensive . . . This will be a worldwide offensive dealing
with the problems of sources of supply . . . wherever they
are in the world.

America, like Britain, Russia and several other superpowers
of their times, has made statements, characterised by hubris,
many times before and since this announcement; but few
have overreached quite so much, and failed so spectacularly
to deliver, as Nixon's words that day.

What followed that announcement, in the US and
the UK in particular, was expenditure on drug law
enforcement, the criminal justice system and prisons at a
level that defies the imagination. Nixon managed to gain
congressional support for the creation of an entirely new
federal agency, the 'Drug Enforcement Administration',
which now boasts around 5,000 agents and has a budget
of over $2 billion. But that is just a small fraction of the
total sum spent in the US alone in an effort to enforce
the policy of prohibition, which is the central tenet of US
drug laws.

With little pause in almost fifty years, spending on drug
enforcement, prosecution and incarceration has gone up
and up, time and again driven by that same moralising
and electoral populism which began much earlier in
US history, as we have seen. In October 1982, President
Ronald Reagan doubled down on Nixon's announcement
of a decade before. In one of the most misguided, divisive
and – in its consequences – deadly political statements of
all time, Reagan managed to tick pretty much every box of

what does not work in criminal justice policy. Stage centre, unsurprisingly, were drugs and organised crime:

> Crime today is an American epidemic. It takes the lives of over 20,000 Americans a year, it touches nearly a third of American homes and results in about $8.8 billion a year in financial losses.
>
> The Federal Government will mount an intensive and coordinated campaign against international and domestic drug trafficking and other organized criminal enterprises.
>
> Millions of dollars will be allocated for prison and jail facilities so that the mistake of releasing dangerous criminals because of overcrowded prisons will not be repeated.
>
> Let this much be clear: Our commitment to this program is unshakable: we intend to do what is necessary to end the drug menace and cripple organized crime.

I have no idea whether President Reagan actually believed this grandstanding nonsense, any more than he believed the equally clichéd lines he uttered in the B movies of the 1940s and 50s in which he found his first round of fame. Whether he actually thought this toxic combination of mass criminalisation and incarceration for drug crimes, supported by a full military operation against those who supply and use drugs, would work, is unknowable and – in the end – academic. What matters is that he acted on those words and, in doing so, thoroughly entrenched the failed approach to drug policy, the effects of which we see today.

In one important sense, Reagan was rewarded for his decision to up the stakes in the War on Drugs. Speeches like that one led him, just two years later, to a landslide election victory that no president has even come close to matching in the decades since (Nixon's margin of victory in 1972 had been even bigger). The 'tough on crime' message is one of the most popular political tropes of all time, both with candidates on the campaign trail and with voters at the ballot box.

Reagan went all out to change the country, and significant parts of the world, and he certainly managed to achieve that objective in respect of drugs, albeit not with the results he predicted. The then First Lady, Nancy Reagan, fully backed by her husband, launched a high-profile 'Just Say No' campaign, seeking to buck the reality of the previous few million years of the human species, and sought to persuade young Americans to stop taking drugs altogether.

The result of all this? In the short term there was a small reduction in the overall volume of cocaine entering the United States. The consequence of such shortages, as in every supply-chain issue brought about by prohibition, weather conditions or anything else, was an increase in the market price of the pure drug, manifested in two ways. First, the price per gram rose on the streets, and second, the purity levels of cocaine in each wrap fell, so that users needed to buy more to get the same effect. Rising prices and disrupted sources of supply meant only one thing: an opportunity for new suppliers to come into the market and make even bigger profits than before.

Drugs being drugs, people being people, markets being markets, the results of Reagan's escalation of the War on Drugs were exactly the same as for every other ratcheting up of prohibition. By every measure – economic, fiscal, criminal, health, social, educational, violence and death – Reagan's strategy made things worse. Far worse.

In Britain, based on many of the same political motives, we have seen exactly the same process, albeit – as ever – on a smaller and less dramatic scale. Since I began defending in drugs cases, at first for low-level users and dealers, later in some of the largest British cases of drug importation ever seen, levels of sentence have increased time and again. In the 1990s a ten-year sentence for drug trafficking, which meant about six years behind bars, was considered to be towards the top of the scale. Since then, a combination of sentencing guidelines and judicial discretion has seen more people in prison for drug offences for longer than ever before.

Sentences of twenty years, in cases of large-scale importation and supply, have become entirely commonplace. Many of those at the top of the supply chain, or at least deemed to be so by the courts, have received sentences of twenty-five years, thirty years or, in a few cases, even more. Even with release on licence halfway through the sentence, periods of incarceration for drug crimes are at record levels. These sentences are often several times higher than those imposed for rape, robbery, serious assault and even, in most cases, the sexual exploitation of children and other paedophilic crimes. On top of the draconian levels of prison sentencing, drug offenders are targeted with some of the most punitive financial penalties of all, often including confiscation orders that some will not be able to repay in a lifetime (and hence they remain locked up even longer in default).

All the while, as the prison vans head off from court buildings with another batch of inmates, the drugs continue to flow and profits continue to be made. The British

National Crime Agency is clear that drug trafficking is the largest source of revenue for Organised Crime Groups ('OCGs' in law enforcement terminology), many of which are also involved in other forms of serious crime, such as firearms dealing, sexual exploitation, modern slavery and illegal immigration. And, the greatest tragedy of all: drug users continue to be exploited, live miserable and unhealthy lives, become exposed to violence, and they continue to die. Thousands of our fellow citizens meet their deaths each year from drug overdoses and the effects of addiction.

The British experience is no different to that of the United States, and everywhere else on the planet; the more resources dedicated to the criminalisation of drugs, including through law enforcement and draconian prison sentences, the higher the profits to be made. We need a complete reversal of current policy, rolling back half a century of failed prohibition and moving to a legal, licensed and regulated drug market. Only such a radical change of approach will finally see a reduction in drug-related crime and death, which will otherwise continue to rise, year on year, as they have for decades.

It is impossible to take stock of just how badly prohibition has gone for the world without considering the actions of President Rodrigo Duterte of the Philippines, who took office in June 2016. He came to power on a platform of all-out assault against the drug traffickers of his country, promising at an election rally in 2015:

> If I became president, you [criminals] should hide. I would kill all of you who make the lives of Filipinos miserable. I will definitely kill you. I do not want to

commit this crime. But if by chance God will place me there, stay on guard because that 1,000 [killed in Davao City] will become 100,000.

Duterte was true to his word. By early 2020, the government had admitted carrying out over 5,000 extrajudicial killings, superficially targeted at drug gangs but leading to the deaths of hundreds of innocent men, women and children from all walks of life, including those on the wrong street at the wrong time. Human-rights groups and independent observers place the death toll at well over 10,000, but Duterte is unrepentant: 'What is my sin? Did I steal even one peso? Did I prosecute somebody who I ordered jailed? My sin is extrajudicial killings.'

Not far behind Duterte is the Russian Federation, which takes a 'zero-tolerance' approach to drugs, in practice meaning violence and cruelty against addicts and sky-high levels of HIV infection, overdose and death. After the Russians moved into Crimea in 2014, they replaced a relatively benign regime of methadone-assisted treatment for heroin addicts with a complete ban on the practice. Users returned to street heroin and began to die in large numbers. Not only that but the police arrived and flooded the main drug-dealing areas with officers who, as one observer described, 'broke arms, legs, everything . . . of course the heroin was still there – just the price went up two, three times'. For those arrested and prosecuted in Russia, even a few grams of cannabis can mean a sentence of fifteen years in prison.

Does all of this reduce the consumption of drugs in Russia? Or the catastrophic health consequences of the prohibited drug trade, especially among intravenous drug users? Or wipe out the organised crime networks responsible for the nation's drug supplies? As in every other country where prohibition has been or is being attempted, the harsher the enforcement, the greater the profits, the more people who suffer and die. The equation is that straightforward.

Yes, we are killing people every day, thousands each year, as a direct product of the criminalisation of the drug supply chain and the perverse outcomes it creates. I could choose any one of these stories, but there is something particularly senseless in the death of a child; a child killed by the laws we have and the way we enforce them.

HOW PROHIBITION KILLED MARTHA FERNBACK

Martha Fernback died of an accidental overdose of MDMA ('ecstasy') at the age of fifteen, one Saturday morning in Oxford. She had taken half a gram of powder but had no idea that it was 91 per cent pure MDMA, meaning that Martha had consumed enough of the drug for up to ten people. Given that this was just the fourth time she had ever taken it, Martha's system had no tolerance for a dose of that strength. She collapsed and was taken to hospital, where valiant and sustained efforts to revive her continued beyond the point when most doctors would have given up.

I interviewed Martha's mother, Anne-Marie, in the course of research for this book, and she spoke of the unimaginable experience of going from being a 'mum of one to a mum of none'. Anne-Marie had been a single parent and it was clear that her relationship with her daughter had been a strong one. She told me what Martha was like as a child and as a blossoming young woman: 'quirky, curious and socially engaged, she campaigned for support for teenage mental health, she would talk to homeless people in the street ... she was very funny and very bright.' She was also a sensible girl and on one occasion took a friend, who was having sex with her boyfriend, to buy condoms in order to be safe. Anne-Marie was keen to make clear that she was not seeking to eulogise her daughter as a saint. 'She could be a little bugger as well,' she told me, with a tone of pride.

'We were very close', Anne-Marie told me, 'and would spend most of our lives together – I not only loved her as a daughter but I liked her a lot.' It was surely the depth of their relationship that allowed Martha to open up, just six weeks before her death, to tell her mother that she and her friends had tried some ecstasy together. They had enjoyed it. No harm done.

Anne-Marie knew nothing about drugs or how to approach the issue with her daughter. She was so angry that Martha had placed herself at risk in that way. Desperate for answers and information, Anne-Marie turned to the Internet and found very little, even on official websites, other than dire warnings of the dangers of drugs cut with 'rat poison', and admonitions to abstain. Armed with what little she could find, Anne-Marie sat down with Martha and explained the dangers she had read of, especially of contamination by adulterants. Little did she know that her ever-sensible teenager had taken to the Internet herself, looking for 'safe ways to take drugs', but Martha had found little useful information either.

Whether due to her own research, the concerns of contamination understandably passed on by Anne-Marie, or just the supplies available on the day, Martha sought out the purest form of ecstasy available, perhaps believing that this would be preferable to contaminants unknown and possibly deadly. And herein lies the problem in an unregulated market. Imagine if you had no way to know if a pint of beer contained 4 per cent alcohol or a deadly 99 per cent – if it looked and tasted exactly the same either way, if there was no label to help, if the landlord had no idea and if you did not find out which it was until after you had drunk the lot. Oh, and if there were no age restrictions at the point of sale.

That is precisely how the drug market works under prohibition, and that is the reason why, in July 2013, Martha Fernback took enough MDMA to fell a horse. Not because she was a wayward child, still less an immoral one; not because her mother was a bad parent – quite the opposite in fact; but because we, all of us, failed to keep Martha safe, by making sure that she would not be exposed to a tiny, unlabelled and unlicensed bag of powder which, in a tragedy beyond compare, had enough chemicals inside it to snuff out her young life. And to leave Anne-Marie as a mum of none.

Born in 1971, little did Anne-Marie know that a few pieces of paper, printed by Her Majesty's Stationery Office that same year, represented a death sentence for a daughter to whom she would not give birth for over three decades. The Misuse of Drugs Act was chapter 38 for 1971 (all Acts of Parliament are given a consecutive 'chapter' number in the year they are passed). MoDA was sandwiched between the 'Welsh National Opera Company Act (repealed)' and the less than intriguing 'Ratings Act'. There were seventy-seven others.

However apparently innocuous – and even well intentioned – MoDA may have seemed to some, Anne-Marie is in no doubt that drug prohibition was the direct cause of death of the wonderful human being that was Martha Fernback.

Anne-Marie cannot help but doubt herself – who could? – wishing she had listened more and shouted less. She questions and regrets her own ignorance and sees it now as her 'primal scream' to ask: 'Why are we not talking about this?' The last thing young people need is a judgemental and moral approach to drugs. There are just too many teenage funerals happening for us to carry on like that. One undertaker even bought a copy of Anne-Marie's book, in which she tries to make sense of the lessons of her grief, to help other parents facing the same overwhelming experience of the loss of a child to drugs.

A woman of limitless courage and deep insight, at the end of our discussion Anne-Marie put forward two simple and unobjectionable ideas from which much can be learned. First, young people should all stay alive until the end of the weekend, whether they choose to take drugs or not. And finally, a moving rhyme: 'Martha wanted to get high, not to die.'

For Martha, you can of course substitute every person who ever smoked a pipe, popped a pill, drank a glass of wine or consumed a drug by any other method invented by man. And those who will utilise other delivery mechanisms, as yet undiscovered, until the end of time.

HOW WE GET OUT OF THIS CYCLE OF DEATH

Martha, daughter of a loving mother, living in the beautiful and historic city of Oxford, with everything to live for. Gary, existing day to day in pursuit of heroin, eventually kicked and beaten to death in a dirty puddle, in a post-industrial town. They were united in two simple ways – each of them died as a result of drug prohibition and neither of them deserved to do so. It was no more right for Gary to meet his death that way, following his decades of addiction to heroin, than it was for Martha, a vibrant girl, full of potential, who just wanted to see what drugs would feel like. Nobody deserves to die a death caused directly and unquestionably by prohibition, and nobody needs to.

Towards the end of the research process for this book, I flew to Geneva, on a mission to witness for myself a very different approach to drug policy. My flight took a route along the whole of Lake Geneva, and from the air I was able to observe the beautifully maintained villas and immaculate chateaux along the water's edge. Switzerland is truly a spectacular country; in its natural scenery of lakes, mountains and pastures; in the tasteful combination of classical and modern architecture of its cities; and, it turns out, in its pragmatic and humane approach to those affected by drug addiction. Conservative and bound by tradition in so many ways, the Swiss have nevertheless learned from experience: that you cannot persecute, arrest and imprison your way out of a drug problem. You have to understand and accept it. Then you might actually get somewhere.

In the 1980s, Switzerland had a major drug problem. Its carefully cultivated image of cleanliness, good order, civilised behaviour and robust good health was under threat. Now iconic photographs of Zurich's open drug scene found their way into newspapers, magazine and television reports around the world. The city's Platzspitz Park had achieved an unenviable rebranding as 'Needle Park', due to the public injection of heroin and other drugs, by up to a thousand addicts, which took place there twenty-four hours a day.

HIV infection rates reached the highest level in Western Europe. All forms of blood-borne disease, overdose and crime were out of control. In other words, Switzerland,

FIGURE 7 An addict searches for a vein, Zurich, 1990

albeit on a far smaller scale, was facing all of the same problems with drug use as the US, Britain and many other countries at that time.

Rather than simply lecturing addicts to abstain, and locking up dealers for longer and longer, the Swiss went a very different way. They took a path that led them, both in the short term and to this day, to one of the least deadly drug scenes for users, and to one of the lowest rates of drug-related crime and violence, anywhere in the world.

For a people known for secrecy, the Swiss were remarkably open in discussing drugs with me during my visit. Those I met came from across the spectrum of involvement in drug policy, treatment and law enforcement. In many ways it was disconcerting. They all agreed. Switzerland, I was told by everyone, had made the right decisions on drugs, and their approach, in particular to heroin users and heroin treatment, had been entirely positive in its impact on Swiss society.

I began by sitting down for an hour – which quickly turned into two – with Khalid Tinasti. A young man of extraordinary intelligence and with an encyclopaedic knowledge of all things drug-related, Khalid is the Executive Secretary of the Global Commission on Drug Policy, whose modest offices are on the third floor of a small building a hundred yards or so from the lakefront, in the centre of Geneva.

Khalid spoke with the clarity and confidence of a true expert, talking me through the sorry history of prohibition and the escalating drug wars of the past half-century and more, summarised earlier in this book. He spoke of the irony that those treaties calling for global crackdowns on drugs were among the most ratified of all, whereas others, on issues as diverse as war crimes and global warming, were far easier for even the major powers to ignore. No rational system, he observed, could impose such harsh sanctions for drugs like cannabis and ecstasy, by way of example, but leave tobacco and alcohol entirely untouched. Even the names of drugs could be used and abused to political ends – the Spanish word 'marijuana' was used in the US, rather than the Latin 'cannabis', to denigrate a drug associated at one time with poor Mexican immigrants.

Khalid believes that, as drugs do not offer opportunity to businesses (or at least until recently in those US states that have decriminalised cannabis), they are seen as offering no economic opportunity. Combined with the relentless War on Drugs narrative, this means that there is no political will or, crucially, great public demand, for reform, at least in the US, the UK and most other developed nations. In Khalid's view, there was only one word for the messaging on drugs from politicians in recent decades – 'propaganda'. He could not think of a society on earth where there was a majority sentiment in favour of radical reform and a move away from the entrenched model of drug prohibition.

Khalid reeled off the short list of more progressive nations, where at least some progress has been made. The Czech Republic, France, Seychelles and Israel have all decriminalised, whether in law or enforcement practice, the possession of small quantities of cannabis. Portugal went further and, in 2001, decriminalised possession of up to a ten-day supply of any drug. The evidence of positive outcomes in these countries, especially as to rates of HIV infection and drug-related crime, is clear – the real way to 'get tough' on the drug trade is to *reduce* criminal sanctions and *increase* harm reduction efforts, including drug treatment and prevention services.

Khalid talked me through the Swiss model and, to begin with, disabused me of the notion that reform was kindled by a feeling of good will towards the addicts shooting up in Needle Park. The truth, less altruistic but no less beneficial in its impact, is that the conservative Swiss objected to two things: first, the reputation of their nation being sullied by global attention on public drug use in its public spaces; second, their streets, parks and playgrounds becoming dangerous no-go areas for the law-abiding public, especially for children. There was a growing concern, too, about the rise in HIV/AIDS in the 1980s. But it was the impact of the drug scene on taxpaying citizens and their families, going about their lives, that was the real catalyst for change.

You see, Switzerland is a democracy like no other. The kind where things can actually get done. Despite its diminutive population of just 8.5 million people, divided into twenty-six 'cantons' – equivalent in many ways to US states – Switzerland is a fully functioning federal democracy, with one added feature – referendums. Unlike the handful of public votes in Britain, and the larger number in the US at state level, notably in California, the Swiss Constitution provides for binding referendums on a host of issues at national, canton and local level. If enough people want something in Switzerland, they will get it, regardless of what their elected politicians may think about it.

As the world was exposed to shocking photographs of the men and women in Needle Park, injecting heroin into their veins in broad daylight, the Swiss did what they do when decisions need to be made – they held town hall meetings and they talked about it. Their politicians wisely came along, too, and they listened. Police enforcement operations against drug users, including in the main railway station in Geneva, were failing to reduce drug use or crime. Overdoses were increasing and the HIV epidemic was going from bad to worse.

Unafraid of personal or moral reprisals, LGBT advocates attended the growing number of public meetings, setting out the case for reform, to save lives as the HIV crisis grew. Sex workers, themselves no longer criminalised in Swiss society, were also able to speak out about the need to focus on health and welfare, rather than to moralise to no avail. Social workers, nurses and doctors, caring for drug users and those infected with HIV, joined the chorus of voices for change.

As the clamour for a new approach to drugs grew louder, first local and eventually federal referendums mandated the introduction of a radical reform programme, at the heart of which lay the principle of harm reduction. By the mid-1990s, Swiss drug policy on the ground was guided by the '4 Pillars' system, designed to reduce the harm of drugs to those who used them and to everyone else. Prevention, Therapy, Risk Reduction and Repression were and are the guiding principles behind the health, regulatory and law enforcement approaches to drugs in Switzerland. The 4 Pillars finally achieved federal legal approval by means of a national referendum in 2008.

There is no moral element to any of it, even 'repression', which is a more familiar concept to us in Britain and the United States. In the Swiss context, repression means reducing the direct and obvious harms of the black market for drugs – from the antisocial impact of street dealing to the drug-related crime carried out by users and dealers alike. It does not mean punishment of dealers for punishment's sake. The policy has been an overwhelming success, as I was to find out when I visited those on the front line of the 4 Pillars system in action, both on the streets and in the halls of power.

In Khalid's view, it is a fool's errand to try to take complete control of drugs, let alone to eliminate drug use in line with the Reagan model. There are only two options – either be proactive and pursue harm-reduction measures along the lines of the Swiss model or beyond, or end up with no choice but to deal with the sort of crisis represented by Needle Park and the HIV epidemic, which led to the introduction of the 4 Pillars.

'We in the West created this problem, all over the world,' Khalid concluded, as I stood up to leave, 'and we need to find a way to solve it. The only solution that exists is legalisation and regulation. Anything else will just make things even worse than they are.'

The next morning, I found myself at a busy intersection, in the shadow of the elevated railway lines close to Geneva's main railway terminal, where heroin was openly injected as recently as the 1990s. My phone mapping had taken me there but I had to call ahead to identify the address I was trying to find. After a couple of minutes, a man and a woman emerged from a box-shaped, two-storey, lime-green building surrounded by low fencing, hiding in plain sight.

Dr Jennifer Hasselgard-Rowe, Executive Coordinator of the Geneva Platform on Human Rights, Health and Psychoactive Substances, approached me with a wave of welcome, alongside Serge Longère, the French manager of the green building in front of me. This was one of thirteen 'safe consumption rooms' in Switzerland, where drug users can bring their drugs and 'works' (needles and other equipment) and inject, snort or smoke in safe and sanitary conditions. The first, in Bern, opened as long ago as 1986.

Serge showed me inside, where he was in the process of setting up for the day. At first glance, there was little to distinguish the reception area from a basic medical facility or even a small British village hall. It was only by looking carefully that the functionality of this place was made clear. Serge showed me the 'needle drop', immediately inside the entrance door, where users could deposit used syringes in return for new ones. Needles were in plentiful supply and hygienically sealed as in any hospital, stored away behind the counter.

Posters on the walls explained, without judgement, the effects of various drugs, on the body and the brain, and a whiteboard gave the times when users could book in for an HIV or hepatitis test, together with various other medical services on offer. There was a shower room, washing facilities, and the store cupboard was well stocked with a variety of supplies, of particular use to those drug users existing on the margins of one of the wealthiest cities on earth; there was a real pathos about the pile of new sleeping bags, boxes of toothbrushes and multicoloured plastic cups sitting on one of the shelves, waiting to be issued to those in need of such basic items.

We walked through into the consumption room itself, dubbed a 'shooting gallery' by the press, the walls a garish shade of lime green; again there was something moving in the bare simplicity and humanity of the place. More impactful still was the sheer utility of everything I saw – practical, useful equipment to keep users as safe as possible, whilst they ingested drugs that in many countries would see them arrested, locked up or worse, just for possessing them.

Spotlessly clean, along one wall were four 'injection stations', each identically equipped with a green plastic chair, a dustbin on the floor lined with a new binliner, a sharps bin for used needles, and a small glass shelf holding antiseptic spray and paper towels. Finally, there was a white injection and preparation table, bolted firmly to the wall at about the height of a writing desk.

Here users could sit and prepare their drugs, with support staff on hand if needed, inject and sit back, while the heroin flooded through their system, bringing that flash of relief, and – yes – pleasure, that they all sought out several times a day. I was told that over a hundred visitors a day came to this consumption room, with most choosing to inject but some using the 'snorting stations' (clean plastic tubes provided) and others using the small 'smoking area', which was enclosed in a separate air-filtered room to prevent smoke reaching the non-smokers (rather like in an airport). All of these methods of ingestion involve some risk, not to mention the dangers from the drugs themselves. This was a 'bring your own' establishment, with users buying their fixes on the streets, so neither quality nor purity was guaranteed.

Accepting that those coming here are going to inject, smoke or snort – whether this place exists or not – has led to a focus on only one thing: keeping them alive and as healthy as possible. Not only are the facilities maintained to a clinical level of hygiene in order to reduce infection risks, but staff will call an ambulance if a drug user needs naloxone, a miracle drug that rapidly counteracts the effects of overdose. Nobody has ever died of an overdose here, and such deaths are relatively rare throughout Switzerland, due to the health-focused approach to drug-taking and the ready availability of naloxone nationwide. HIV and other infection levels are now amongst the lowest in the world.

I sat down with Serge and asked him about the impact of the consumption room. He was surprisingly frank that there were still many users who did not come, who lived completely 'outside of the system'. There were still drug dealers too, although mostly small-time, and Geneva did not have the gang turf wars and violence associated with similar-sized cities elsewhere. There were still overdoses in the city – nobody was pretending that all the problems had been solved.

Serge was in no doubt that drugs should, as a minimum, be completely decriminalised, and he pointed to the hypocrisy of alcohol and prescription drug use when compared with the treatment of those taking street drugs. He had no doubt that the effect, even with facilities like his own, was to marginalise and exclude users of illicit drugs from mainstream society.

I left under no illusion about two things – that compassion and support are the only humane ways to address drug use and that, even in one of the most pragmatic and enlightened nations on earth, in terms of drug policy there is still a long way to go.

I next met with the Deputy Head of the Judicial Police, Jean-François Cintas, who was in charge of drug enforcement in the city. He proudly showed me graphics of the 4 Pillars and made clear that there was still a place for repression of the drug trade, alongside the other three priorities of the system. I was impressed by his lack of moral judgement of those who took drugs, unlike many police officers I have spoken to in Britain and the US. Jean-François smiled when he told me of the tests of the sewers, which revealed higher concentrations of controlled drugs, especially stimulants, during the main university exam periods in Geneva. There is clearly no single stereotype of what a drug user looks like, or why he or she turns to chemicals in the first place.

'There is no way we can stop drugs coming into Switzerland,' Jean-François told me. 'Drugs arrive from everywhere. It's a business and people are human.' Drug 'mules', usually poor couriers with drugs strapped to their bodies or swallowed in precarious plastic wrappings, arrive in large numbers by air, bringing cocaine from South America. Most get through. Vehicles are driven overland from Africa or the East, entering Europe at its weakest external entry points and then straight into Switzerland, across the open road borders from Italy and France.

The dealers themselves, I heard, are a fairly unproblematic lot, and gang violence is virtually unknown. In Geneva, West Africans and South Americans control the cocaine trade, alongside Albanians who specialise in heroin, with North Africans taking care of cannabis. 'They respect each other,' Jean-François observed, with a tone of professional admiration. 'What the public care about,' he continued, 'are things that interfere with their lives or poison their kids, which becomes a political issue.'

So, did the Deputy Chief of Police support the legalisation of drugs, which would perhaps put him out of a job once and for all? The answer was a firm 'No'. He was against drug legalisation, but not for moral reasons. His objection was more practical – 'If we legalise drugs in Switzerland, we will be deluged with addicts from France, Italy, all over the place. It's happened already to some extent as drugs are much cheaper here.' So it was not the principle of legalisation to which Geneva's most senior drug cop objected, but the incentive it would create for an influx of the sort of immigrants that Switzerland was not keen to attract – drug tourists.

Having heard from the police a description of relative equilibrium and peace in the drug trade, with broad support for the public health focus of the 4 Pillars, I took a short taxi ride to the Ministry of Justice, where I was shown to the spacious office of the Attorney-General, Olivier Jornot. Floor-to-ceiling windows looked out on the neat cityscape and the snow-capped mountains, just a short drive away. We sat at his vast glass-topped conference table on the sort of black leather chairs that mean business.

Olivier Jornot is a man of substance. A practising lawyer for over fifteen years, he had entered cantonal politics before being appointed to complete the term of the previous Attorney-General, seven years earlier. He then stood for election – it is a directly elected office – on a conservative ticket and won by a landslide against a left-wing opponent. Monsieur Jornot exudes conservative from every pore. Around fifty years of age, balding and solidly built, dressed in an immaculate dark suit and tie, this is a man who takes his official duties seriously. And yet, when we spoke of crime and drugs, he was quite accepting as to the limits of what could be achieved by law enforcement and the criminal justice system.

'You have to say you will be "strong" when you stand for election to a role like this,' he said. 'The public don't want to think you will be nice to criminals.' That said, he had campaigned, at the last election, against the use of prison as a sentence of first resort, appealing successfully to Swiss pragmatism and, unlike my experience in the US and the UK, to *evidence* rather than *emotion* in sentencing policy. 'As Attorney-General, I am not just a prosecutor but a protector of public liberties for everyone, and that means taking a fair approach, not a punitive one.'

In Monsieur Jornot's view, Swiss people were not in favour of drugs at all, and it would be unwise for a politician to stand on a pro-drugs platform. Legalisation, even of cannabis, had been firmly rejected in a referendum and there was no clamour for a more liberal approach. The 4 Pillars had come about because of the impact of drugs on the public consciousness, partly through the infamous images of Needle Park, but mainly because of the impact of drug consumption in streets and public places. It was not hard to persuade the rational Swiss of the merits, first of consumption rooms to take users off the streets and reduce crime and disorder, and then of Heroin Assisted Treatment programmes, where state clinics provide drugs directly to users, under medical supervision.

In Swiss terms, this represented both a radical change of policy and an eminently workable solution. Yes, it meant enabling addicts to obtain and use heroin, but, more importantly, the policy created ground-breaking improvements in public health and dramatically reduced the worst side-effects of the drug trade. Monsieur Jornot pointed with pride to the decision of the Swiss Supreme Court to define addiction as a disability, thereby affording heroin and other drug users the same rights and legal protections as those with any other form of disability. 'They have the right to treatment, so that they can have jobs, relationships and families like everyone else,' he explained.

Everything about the approach to drugs in public was based on common sense rather than dogma, as I was soon to see for myself. Although drug use remained technically unlawful, there was a consensus of public opinion to leave users alone and, even in terms of low-level dealers, to disrupt their activities only when it affected the safety or wellbeing of the public going about their daily business. 'If they are blocking the steps into an apartment building, people will call the police, otherwise it is live and let live.'

So, I asked, would Monsieur Jornot go further and campaign for even more radical reform next time around? (He had an election coming up.) Whatever his personal view, he told me – and he considered prohibited drugs no more inherently immoral than alcohol – he could not publicly campaign for drug legalisation. There were two reasons – each of which made sense, at least in this country of gradual change – first, he wanted to be re-elected, and, second, he did not consider it within his role to push for social and political reform. He was there to enforce the laws, not to set the agenda for the sort of change that full drug legalisation would represent.

'Anyway,' he concluded, when our time was up, 'our system basically works. There is not much I would change.' That is not a comment I have ever heard in Britain and is the precise opposite of everything I have heard in the US on the subject of criminal justice. The Swiss, I have no doubt, are doing many things from which we could learn.

I was escorted from the Justice Ministry by a media minder, a young man whose fluent English was subtly inflected with a Welsh accent, alongside the more obvious French tones. It turned out that he was half Franco-Swiss and half Welsh – a real citizen of Europe. On our way down in the lift, I told him that I had never before met a senior politician, official or law-enforcement officer who believed there was little room for improvement in the criminal justice system. 'It is true,' he replied. 'Everyone pretty much gets along, even the drug dealers. Do you want to come and see the open drug market for yourself?'

I processed the suggestion for a moment. We were in the Ministry of Justice, where I had spent several hours with the head of criminal prosecutions for the city. I had been with the head of enforcement for drugs for the Judicial Police. And I was being offered a guided tour of the local drug market by a ministry press spokesman. This was not something offered by the police and prosecutors of Alabama, nor by those in London, Manchester, or anywhere else in Britain.

'Of course!' I said. And off we went. Just three stops on the tram from the Ministry, maybe five or six minutes, and we alighted in a mixed residential, office and retail district, marked by smart modern architecture. Scandinavian furniture shops, stylish boutiques and coffee shops lined the streets. We left the main avenue and walked for no more than 50 yards down a wide road, overlooked by apartment buildings through whose large windows the expensive furniture of the wealthy inhabitants was unmistakable. 'Nice area,' I said to my guide. 'Yes,' he replied. 'Millions of francs for some of these apartments.'

On the street corner, eyeing us with mild and unobtrusive interest, were two West African men, late twenties or so, casually standing against a wall. 'They will offer you drugs,' I was told. And they did. At exactly that moment, a smart blue Volvo SUV was backing into a parking bay, right outside the entrance to one of the luxury apartment buildings, a road's width away from the two dealers. A young woman emerged from the driver's door and went to the back of the car. She opened the rear doors and unbuckled a toddler from a car seat, before extracting a buggy from the boot. With a slight nod in the direction of the two black men, she strapped in her son, helped an older child – possibly five or six years old – from the car and strolled casually away.

This was more shocking to me than almost anything I had seen on my travels, save for the sight of the poor souls behind the cracked glass of an Alabama jail. I told my minder that I could not believe my eyes. Drug dealers were operating openly in a public street, in a smart neighbourhood, alongside the daily lives of what were obviously the young families of the Swiss middle class. And nobody was calling the police or scurrying away in fear.

My guide shrugged as if to say: 'So?' What he then told me was equally surprising but, reflecting on it without our instinctive prejudices, his words make perfect sense. 'Everyone just gets on here. The dealers even attend town hall meetings. People know exactly who they are. If the local residents have a problem with someone blocking a doorway or getting too near a school, the dealers will sort it out and make sure it doesn't happen again.'

'What about gang wars, stabbings, shootings over territory?' I asked, thinking back to the wall-to-wall news coverage of knife crime in Britain and the staggering death toll from drug-related gun violence in the United States.

'We don't have those problems here,' said my guide. 'I think people just want to live their lives; not create those sorts of problems for themselves.'

Before I came to Switzerland, I had expected to hear of a more enlightened approach to drugs, but I did not think that open street dealing of every form of substance would be tolerated, right outside the homes of Swiss families, without interference or even complaint. This was pragmatism in the extreme. The next person I saw had no doubt that legalisation should be the endgame. 'We need to stop this stupid thing – prohibition – and stop with this stupid A, B and C classification of drugs. We need coherent regulation of all substances,' I was told by Dr Barbara Broers.

'BANNING DRUGS IS STUPID' – DR BARBARA BROERS

Dr Broers is a remarkable woman and, without doubt, the most charismatic, persuasive and informed person I met on my travels for this book. A psychiatrist for over thirty years, she is head of the Dependencies Unit at Geneva University Hospitals. Offering treatment for every form of addiction – from gambling to crack – the unit takes up an entire floor of a modern medical facility, across the road from the imposing main hospital building.

After qualifying in the 1980s in her native Netherlands, Dr Broers worked in the heart of the drug-using community of Amsterdam, which was suffering acutely from the impact of the HIV/AIDS epidemic. She has no time for prison sentences for drug crime – 'What's the point?' – and no doubt, after three decades of working with addictions, that 'There will always be demand, so someone should provide a supply. It's that simple.' She pointed to our freedom to consume French fries and ketchup, sit in front of the TV and 'eat ourselves to death', to support her view that the attempt to control just one form of objectively 'unhealthy' behaviour was irrational and misguided.

With not just HIV but hepatitis ravaging the intravenous drug-using community, the Dutch authorities introduced the then revolutionary idea of a needle-exchange programme as early as 1983. Shortly after that, Dr Broers moved to Geneva, just as reform began to arrive there. Needle exchanges were in place by the late 1980s, methadone treatment for prison inmates arrived in 1991, the Heroin Assisted Treatment ('HAT') programme in 1995, and the consumption room, which I had visited earlier, in 2001.

The Swiss government has established an 'Addictions Commission' to coordinate services across all forms of addiction, removing the artificial barrier between prohibited substances, alcohol, tobacco and other forms of addictive behaviour, such as gambling. Bringing together services and experts from policing, education, social services, state ministries, medicine/psychiatry, NGOs and civic organisations, the Commission's purpose is to advise government on how best to reduce the harm from addiction, to patients and to everybody else.

Not every recommendation is accepted straight away, but at least there is a channel for expertise and resources to be brought together and put before a minister with the power to get things done. 'For a long time, the Commission advocated drug testing, to allow people to find out what they were taking,' Dr Broers explained, 'but it took a lot of time to get it through and there was a lot of resistance to the idea. Now it is in force and it saves lives.'

Even the Heroin Assisted Treatment programme itself, now a world beacon of best practice, operated in the guise of a 'trial' for well over a decade. It only became a permanent part of the Swiss legal and medical approach to drug addiction as recently as 2007, following approval by referendum.

I asked Dr Broers, what model of legalisation of drugs she would favour. 'Not the US commercial model for cannabis supply,' she replied. 'That is all about money and not in any way about public health. That is barely more sensible than prohibition.' She favoured complete regulation and licensing of the supply chain, separating the medical use of drugs, for pain relief or mental health conditions for example, from what she called 'non-medical' use, objecting to the term 'recreational drugs', which she believed disguised what, in truth, was often self-medication rather than 'fun'.

For Dr Broers, the keys to drug policy were transparency for the user, both as to the risks and what exactly they were taking, and state control of drug supply at every level and in every detail, so as to ensure that a parallel black market would not operate alongside the legitimate market. 'In an ideal world, nobody would take drugs, smoke, drink alcohol – of course they are harmful – but people do all these things. Who am I to say that someone who takes steroids to build muscle shouldn't have access to a safe supply? He will likely still be healthier than if he stayed at home on the couch.'

On one particular topic, Dr Broers brought a new perspective, focusing not merely on the harm to wealthy nations like Switzerland from drug prohibition, but the consequent impact of a criminal supply chain on those nations where most drugs are produced and through which they are trafficked. She spoke of the tens of thousands of deaths in countries like Mexico and Colombia, in enforcement operations or wars between the rival cartels. 'We need a global health policy around drugs,' she said. 'We are responsible for those deaths and, if we do not legalise drug supply, it will not stop.'

Dr Broers spoke movingly of the compassionate approach to drug withdrawal and treatment, even in the prisons of Switzerland, where she had seen many patients in the course of her career. In some cases, she felt that the inmates gained a net benefit from a short period inside, to get access to a drug treatment programme, health checks and other medical intervention. Her bigger concern was the danger of relapse and overdose after release, once they had detoxified in the prison environment. 'We would send them out with a low dose of methadone, even if they were clean. Better that than a fatal dose of street heroin on the first day out.'

It must take quite extraordinary reserves of resilience, courage and energy to remain so passionately committed to patiently treating the addicted, and arguing for radical reform, in the face of so much death and addiction over so many years. To me Dr Barbara Broers is nothing less than a heroine, and policymakers around the world would do well to listen to her views.

I had one last visit to pay before I left Switzerland, to the Heroin Treatment Programme itself, which I found in an anonymous building in one of the less salubrious parts of the city. I arrived during the evening clinic and was shown to the waiting room – once again just like a GP surgery at home, but with a decent coffee machine – and sat among the 'patients', as they waited their turn to consume pure pharmaceutical-grade heroin, just down the corridor.

Two men, somewhere in their thirties, sat patiently scrolling through news feeds and social media on their phones, waiting their turns. They were better dressed than the addicts scattered in large numbers on the streets of every British city; cleaner, certainly not on the verge of collapse or death. A woman of indeterminate age – thirty-five, forty, fifty? – added several sachets of sugar to a cup of milky coffee and paced the room, clearly in need of a fix. She mumbled to herself and glanced every few seconds at the reception desk, waiting with palpable anxiety for her name to be called. She was next.

The Chief of the Centre, a young psychiatrist by the name of Dr Aline Bervini, came to find me and gave me a tour of the facility. She was barely out of medical school but had been running the place for over a year, leading a small team of nurses and auxiliary staff, alongside just one other full-time doctor – 'Budget cuts,' she observed.

Dr Bervini took me straight through to the dispensing area, behind the counter and then into the drug-storage room. There was a heavy-duty industrial safe, embedded into a concrete base and bolted to the wall. Inside, I saw bottle after bottle of heroin in liquid form, together with boxes of heroin tablets of various doses, all neatly shelved and labelled. In another area, a nurse sat at a counter, carefully filling syringes with precise quantities of the liquid drug, recording each dose on a computer. Not a drop would go astray.

Each filled syringe was handed to a user to take into the clinic's own consumption room, into which Dr Bervini and I went next. Much smaller than the 'bring your own' facility I had visited earlier in my trip, the room had eight injection stations, overlooked by a nurse. Each of the sixty patients who visited twice a day – for a morning and evening dose – was allocated a small section of shelving unit, to store drug works, a toothbrush, not much else. Nurses were an unobtrusive presence in plain clothes, on hand to help if a user could not find a vein or to intervene immediately with naloxone in the rare case of an overdose.

I was a little surprised to hear that the staff actively assisted in finding injection sites, but this was very much part of the service: 'We don't want infections, serious damage to veins or arteries,' said the nurse. 'Remember, we are not here to judge them for their use of drugs but to help them do it as safely as possible.' This was a practice as far from the populist garbage about the 'moral failings' of drug users – spouted by Nixon, Reagan and so many others – as it is possible to imagine.

One female patient was seventy years old and had been injecting drugs for so long that there was absolutely nowhere left to insert a needle. As with many others, she was not only addicted to the drug itself but to the physical *act of injection*, hence the option of taking her dose by tablet would not satisfy her needs. The solution will, I am sure, surprise readers as much as it did me when I heard about it from Dr Bervini.

After many meetings of ethics committees, amongst both the psychiatric and the surgical branches of the medical profession, it was agreed that the patient would have a tube surgically inserted into a vein in her neck for the sole purpose of providing a viable and safe injection site for heroin. Not only that, but she was physically incapable of attending the clinic in person, to collect and inject the drug. In order to meet her needs, clinic staff visited her at home up to three times a day, taking with them a syringe of heroin each time, a clean needle, and a dose of naloxone just in case. So it was that a Swiss surgeon operated on an elderly heroin addict, and one of the world's first Heroin Assisted Treatment centres ensured that its patient could receive her fix, as safely and humanely as possible, for as long as she chose.

Dr Bervini told me of other patients who dropped in on their way to work or college, still on heroin but otherwise able to go about their lives: a young woman pianist, forced by her father to play to such a degree of perfection that, when she once missed a single lesson, he smashed her piano to pieces. She never played again and rapidly spiralled into addiction. A young man, who became addicted as a student, failed his exams and dropped out. With support from the unit, he is now on track to graduate. 'Without this programme he would be back on the streets,' Dr Bervini told me, 'and before long he would be dead.'

Dr Bervini was in no doubt that HAT was the 'gold standard' of drug treatment, and the majority of patients stopped using heroin altogether after a time. Even those who remained on the drug for a long period of time were less victimised, more likely to maintain work, studies, family life, much less likely to die a premature death. Some, like the seventy-year-old patient with the injection tube, might never come off drugs, but at least they were as safe, healthy and happy as possible.

'My patients are *auto-stigmatised*. They have been told so many times that they are worthless that they believe it themselves,' Dr Bervini concluded, 'but this programme shows them that they are no different to anyone else with a long-term illness. They deserve compassion and help.'

I left Switzerland, the plane banking to provide a spectacular view of Lake Geneva once more. I had been convinced that the country can teach us lessons about drug policy, which we in Britain and elsewhere desperately need to learn.

A small chink of light has appeared in the United Kingdom, in Scotland, where rates of drug deaths are higher than anywhere in Europe or even the United States, with around 100 people dying each and every month. In November 2019, it was announced that the UK's first Heroin Assisted Treatment programme would open in Glasgow, providing medical-grade heroin to as many as 500 of the most vulnerable users. Could it be that we in Britain are taking a first, faltering step away from the darkness of moralistic prohibition and into the light of reform, focused not on condemnation but on saving lives and making our streets safer for everyone?

According to the British National Crime Agency, opium production in Afghanistan and cocaine production in Colombia are at record levels. With supply plentiful from the producer countries, the purity of street drugs is increasing, prices are falling, and the risks of addiction and overdose are also going up. Users exposed to high-purity drugs are, of course, more likely to overdose, but, for those who survive, more and more heroin or cocaine is needed each day and, for an ever-greater number, this means turning to one of the purest forms of drug of all – crack cocaine, which drives violence on to the streets like no other substance.

With competition for customers at record levels, drug gangs engage in deadly feuds, often involving knife and gun murders as they battle for territory. Britain has seen an explosion in such deaths in recent years, with forty-two killed by gang violence on the streets of London in 2019 alone, many of them children and teenagers. The established city markets are so saturated with supply that gangs have branched out nationwide, via so-called 'county lines' operations. These new supply routes exploit thousands of children and illegal immigrants, forcing them to act as couriers to deliver drugs to smaller towns and to collect the profits from local dealers for the return journey. The violence of the city streets is now playing out in ever-smaller towns, from one end of the country to the other, as the gangs continue their territorial battles.

The NCA regularly trumpets record-breaking seizures of drugs, including well over 100 tonnes of cocaine and 5 tonnes of heroin in one year alone. And yet, more and more drugs get through and, as we have seen, purity rises, prices fall and violent competition escalates. Social media are being used for mass advertising campaigns to attract new and ever-younger customers, with 'free samples' and 'two-for-one' deals on offer from competing suppliers looking to build contact lists for their target markets. App-based taxi services have become the unwitting last stage of the delivery networks, transporting gang members, victims of exploitation and the drugs themselves.

Around the world, trillions of dollars have been spent on 'the War on Drugs', in pursuit of an irrational and debunked moral agenda that has caused death and human misery on a scale rarely seen outside of times of war, famine and plague. Most governments seem intent not only on continuing this failed policy of prohibition but on increasing the use of law enforcement, the criminal justice system and imprisonment as first-line strategies, hugely expensive both in money and in lives.

All the while, people of every race, in every age group and from every corner of the globe are dying needless deaths. Drug prohibition connects Martha Fernback, the children stabbed on the streets of London and shot to death in Atlanta, Juarez and Manila, with the dark events that brought a northern English jury into court to deliver its verdicts on the murder of Gary Jones.

Andy was found guilty of Gary's murder, in effect of arranging a vicious punishment beating that went too far. Rick and another of the men were convicted of manslaughter, the jury accepting that they had participated in the attack that caused Gary's death without the intent required for murder. The young teenage defendant was acquitted of all charges, given the benefit of the doubt, and he avoided a sentence of detention for life.

And as for my client, Sharon; after six months in a women's prison, she too heard the words 'not guilty' from the foreman of the jury, marked by a respectful silence in the courtroom. I turned to look at her, just a few feet behind me in the secure glass dock containing all the defendants. The blood had drained from her face and tears rolled freely down her cheeks. Three hours later she would be home with her children, but this could hardly be called a victory for anyone. A man was dead; Sharon's brother was beginning a life sentence; the father of her children would not be free to put their children to bed for many years to come. The ripples from the death of Gary Johnson would be felt for lifetimes.

WHY?

Why does this madness of prohibition continue? Why could Gary Johnson not receive a reliable supply of heroin within a caring and therapeutic setting like Geneva's? Why could Martha and her friends not experiment with ecstasy tablets, aware of what they contained, strong enough to get high but not strong enough for one of them to die? Why can't the drug farmers and processors of Mexico, Colombia and Afghanistan carry out their trade under official licence, without the daily risk of violent assault, a lifetime in prison, and of being shot in the head? For that matter, why can any of us not choose to smoke some weed, snort some coke or take a pill without the need to turn to some of the most dangerous and exploitative organisations on the planet to obtain supplies?

The straightforward answer, even in the more progressive countries on earth, is politics. Our politicians do not believe that they will win power on a platform of radical drug reform. And certainly not by advocating, as I do, the wholesale legalisation and regulation of the production and supply of drugs, to bring cannabis, cocaine, heroin, MDMA – and all the rest – into line with their chemical cousins: alcohol and nicotine.

Worst of all, no matter what the facts, no matter how clear the evidence, our politicians are probably right: cracking down on drug dealing, advocating a 'Just Say No' message to our young people, locking up the bad guys, all are much easier to sell to voters than the truth – that prohibition, not drugs, is the real killer; of Martha, Gary and all the rest. Whether we accept it or not, as long as we live in a democracy, we all have their blood on our hands.

4

Why children are never criminals

In the years before I applied to take Silk – an ancient rank of the English Bar, which involves appointment as one of 'Her Majesty's Counsel' and the right to use the suffix 'QC' – I sought out the most difficult and challenging cases I could find, regardless of the level of fees on offer. The reason was simple – in order to succeed in the year-long 'QC Competition' of 2012, I had to demonstrate excellence across a wide range of legal skills and personal qualities. This was to be achieved with direct evidence from up to a dozen cases, undertaken in the two or three years before the application. It was the hardest process I have ever been through.

The more complex and sensitive a candidate's caseload, in the period under review, the more likely that he or she would be able to put forward evidence of excellence in all of the categories.

For me, this search for the 'right' cases took me outside of my established practice. Throughout my almost twenty years as a criminal barrister, my work had been concentrated almost entirely in the fields of serious and organised crime – especially major drug-trafficking cases – and complex financial crime, such as money laundering and fraud. It had been some time since I had defended charges of rape, sexual assault and indecency, but such cases involve the sort of difficult judgements and skilful handling that are so important to a successful application for Silk.

When I first decided to make the application, I spent time with my Senior Clerk, David Wright, who had successfully supported many barristers in their quest to become a QC. We discussed the cases he would seek out for me as the period of review unfolded.

It was not long before he called. 'Mr Daw, I have a case which I really think you should look at,' he told me. 'I will send you the details by email but, in a nutshell, it is a child charged with raping another child.'

I read the police summary of the case with the practised unemotional objectivity essential to any good lawyer. My client, who became 'Boy W' for the purposes of the prolonged court proceedings that were to follow, was twelve years of age. He had learning disabilities that placed him well below average, meaning a mental age of no more than nine or ten. He was charged, alongside his eleven-year-old – but more mentally mature – cousin, with the rape and sexual assault of a five-year-old boy; the child of a friend of the family.

By the time I was asked to take on the case, the two young defendants had already appeared before a Youth Court and had been transferred for trial in the Crown Court, where all serious crimes in England, up to and including murder, are tried by jury; at least in the case of adults. It is rare for children, let alone children this young, to be sent to the Crown Court at all, even for a charge as serious as the rape of a child, which carries a maximum sentence of life imprisonment (or 'detention for life' in the case of a juvenile). A preliminary hearing in the Crown Court was imminent and the solicitors, looking to instruct a barrister in the case, needed a decision. I accepted the brief the same day.

The full case papers arrived a few days later and I read the detailed evidence in the case. The two older boys regularly played together and were frequently at the home of the family where the five-year-old lived. Their games had become inappropriate, with sexual language used by the older boys in particular. One day, the five-year-old boy told his mother that, more than once, the eleven-year-old, encouraged by my client, had penetrated his anus with his penis.

The mother had taken things up; first with the parents of the two accused boys, and then, after discussion in the family, with the police. That triggered a formal criminal investigation, involving video-recorded interviews under caution and all of the other processes to which an adult suspect would be subjected. On wise legal advice, neither of the boys said anything during the interviews, but instead sat silently, swinging their legs under their chairs in the interview room.

It had been many years since I had last represented a child, and then it would have been for street robbery or perhaps burglary when I was starting out as a young lawyer, occasionally defending in the Youth Court. I had been involved in murder cases with teenage defendants before, but never had I defended a child of this age for a crime of such an intrinsically adult nature as rape.

Something about the whole thing did not feel right, even before I met my client. He was, by that stage, under the care of social workers and outside of mainstream education, in part as a result of bail conditions imposed by the courts. I met him in my chambers with a social worker and solicitor present. It was a very bizarre situation indeed. The boy could barely communicate, bar muttering some words about his hobbies (he had few) and what he liked to eat (pizza). He denied any sexual activity with the young child but was more vague about the behaviour of his co-defendant, although he never made any specific allegation against him.

After a short time, it became clear that this was about as much information as I was going to get from my client. I asked him to take a seat in the waiting room, where one of the receptionists found him some biscuits, while I spoke to the social worker and the solicitor. 'What on earth is this boy doing in an adult court?' I asked, rhetorically, as each of them nodded seriously in agreement. 'It just cannot be the right way to handle things.'

I did what all sensible lawyers should do when faced with an apparent injustice and went back to basics. I read the law on children and young offenders in the criminal justice system. In particular, I wanted to understand how it was that these boys, and my client in particular, had ended up in an adult court, which would mean a public trial for all the world to see, with only the small mercy that their names could not be reported in the press.

I dug into what had happened at the Youth Court and found what I believed to be a legal error in the procedure. Rather than assessing them individually, the magistrates had considered the two defendants together when deciding if the case met the criteria for being sent to the adult court for trial. This meant that my client had, in effect, been transferred to the Crown Court not because of his own actions but because of the more serious allegations against his co-accused. It created a possible legal avenue to have the case sent back to the Youth Court.

I called my instructing solicitor and told her of my opinion. She was delighted. 'There is no way this child should be put through this, at this age, with all of his problems,' she said. I began drafting an application for a Judicial Review of the magistrates' decision to send my client to the Crown Court for trial.

Before we got to the High Court for the Judicial Review proceedings, we had to attend the preliminary hearing in the Crown Court. Even readers who have not been to a Crown Court will be familiar with the general layout and the ceremonies to be observed, together with the antiquated court dress of all of those involved in the proceedings. For an adult defendant, the Crown Court can be an intimidating place. For a young child it must be terrifying.

The default setting is for the judge to wear full robes, including horsehair wig, gown and purple sash, for the court clerk and court ushers to be robed as well, and, of course, for the barristers to wear their own gowns, wigs, stiff court collars and 'bands' – two rectangular pieces of starched cotton fabric, tied to the collar and popularised in the late 1640s.

Boy W was due to appear before a senior Circuit Judge, formerly a QC himself, who had begun his career in a different legal era. Nobody had informed him that courts were supposed to make allowances for child defendants and seek to make the proceedings as unintimidating as possible so as to avoid unnecessary distress. Before my client was brought into court for the hearing, I stood to ask the judge if we could at least remove our wigs and if the two boys could sit with their parents or social workers, rather than in the Victorian dock of the court where they would be behind a heavy glass security screen with two burly prison officers.

'I'm sure they will be fine,' insisted the judge. 'It will only be a few minutes.' He brushed aside all protest and called the case on. A few seconds later and there they were, these two young boys standing in the dock behind me, looking around anxiously for a friendly face. Boy W did not immediately recognise me with my wig on so I gave him a nod and quick thumbs-up to let him know I was there and that it would be OK.

The judge was right about one thing: the hearing was over quickly. I told him about the Judicial Review claim which, if successful, would render the Crown Court proceedings unlawful and, therefore, null and void. He grudgingly agreed to adjourn the proceedings without arraignment (a formal plea from the defendants) pending the outcome of the Judicial Review.

I found my client with his social worker, in a small conference room outside the court. I explained to the boy what had happened but, despite my best efforts, I am not sure he understood much of it. 'Are you OK with everything?' I asked. He shrugged but said nothing. I made eye contact with the social worker and wordless acknowledgement passed between us – this was all we were going to get out of him.

If the Judicial Review claim failed, we would be back here again a few months later, when Boy W and Boy Y would both stand trial for rape. A trial in which they would be at risk of leaving the court building not by the main exit but, accompanied by custody officers, to begin a sentence of detention, possibly for years.

'THEY KNOW THE DIFFERENCE BETWEEN RIGHT
AND WRONG AT THAT AGE' – A TWITTER USER,
JANUARY 2019

On 16 February 1814, five children were convicted of
the then capital offence of petty theft at the Old Bailey,
the most famous criminal court in the land. They were
sentenced to death. A public hanging took place in
London, during which the children were executed at the
same time. There was nothing exceptional about such
an event, not even the fact that all five of those who fell
through the trapdoor to their deaths were under the age
of thirteen. The oldest was twelve; not even a teenager.
The youngest of them was just eight years old, still
comfortably above the age of criminal responsibility at
the time, which was set at seven!

The prisons of the era were full of children, who were
treated no differently from adult offenders. It is easy to
imagine the forms of abuse those children suffered, confined
alongside rapists, murderers and hardened criminals of
every other ilk.

In the decades that followed, things changed a little.
A Society for the Improvement of Prison Discipline and the
Reformation of Juvenile Offenders was formed in 1817, with
the objective of distinguishing between the 'young offender'
and the 'hardened adult criminal'. A few years later, in 1823,
a new convict 'hulk' (prison ship) was introduced to house
child prisoners separately from their adult counterparts.
Still, most children continued to be locked away in exactly
the same institutions as older prisoners.

In 1838 the first land-based penal establishment for
children was opened at Parkhurst on the Isle of Wight.

Separated the children may have been, but the conditions of their detention were as unpleasant and repressive as any others in the prison estate.

By the 1860s, there were dozens of certified 'reformatories' and 'industrial schools' set up to house children – including both those convicted of crimes and those considered 'vagrant, destitute or disorderly'. Still children were processed through the courts exactly like adults until, in 1879, the Summary Jurisdiction Act provided for those under sixteen to be tried in magistrates' courts, with much lower levels of sentence than adults received for the same crimes at that time.

Despite admirable, if typically patrician, efforts in the 1890s to change the ethos around children in the criminal justice system, the central theme – that young people were criminals like any others and deserved punishment – continued to guide sentencing policy into the twentieth century. In many ways, it still does.

Probation supervision in the community was introduced in 1907 and many thousands of children, from as young as eight years old, came under the jurisdiction of probation officers. Those under fourteen were eventually removed from the adult prison system in 1908, which marked the beginning of the 'borstal' era, named after the town of Borstal in Kent where the first 'juvenile reformatory' was built.

By the 1920s, tens of thousands of children had been sent to borstals, and some continued to be hanged in public less than a century ago.

The Children and Young Persons Act 1933 introduced the first 'juvenile courts', with specialist magistrates handling cases, the age of criminal responsibility raised to eight, the abolition of capital punishment for children under eighteen and, for the first time, an obligation imposed on the courts to take 'primary account' of the welfare of the child.

An attempt to increase the age of criminal responsibility to fourteen was abandoned by the incoming Conservative government in 1970, when a new era of 'getting tough' on young offenders really began to gather momentum. The number of juveniles locked up each year quintupled between 1965 and 1980. Those earlier faltering steps towards a welfare-based approach to youth justice had well and truly come to an end. Utterly contradictory policies towards young offenders prevailed in the 1980s and 1990s, veering from the exploration of non-custodial alternatives to increased sentence lengths, introduced by the Criminal Justice and Public Order Act of 1994.

Despite a reduction in the number of young prisoners in recent years, some innovations, such as *mandatory* detention for young offenders for certain weapons offences, have once again seen the return of the 'get tough' approach. At no time in recent history have the conditions inside Young Offender Institutions been more oppressive and violent than they are in 2020. Considered by many to be even more dangerous than adult prisons, establishments like Feltham YOI, west of London, closely replicate the feral violence of custodial institutions in the Victorian age.

As one inmate put it after his release, 'Literally every day I was there, you'd see a fight. It just happened all the time, literally all the time.' Another young man who was sent to Isis YOI, not far from London City Airport, spoke of the sort of violence that erupted there. 'Someone got stabbed in the neck in the shower. It was very gruesome and horrifying for me to see all the blood spurting out and someone on the floor nearly dying.' There is a suicide in a British Young

Offender Institution almost every month, and self-harm is at epidemic levels.

For one teenager, Zahid Mubarek, Feltham was to mark the end of his young life for a different reason. Zahid was serving his first and only custodial sentence, for stealing some razor blades (value £6) and 'vehicle interference'. Towards the end of his sentence, Zahid was allocated a new cellmate. Robert Stewart was a 'psychopathic and violent racist', who had already been involved in killing another inmate before he was placed with Zahid, who spent the last days of his life in constant fear.

The prison officer who made the decision to place Stewart with Zahid apparently knew nothing of the previous murder. Nobody noticed that, slowly but surely, Stewart was dismantling a table in his cell. He eventually managed to separate one of the table legs and, on the very day that Zahid was due to be released, Stewart battered him nearly to death in his sleep. Zahid's uncle, who saw him lying in a hospital bed, clinging to life, realised that there was no hope. 'His injuries were so horrendous, I knew he would not be able to survive them,' he later recalled.

An inquiry into Zahid's death heard that some of the officers at Feltham had engaged in a practice known as 'gladiator' or 'colosseum', in which black or ethnic minority inmates were deliberately placed with known racists. It was said that bets were then placed on how soon violence would erupt in the cell.

So much for civilised twenty-first-century Britain. This is the society we have created and, just as with prison policy across the board and our approach to drugs, we have got it completely wrong. Not only are Young Offender Institutions places of misery, violence and death, but they also have precisely the opposite effect to that which is claimed by their advocates. YOIs, and in fact youth custody centres and juvenile facilities all over the world, are among the most effective methods ever invented to *increase* rates of reoffending and *worsen* levels of crime by young people.

One former inmate, 'Jason', spoke of his stays in seven different institutions between the ages of fourteen and seventeen. 'At first it was a bit of a shock to the system not having your family around, and then I got used to it,' he said. Jason's time inside was not put to waste. 'How to weigh up drugs and sell them, how to make a profit on them, car theft. I've learned how to fight in jail. You've got to fight quick; it can only last a couple of seconds before you get stopped, so you've got to fight better. You go for hurting as soon as possible – fighting, kicking, biting, together.'

Young Offender Institutions are not only 'universities of crime' but a form of medieval survivalism, played out in gyms, corridors, dining halls and, for some of the most tragic victims of all – like Zahid – in bed, fast asleep.

POLMONT YOUNG OFFENDER INSTITUTION

Who are these young people – children in many cases – who end up behind the walls of such places; prisons in all but name? On a cool and breezy day in the summer of 2019, I left Glasgow with a BBC film crew to make the short journey east along the M80 to Her Majesty's Young Offender Institution Polmont, on the outskirts of Falkirk.

We had been granted 'access all areas' by the Scottish Prison Service and the Governor of Polmont to film for a television series on criminal justice. It was my first experience of presenting a series for television and, under the guidance of my talented BBC producer, Paul Connolly,

I was able to explore every corner of the criminal justice system: from policing, to the courts, to prisons, to the experiences of both hardened criminals and the victims of serious crime.

The specific reason for visiting Polmont, apart from the more open attitude of the Scottish government towards the media, was that the entire philosophy behind youth justice in Scotland is different to that south of the border. Scotland's justice policy is devolved from London to Edinburgh and has taken a very different course from England's in recent years.

The ethos of the Scottish system is one of welfare and rehabilitation. This begins with a small point of nomenclature, applied to those detained behind the walls of institutions like Polmont. They are given the non-judgemental label of 'young people' and are never referred to as 'inmates', let alone 'criminals'. Which is not to say that some of them have not engaged in activity that has caused the most extreme harm to other people. Indeed, a number of those I met were convicted murderers.

At the time of my visit there were several hundred young people in Polmont, aged between sixteen and twenty-one. The younger group, children by any definition, were kept separately from the older teenagers. After passing through the security checkpoint, I began my tour. My escort was Hugh, an affable veteran prison officer with thirty years on the job.

Despite the stated underlying aims of the institution and the whole system, Hugh was dressed like any other prison officer. He wore the same full uniform – of black trousers, white shirt, epaulettes with name and service number – as officers of Her Majesty's Prison Service all over the United Kingdom. And the buildings themselves were indistinguishable in any material way from the establishments that house adult prisoners.

This became most clear to me as we passed along steel-covered walkways and into one of the units in which the young people were confined. Gate after gate had to be opened by the central control room, just as in Belmarsh and – for that matter – in Alabama, until we finally entered one of the 'wings'. Having read much about the comparatively liberal ethos of the Scottish system, I was disappointed to see that the internal design was identical to that of British prisons I had visited before and to those used countless times as the settings for television dramas.

The wing, around a hundred yards or so long from end to end, was divided into two by a central security control area, manned by officers and staff. On entering the control area from the outside, via a heavy-duty prison-issue steel door, I found myself effectively caged in by floor-to-ceiling metal barriers. Each of them had a large locked gate in the centre, through which access could be gained to the wings, where the cells were located.

Hugh led the way, using the keys from his enormous keyring at each step of the way. He explained that the inmates were in workshops and education, as it was the middle of the morning. They were not locked up at Polmont during the daytime. One of the young men had been excused from educational classes that day so that he could speak to me.

Andy was serving a long sentence for a serious assault committed outside a pub. He had been drinking heavily when someone told him that there was a paedophile outside. Andy and his friends went looking for this man, giving no thought to the rationale for doing so, let alone to the possibility that the information might be flawed. The alleged child abuser was pointed out to them and, without pause for reflection, Andy launched a ferocious attack, punching the man heavily in the face.

He neither noticed nor particularly cared about the fact that the victim was wearing glasses. The lenses were smashed inwards by the force of Andy's blows and fragments of glass punctured one of the man's eyeballs. The injury was so severe that the victim was rendered blind in one eye. Mercifully the man retained the sight in his other eye but, as Andy acknowledged without hesitation, both men's lives were changed for ever in the few seconds of rage that led to the attack. For Andy, there was a further irony, as it emerged that his target was not only the victim of a life-changing assault, but it was also a case of mistaken identification. The man was not a paedophile after all.

I confess that Andy seemed at least as agonised by the fact that he had missed out on the chance to teach a sex offender a lesson as he was by the harm caused to another human being, or his own fate in being locked up as a result. It is a cliché – but no less accurate as a result – that paedophiles are fair game for attack by those in prison for less emotive crimes. For all of his progress and learning – of which more shortly – Andy really did not see that committing a vicious assault outside a pub was never a wise or justifiable course, whoever the target might be.

With the camera crew behind us, Andy showed me around his 'gaff', making clear that the word 'cell' was not part of the Polmont vocabulary. I walked through the heavy steel door into what was, by any rational definition, a prison cell. It was a little larger than Nelson Mandela's cell on Robben Island, but not by much.

With barely room for Andy and me, let alone a cameraman and sound recordist, we spent a few minutes looking around. A small single bed to the left, a desk with small television and PlayStation to the right, shelves laden with a large selection of shower gels in every colour of the rainbow, like a mural of toiletries – 'An artform in Polmont,' Andy told me – and a few small photographs of those 'on the outside', stuck to the walls. 'Is this your family?' I asked.

'No' really,' Andy replied, in a thick Scottish accent, 'Jus' ma friends an' that.' I looked closely and saw that there were indeed no older people, no family scenes; just groups of teenagers – at parties, in pubs, out and about enjoying themselves, doing what Andy had not been able to do in the months he had been at Polmont. And what he would be unable to do for many more months to come.

We left Andy's gaff, which was spotlessly clean and neat to a military level of discipline, to sit in the corridor outside, at one of the heavy metal tables bolted solid to the floor in another echo of Mobile County Jail. Andy seemed unfazed by the cameras following us and opened up as much as I suspect he would have done were he not being filmed at all.

He had been arrested several times, before the assault that led to the charges that landed him in Polmont this time around. He had been in and out of the juvenile justice system since his early teens. Drugs, booze, antisocial behaviour and a virtual absence of direction were all features of his short life. I asked him about his background. 'Some people have a mum and dad, family support, someone to make them go to school and do their homework – did you have any of those things?'

'Nah,' he replied, a pained expression on his face. 'But I cannae blame that for what I done to that guy. I done it myself and I'm responsible.' It was hard to tell if Andy had ever reflected on his lack of role models and support growing up, or if he even knew what a more advantaged childhood would look like. Let alone one where education, careers and affluence are expected as the norm. I also wondered whether he really assumed personal responsibility for his actions, as he claimed, or whether he was repeating back the words of a course leader in a dozen anger-management workshops – was he just saying 'the right things'?

Though I sympathised with Andy's case, I could not shake off what seemed to be his greatest regret; not at bursting a man's eyeball in principle, but in failing to blind a child sex offender – an opportunity missed to exact some street justice on someone he considered a deserving target. Statistically, whatever his statements of good intentions, the likelihood is that Andy, and most of those incarcerated as teenagers, will be back again before long, soon progressing to Scotland's adult prisons, which are as inherently self-perpetuating and violent as any others in Britain. Even in the most enlightened of youth-custody regimes in the country, the outcomes, in terms of reoffending and reincarceration, are extremely poor.

My tour of Polmont continued with visits to workshops, providing skills for the outside world. 'For some of these young men, this is the first time they have really been responsible for anything,' one course coordinator told me (she was leading an animal workshop called Paws for Progress). I watched Ross, seventeen, serving three years for robbery, as he led Elvis, a feisty young black and white terrier, around some traffic cones. Ross appeared entirely absorbed in the dog, exuding a look of confidence and satisfaction – punctuated with a smile as the dog performed as instructed.

And yet, the pathos of it. Ross was bordering on adulthood and this was the most rewarding thing – the *purest* activity – in which he had ever engaged: leading someone else's dog around a line of traffic cones, once a week for an hour or so, behind a massive concrete prison wall, under the all-seeing eyes of the security cameras and the scrutiny of uniformed guards at all times.

We visited a new building, of which the administration and the Scottish authorities are understandably proud. Still within the walls of HMYOI Polmont, the Learning Centre stands apart from the older infrastructure of the institution, marking both a physical and psychological 'escape' from the custodial regime. The entire two-storey building is flooded with natural light, modern in design and marked by colourful choices of paint and furniture colours. It compares favourably with the state comprehensive school that I attended in the 1980s and had the atmosphere of a well-funded sixth-form college or university department.

A central meeting area was informally arranged and had tables and chairs that were not attached to the floor. Around the sides were a dozen or more offices, workshops and classrooms of various sizes. The education staff were civilians, a mixture of men and women, and they wore casual clothes, much like the teachers and lecturers of any college with a teenage student body. We were shown into a large room, which had been set up to demonstrate the project work of some of the young people, in subjects as diverse as basic personal finance, drama workshops, history and art. The standard of work was high and those responsible had clearly taken pride in its execution.

The administration had arranged for ten of the young men, including Andy, to sit with me to discuss their work in the education unit and, with no censorship of any kind, their life on the outside and the crimes that had led them to Polmont. As they arrived, one of them approached me with a warm smile, clearly excited at the prospect of a television interview and the break in routine that it represented. Nathan proudly showed me a finance project he had produced and told me how much he enjoyed coming to the education unit and the things he had learned. The cameras were not rolling at this point, as the crew was still rigging the room for light and sound.

'How long are you in for?' I asked Nathan, thinking that he looked too young, happy and generally positive to have much time left to serve. 'Seventeen years at least,' he said, with a shrug. My producer, Paul, overheard this and, as we moved on to another of the group, looked at me with a raised eyebrow at the length of sentence involved. 'Murder,' I mouthed to him, knowing that there was no other crime in Britain for which a teenager – Nathan was eighteen at the time I met him – could be locked up for such a long time. I was right, as he was soon to confirm when the whole group assembled in a circle of chairs, close to the displays of their work.

I had deliberately dressed down for Polmont so as not to intimidate the young people with the formality – and almost entirely negative associations for them – of a suit and tie. Wearing jeans, trainers, a T-shirt and casual jacket, I sat alongside two of them, and the cameramen operated invisibly around the group, a boom microphone held aloft and out of shot.

I asked them about their education. None of them had remained at school past the age of around fourteen; several had left long before that. I asked a sixteen-year-old, who had already been in youth custody for two years, when he had last been in any form of education. 'Primary school,' he told me. 'Then I was on the streets – I always carried a knife from the age of eleven.' As he told me this, he was smiling and laughing, possibly showing off a bit, but I could not help my reaction, telling him: 'I honestly don't see what's funny about that.'

'It's no' funny,' he said. 'It's jus' the way it is.'

The moment of tension passed and the group opened up. One young Nigerian drug trafficker, serving a long sentence, told me that he could not believe the levels of knife crime and violence among young people in Britain.

Most of these young men had a history of exclusion from school, periods in care, frequent arrests, engagement with the criminal justice system, drug and alcohol use from as young as eleven. Parental influence – in fact any form of positive adult role model – had been almost entirely missing from their lives. They enjoyed and obtained value from the diverse range of educational and training opportunities at Polmont, although some felt that we might not have been shown the more unpalatable sides of life there during the filming. 'You should come to our unit,' one of them said. 'It's a shithole.'

I am sure there are millions of voters – and thousands of angry tweeters – out there who think: 'Quite right, it's not supposed to be a holiday camp.' This is an unshakeable sentiment in the public consciousness, and particularly so when it comes to young offenders, seen by many as a source of relentless misery to law-abiding citizens; in their homes, on public transport and on the streets. I am no apologist for violence and antisocial behaviour. My views on children in the criminal justice system, just like my views on the use of prison and the prohibition of drugs, do not arise from some 'soft' liberal perspective. Quite the opposite – I am interested only in the hard facts as to what does and does not work in reducing crime, improving lives and, first and foremost, preventing as many people as possible from becoming victims.

On that note, I asked for a show of hands around the group of young men at Polmont. 'Do you think this will be the last time you ever go inside?' I asked.

After a moment's hesitation from some, every one of them raised a hand. Sadly, almost every one of these young men was deluded. Good intentions from children and young people locked up in custodial institutions, however enlightened the regime, are almost never carried through on the outside. Without for a moment denigrating the extraordinary commitment of the staff and the admirable policy priorities of the Scottish government, the simple truth is that most of the young men in that room will be in and out of Polmont until they 'graduate' to the full adult experience of prison. From there, as we have seen, for most, all prospects of a law-abiding and productive life will be lost.

There was one further 'personal development' project for me to see, outside the education building. Two of those I met were enrolled on the prestigious Duke of Edinburgh Award scheme, a longstanding charity that 'works with organisations across the UK to help young people gain essential skills, experience, confidence and resilience to successfully navigate adult life'.

These young men were serving long sentences for violent offences, but during their time at Polmont both had become mentors for others and embraced the discipline and challenge of the Duke of Edinburgh scheme. How, though, could they engage in one of the most important activities required – camping outdoors? They were in prison.

They showed me outside to an enclosed yard – customary high fencing on all sides and 'prison' walls behind that – in front of which was a small patch of grass, possibly half the size of a tennis court. If the sight of a young inmate, patiently leading a dog around traffic cones, had carried with it an element of pathos, the proud display here took things a step further. The two young men showed me the skills they had learned on the DofE programme, smiling broadly as they did so. There, in the bright sunlight of a Scottish summer afternoon, were two single-person tents, skilfully erected and each accompanied by a small gas cooker, firewood and various other camping equipment. This is where they would spend the required number of nights to demonstrate the skills needed to pass the 'expedition' requirement and to qualify for a Bronze Award. Under canvas, under the Scottish skies, at least a hundred yards and a dozen layers of security away from freedom.

The Governor of Polmont is Brenda Stewart, a veteran of the prison service and a woman brimming with empathy, compassion and common sense. Her accent has a lyrical and gravelly quality, which somehow combines poetry and steely discipline in the same package. There are few people in British criminal justice with greater front-line experience of dealing with children and young people than Brenda Stewart.

She was incredibly open and frank. 'These young people have committed offences, some of them serious ones, but they are victims too,' she explained. The Scottish authorities, with Brenda's support at Polmont, had spent a great deal of time analysing the backgrounds of those who were arrested, prosecuted and ended up in custody. The life experiences that this research had uncovered shocked me to the core.

Most of those I had met at Polmont had been excluded from school, many of them never to return. More disturbing still was the degree of their exposure to trauma the likes of which most of us will never experience even once in a lifetime, let alone several times. 'Many of the young people here have directly witnessed a traumatic death,' Brenda told me, 'meaning either a drug overdose or a death from violence – a murder. Some of them more than one.' She reeled off a list of other life experiences that lay behind the stories of the young people in her custody and care – imprisonment of one or both parents, exposure to domestic abuse, drink and drugs from a young age, homelessness, life in the care system and, of course, child poverty.

Brenda spoke passionately of the need for a holistic and compassionate approach to children and young people. She told me that we need to address the complex web of trauma and other negative factors that act as catalysts for criminal behaviour, leading inexorably to longer and longer periods of incarceration. Only by focusing resources on the whole child, Brenda believed, and not writing young people off as a lost cause, could we begin to make Polmont and other Young Offender Institutions obsolete.

'What about punishment?' I asked.

'These young people have been punished; being in here is punishment enough. We need to focus on what happens when they leave,' she replied.

Brenda's view is supported by countless sources. The Howard League analysed teenagers in the criminal justice system and found that those from children's homes were at least fifteen times more likely to be criminalised than others of the same age. It is inconceivable that, by sheer chance, some of the most deprived and damaged young people in society just happen to be overwhelmingly more criminal by nature than the average.

As we left Polmont, I reflected on the whole experience. There was a lot that was right about the ethos I had seen in practice during my visit, but even a small amount of digging revealed that, in the end, the incarceration of these young people still amounted to a form of life sentence. Most would never really be free, even when they were released back onto the streets. Once inside the criminal justice machine, the inmates of Polmont, just like those elsewhere in Britain, would, by and large, be trapped there for good.

THE FAILURE OF CHILD CRIMINALISATION

'Recidivism' – meaning the tendency to reoffend – is a word that is largely confined to criminology lectures, official statistics and the occasional government report. It is not a headline-grabber, like 'hooligan', 'thug' or 'teen gangster'. Few politicians get excited about statistics, still less about those that tend to undermine the prevailing public mood when it comes to election time. Perhaps even some of the readers of this book, with an above-average interest in criminal justice policy, may have read the word 'recidivism' with a guilty lack of enthusiasm.

You could be forgiven for doing so, when politician after politician advocates a 'crackdown' on 'antisocial behaviour', 'gang violence', knives and even 'feral youth'. In response, many elements of the news media duly oblige with copious acclamatory reports of such policies. Voters respond with approval in large numbers in the ballot box, in Britain and elsewhere, and Parliament duly obliges by passing harsh sanctions for children and young people, whatever party is in power.

In the US, mandatory custodial sentences have long been a feature of the sentencing of children, as we saw in chapter 2, even in some cases leading to the imprisonment of those under eighteen for the rest of their natural lives. In England, we have been steadily moving in the same direction, as politicians respond – slavishly and without reason – to each round of media coverage of a youth 'crime wave'. Escalating incidents of knife violence in recent years, specifically those involving young people, have led to the introduction of a mandatory custodial sentence for a first offence of threatening someone with a knife or a second offence of possessing one. The use of evidence, or of any form of analysis of what actually works to reduce youth crime, always gives way – in the end – to populism.

In 2019, British Home Secretary Priti Patel took the 'tough on crime' rhetoric to a new level in British politics when she said that she wanted people, including young offenders, to 'literally feel terror' at the thought of what would happen to them if they committed a crime. She has advocated increased use of custodial sentences, aggressive police action against young people on the streets in the form of greater use of 'stop and search', and a zero-tolerance approach to cannabis possession. Ms Patel even went so far as to promise her supporters that she will win 'the war on crime'. What an extreme of hubris, jingoism and arrogance.

Throughout all of these waves of media and political tub-thumping about youth crime, and subsequent policies on child sentencing, one thing above all shines through.

Recidivism. Yes, just as with the imprisonment of adults, the criminalisation – and incarceration – of young people simply *does not work*. I have lost count of the times I have patiently and calmly used unambiguous evidence to that effect, to be met with a shrug of the shoulders and an admonition to 'think of the victim', 'protect the public' or 'impose punishment'.

I am coming to the evidence, but this is the headline – criminalising children causes *more* crime and *more* victims. Locking children up even more so.

Prison and drug reform are important to me, but a sea change in our handling of troubled children, in society as a whole and not just in the criminal justice system, is the most important issue of all. Despite all of the media coverage around antisocial behaviour, knife crime and young people, we have actually seen a sharp decline in the overall number of recorded crimes committed by children.

As with all recent crime figures, there has been a huge distortion in Britain as a result of dramatic reductions in police numbers and in the funding of the criminal justice system, including the courts, prosecutors and defence lawyers. One explanation for falling crime rates in certain categories is undoubtedly that there are fewer police officers to make arrests, fewer prosecutors to bring charges and fewer courts to sentence offenders.

But, on any view, the figures show that reduced use of custody does not result in big increases in crime by children. Quite the opposite.

The Prison Reform Trust's annual 'Bromley Briefing' sets out in stark terms the countless dangerous, unfair and irrational outcomes of the child justice system. Despite a dramatic fall in the overall number of young people under eighteen in custody (70 per cent since 2009), the number of crimes committed by that age group has fallen *even more* (75 per cent). This hardly suggests a link between *increasing* the incarceration of the young and *reducing* youth crime. Young inmates are many times more likely to have been in the care system than other children, which surely calls out for attention to what happens in care as a top policy priority, rather than simply locking up even more care leavers.

Tragically, in what amounts to a stain on Britain's national life, the proportion of young ethnic minority people in custody has increased in the past decade, along with assaults, use of physical restraint and self-harm incidents. In fact, the total number of violent incidents is higher than when there were three times the number of young inmates as there are today. We are brutalising children every day, all in the name of getting tough on crime. The media, politicians and the public are mostly looking the other way. Hundreds of the most damaged and vulnerable young people in our society face the daily risk of violence, self-harm and death, and we are all allowing this to happen; some even applauding it.

But surely putting children through this dystopian nightmare must 'teach them a lesson', whatever the sentence? Dragged through the courts, given a dressing-down by the judge, treated like what they are – criminals? Who would want to go through that twice? Or more? The answer is, of course, that nearly all of them end up back in the system, not twice but countless times, and those who receive the 'toughest' sentences do so the most.

Official figures show the shocking and shameful truth about the criminalisation of our children. Over 40 per cent of those young people subjected to the criminal justice process reoffend within twelve months. Imagine if a manufacturer were building cars that crashed at a rate of 40 per cent a year, due to a design flaw. There would be an uproar. Vehicles would be subjected to factory recalls, safety certificates would be withdrawn and the offending business shut down by public demand. But the average young offender crashes not just once, but reoffends a staggering *four times*, after being sentenced by the criminal courts. With that shameful rate of failure, the youth justice system should be demolished altogether and rebuilt from the ground up.

The plain truth is that the 'tougher' we get on young people, the more crimes they commit and, beyond contradiction, the more victims we create and the greater the quantum of human misery for our society.

ONE BOY'S JOURNEY TO HELL AND BACK

> 'You will never be anything!'
>   – Crown Court judge

Gethin Jones is a man of wisdom, insight and compassion. He has an insider's bitter understanding of life in care, youth justice, drug addiction and prison. In many ways, his story expresses all that is wrong with the criminal justice system when it turns its firepower on the young.

I spoke to Gethin in late 2019 as I approached my fiftieth birthday. He and I are around the same age. In terms of our life journeys, that is where the similarities largely end.

Now smartly dressed, balding, but looking every inch the successful professional that he is today, Gethin Jones's start in life could not have been more different, as he told me when we spoke.

He was born into a family already involved with social services. Gethin's mother, a single parent to four children, had spent her own childhood in care and struggled with learning difficulties. With hindsight, Gethin understands that his mother's own history and struggles made it impossible for her to relate to her children in an ideal and entirely nurturing way. Without a hint of blame, he observes that he simply did not have the sort of family relationships and support that a child needs in order to thrive. Gethin soon found himself ensnared in the criminal justice system.

Gethin's first conviction was at the age of eleven, due to what he describes as 'erratic behaviour'. A predictable pattern ensued: a year later he was in the care system; by thirteen he had been expelled from school; at fourteen he was sent to youth custody for the first time, came out, went back in, and before he knew it his childhood was gone for ever. He had spent most of his teens 'behind the door'. And then things really took a turn for the worse.

Gethin reached the age of twenty and had not once seen a child psychiatrist, psychologist or any other professional with the time and skills to find out what was going on and to help him find a different way to live. Having been told by everyone in authority, throughout his childhood and teenage years, that he was destined not only for failure but for prison and drug addiction, it was not surprising that the predictions came true.

Gethin recalled one occasion when he was released from a Young Offender Institution on a Friday, stole some cigarettes from the petrol station on the Saturday, was arrested and in a police station over the weekend, before being remanded back to custody by the magistrates' court on the Monday morning. No matter the order made against him by the courts, Gethin would breach it and go back inside.

As soon as he 'graduated' to adult prison, Gethin found heroin, having never taken it 'on the out'. The drug became his driving force for the next decade and he entirely gave up on any way of life beyond heroin, crime and prison. The most terrible irony of all is that his fierce intelligence was never extinguished. He knew exactly what he had become and why. Appearing before yet another court at the age of twenty, to receive yet another prison sentence, he told the judge: 'What you see before you is what you created.' He had a point.

The judge disagreed, dismissing all talk of rehabilitation, of giving Gethin a chance to pursue training and employment of some kind. 'You are a professional criminal,' he pronounced. 'You will never be a bricklayer or a plumber. You will never be anything.'

This was the verdict of the criminal justice system on Gethin Jones, a young man barely out of his teens. You can almost hear the cheers for the judge's remarks from a certain brand of politician, from much of the media and, yes, from plenty of voters at election time.

Heroin took hold of Gethin and was both available and, by the time he became hooked, acceptable as a form of escape in the prison environment. He explained how this had come about from a history of disapproval of 'smackheads' among the general prison population, for whom smoking cannabis had long been a more tolerated form of drug use. 'In the mid-90s, they introduced mandatory drug testing and that led to an explosion in heroin use in prison,' he explained. 'It only stays in your system for a couple of days, whereas weed is there for weeks.' Yet another perverse manifestation of the law of unintended consequences in the criminal justice system – a generation of heroin addicts, created directly by a testing policy that had been given no real thought before it was introduced.

Years passed and Gethin got out and went back in, much of his third decade of life also spent inside. He noticed a change over the years. 'It used to be eighty per cent career criminals and twenty per cent addicts and the mentally ill,' he told me. 'Now it's the other way around.'

In his late twenties, believing that his life 'would never be more than a bag of gear, a prison cell and a council estate', Gethin 'was a cornered animal and [his] soul was dying'. Miraculously, after receiving yet another prison sentence, this time of four years, he met people who, for the first time in his life, 'treated [him] with respect and care'. Caring staff on the inside were followed by engagement with services, official and voluntary, after he was released from that sentence. Six long years later, Gethin had completed what he describes as his 'whole rehabilitation journey'. He was well on his way to the age of forty by this stage – childhood, youth, young adulthood mostly behind him.

There is only one feature of Gethin's life that sets him apart from the majority of other children arrested, criminalised, brutalised and institutionalised by our criminal justice system: he managed eventually to escape. He now runs a successful business, 'Unlocking Potential', which draws upon his own experiences to provide training, mentoring and commercial services, aimed at inspiring others and supporting projects to engage with offenders of all ages in ways that might actually make a difference.

Gethin is in no doubt that what he said to the judge all those years ago is the truth. The criminal justice system that judge represents – which operates on behalf of us all – is what created Gethin the child, Gethin the young offender, Gethin the addict, Gethin the adult criminal. It is the same system that created all the young men I met at Polmont and almost all of the clients I have acted for over the years, some of whose stories are laid bare in these pages.

Gethin believes that a legal and safe supply of drugs, access to counselling, addiction services and appropriate forms of therapy would have a huge impact on young people in the criminal justice machine, particularly those who have passed through the care system and experienced trauma in their lives.

He spoke of a fourteen-year-old child 'criminal', recently 'named and shamed' in the press for antisocial behaviour. The boy had become 'feral' at the age of five after his mother died. His father had cancer. The boy was highly aggressive and had, unsurprisingly, entered the criminal justice system. 'Where were we when he was five?' Gethin asked, rhetorically.

The only thing that mattered to Gethin was safety, both for the child and for the rest of us. He had no doubt that it was possible to offer security for the damaged children crossing the radar of the police, and that those leaving care in particular needed to receive huge financial investment, just to provide the basis of a stable adult life. The shameful truth is that we spend almost nothing on the sorts of services needed to support young people through the most troubled of times, to pick them up when they fall, and to provide them with the basic equipment to enter adulthood as fully functioning members of the community, rather than as pariahs, blighted for life by the label 'criminal'.

We nevertheless pay hundreds of thousands of pounds to process many of these children through the criminal justice system and to warehouse them for years; more if they end up graduating to adult prisons, as most of them do. Indeed, we happily condemn damaged children – at enormous expense – to hellholes like Feltham, where they are more likely to be assaulted or killed than to find an escape from the revolving doors of courts, prisons and addiction.

If the prohibition of drugs and the imprisonment of adults are two forms of insanity, the criminalisation of children is madness beyond belief.

AN ESCAPE FROM MADNESS

In Luxembourg this chapter would not need to be written at all. The age of criminal responsibility coincides with the age of majority. The eighteenth birthday of every Luxembourger marks the point of 'full legal capacity and full responsibility for the young person's actions'. Luxembourg's law on this subject begins with this simple proposition:

> *The minor who is the perpetrator of criminal offences cannot as a matter of principle be sentenced to a criminal sentence.*

A minor is a child, and a child in Luxembourg is anyone below the age of eighteen. There is no concept of a 'young offender', as some form of intermediate stage of criminality between the complete innocence of the very young child and the mature culpability of adulthood. In Luxembourg, they do not train their children to become entrenched criminals from as young as ten, in the way that we and our American cousins do.

The 1992 law has one overriding objective – the protection of the child.

This is achieved by means of confidential interventions in closed youth courts with no formal legal procedures or even – in most cases – lawyers at all. The proceedings never result in the details of the case, let alone the identity of the child, entering the public domain. Nowhere is the concept of punishment mentioned at all. Where a child behaves in a way that might – in other nations – result in a criminal sentence, the only options are reprimands, educational assistance programmes, engagement in philanthropic activity to help the community, and in a few extreme cases placement in the security unit of a socio-educational centre.

This law came into force following the United Nations Convention on the Rights of the Child 1989, which set out universal rights for all children, such as the right to be protected from abusive treatment, the right to an education and the right to family life. The United Kingdom is a signatory but we consign our children to the formal criminal justice system with wilful disregard for the Convention's most fundamental principles, not least in places like Feltham.

I am in no doubt that we in Britain – and even more so the authorities in the United States – routinely breach the UN Convention in our criminal justice systems, day in day out. It is one of the great and largely hidden scandals of modern times.

Luxembourg is a small and sophisticated country, with high levels of income, education and social welfare provision. Perhaps they can afford to give their children greater legal protections, higher standards of welfare and more intensive intervention than a large and diverse country like Britain? I am sure there are those who will make that argument. To them I say this – we cannot carry on as we are, condemning thousands of the most vulnerable children in society to a lifetime of crime, drugs and prison. We cannot afford the grotesque human and financial costs of our criminalisation of children, and we must not perpetuate the impact it has on the fabric of our society and on our social conscience.

Ten years old is one of the youngest ages of criminal responsibility in the world, never mind in the developed world, despite all our advantages of wealth, education and the rule of law. Dozens of countries have chosen older ages, including in places not otherwise regarded as bastions of human rights. A small selection makes the point:

Country	Age of Criminal Responsibility
Albania	14
Austria	14
Denmark	15
Finland	15
France	13
Iceland	15
Saudi Arabia	12
Spain	14
Sweden	15
Vietnam	14

Many other nations approach children who come into contact with the police and the criminal justice system in a very different way.

In 1994, in a small Norwegian town, five-year-old Silje Redergard was beaten to death by two six-year-old boys. The case has obvious parallels to that of James Bulger. How the boys were treated after the incident could not be more different from the UK approach. The age of criminal responsibility in Norway is fifteen, so the killers could not be branded criminals. Their names were never made public, the media did not brand them 'evil', and they received extensive psychological treatment, intended to permit them to lead fulfilling, crime-free lives.

This compassionate, welfare-based approach to children who break the law is not unique to Norway. Many other countries stand in stark contrast to England and Wales. You do not have to travel far to find them – for example, the regime in Spanish young offender institutions is very different to that in Britain. In La Zarza 're-educational centre' for young offenders in the south of Spain, the only time children are in their rooms is for a forty-five-minute siesta and overnight. In Feltham Young Offender Institute in London, they can be kept in their cells for up to twenty-three hours a day.

Luxembourg, Norway and Spain all have lower rates of youth crime, violence, incarceration and death than the UK. The evidence from around the world is overwhelming. The more you invest in children – before, during and after the period when they first break the law – the more likely they will be to never see the inside of a courtroom in later life, let alone a prison cell. The more you criminalise them, the more crimes they commit.

WHAT HAPPENED TO BOY W

The High Court judge, dressed in the sombre black robes of the Administrative Court, hearing the Judicial Review claim on behalf of Boy W, was not happy. Our challenge to the decision to send Boy W to the Crown Court for trial was based on the argument that he should have been considered separately from Boy X (whose involvement was much more serious). The issue had not been raised at the time of the decision in the magistrates' court and judges do not like it when a new point is raised for the first time on appeal.

Nobody had apparently asked the magistrates' court to consider whether Boy W met the criteria for his case, separately from that of Boy X, to be sent for trial in the Crown Court; wigs, gowns and all. Had they done so, and had the magistrates gone through the proper procedures, said this most eminent of judges, the decision might well have been a lawful one, and Boy W would likely have been placed before a jury for trial, aged twelve (in body if not in mind).

But the court's hands were tied. The law had not been observed. The sending of the case was therefore unlawful, null and void. It was quashed. That meant that Boy W was no longer before the Crown Court at all. He was back in the Youth Court, right at the beginning, and his situation would have to be considered all over again, applying the law correctly, both by the prosecution and the magistrates.

I spoke to the QC for the prosecution after the hearing, a decent man I have known for over twenty-five years. He had read all of the reports on Boy W and could see that the evidence of criminal behaviour by him was slim at best. Ever the professional, he made clear that the decision as to the next steps was ultimately for the Crown Prosecutor in charge of the case, but the QC could see that the criminal justice system might not be the best place for this sorry case to be played out to its conclusion, let alone with the ceremonial formality of the Crown Court.

A few weeks later I received news that the criminal charges against Boy W had been dropped. He was under intensive supervision by social workers and there was a plan in place, both for his welfare and for that of all the other children involved in the case. This decision had been reached in discussion with the parents of all the boys, including those of the five-year-old. Boy W would not need to go through the baffling trauma of giving evidence via video link to a court. There would be no trial.

Sanity had, in the end, prevailed; at least this once.

5

Why people are neither good nor evil

'That door opens up a world where we do not lock up and throw away the key. Where we do not slash prison budgets, and where we focus on rehabilitation not revenge. Jack believed in the inherent goodness of humanity, and felt a deep social responsibility to protect that. Through us all, Jack marches on.'
                            – David Merritt, father of Jack Merritt
                                                       (deceased)

By the time you read these words, for most of you Jack Merritt will probably be little more than a statistic. You may have a dim memory of the white heat of media coverage in the frenzy of the 2019 British election campaign, months or years in the past. Jack Merritt, twenty-five, and Saskia Jones, twenty-three, volunteered for a charity by the name of Learning Together. The organisation brings together some of the brightest and most educationally advantaged young people in the country, graduates of elite universities like Cambridge – Saskia and Jack among them – with ex-offenders, so that each group can be enlightened and enriched by the other.

In late November 2019, Usman Khan, twenty-eight, attended a Learning Together event at Fishmongers Hall, adjacent to London Bridge, and stabbed Saskia and Jack to death. Less than a year earlier, he had been released from prison, where he had been serving time for terrorism offences, centred on an inchoate plot to blow up the London Stock Exchange and to carry out attacks on other public buildings. Khan and his fellow defendants at their trial in 2012 evidently possessed more ideological conviction than bomb-making skills or technical capabilities. Their fantastical plans were disrupted without difficulty by the police and security services.

Following Khan's sentence by the trial judge to an indefinite period of 'Detention for Public Protection' – in effect a life sentence, requiring an application for parole – the Court of Appeal later substituted an 'Extended Determinate' sentence, that provided for Khan's 'automatic release' after serving eight of the sixteen years imposed by the sentence. That ruling began a chain of events that ended with the death of Khan's two young victims in November 2019. He was released straight back onto the streets from one of Britain's highest-security 'Category A' prisons, HMP Whitemoor, a bleak establishment that I have visited several times and to which we will return.

Khan had been in custody for exactly 70,128 hours. His sentence was spent almost entirely in high-security conditions and with no more than a tiny number of those hours used to address the reasons why he had become radicalised or to send him back into society with a new outlook. For the great majority of his time, Khan was warehoused, dehumanised and, perhaps most alarming of all, completely ignored by all but his fellow inmates, many of whom were happy to encourage the ideology behind his past crimes, the same warped view of humanity that subsequently guided his last acts of all – the murders of Jack Merritt and Saskia Jones.

Khan claimed to the authorities, until the day he died, that he had been 'deradicalised' and was no longer a threat to society, although there was little concrete evidence of that, beyond his words. At 1:55 p.m. on 29 November 2019, he walked into Fishmongers Hall and stabbed and slashed Jack and Saskia to death, before making his escape onto the street, where he was tackled to the ground and disarmed by members of the public. He was wearing a fake suicide vest – a pathetic but informative reminder of the limits of his terrorist skill set. At 2:03 p.m., armed police officers arrived and shot Khan dead as soon as they had a clean line of sight.

The killings took place at the height of election fever, and politicians on all sides were quick to take to the airwaves. Prime Minister Boris Johnson gave his view shortly after the murders: 'I think that it probably is true that people can't be rehabilitated, and I think it varies very widely. There are unquestionably some cases that are just too tough to crack and alas he appears to have been one of them.'

As the facts of the case began to emerge in more detail, the bitter irony of the whole sequence of events came into focus. Khan had certainly not been deradicalised or rehabilitated, despite the tens of thousands of hours during which he was under the total control of the British state, which had the power to place him where it wished, with whom it wished, and to direct every minute of his day. It is difficult to imagine a clearer example of the failure of the present approach to imprisonment than Khan's

I found a video online of Khan; a short BBC interview filmed several years before the crimes that led to his incarceration for eight years. He was sixteen or seventeen when his family home was raided by the police; fresh-faced and barely able to carry off the fluffy beard that he was beginning to grow. Wearing both an Islamic headscarf and a hooded tracksuit top, he spoke with a voice newly broken, still a hint of boyish high pitch about it, to tell the reporter: 'I've been born and bred in England, in Stoke-on-Trent, in Cobridge, and all the community knows me and they will know, if you ask them, they will know like these labels what they're putting on us, like terrorist, this, that, they will know I ain't no terrorist.'

Whether or not Khan had already then begun to engage in earnest in the discussions of bombing and death that led him to commit a double murder, he looked to be precisely what he was: a foolish child, plainly seeking an identity beyond the Midlands pottery town in which he had lived his short life. But, as it later emerged, he had turned not to football, to college, to a job at McDonald's, nor to any one of the host of innocent ways in which he could have spent his time. Khan had been drawn to the magnetism – for that small minority of disillusioned Muslim boys – of jihad. In more basic terms, he had been brainwashed.

Other photographs emerged, including stills from police surveillance footage two years or so after the BBC interview, in which a more mature Usman Khan is depicted in deep discussion with his eventual co-defendants at trial. The conspirators were all arrested in 2010 in connection with

FIGURE 8 Usman Khan (circled) as a teenager in 2010, at the time he was planning terrorist attacks

their grandiose plots against the British public. Khan, then aged just nineteen, was charged with the terrorist offences of which he was later convicted.

Shortly after the 2019 killings, the identity of Khan's victims emerged, and before long their faces appeared on every news website and television report. One of the most popular images comprised side-by-side photographs of Jack and Saskia: both in their academic robes; he holding up his Cambridge degree certificate; she standing proudly before a college building. In every image, they were the picture of vibrant, unstoppable youth, smiling at their good fortune. The world was theirs for the taking.

The news media found the narrative easy at first. The subliminal message was clear – dangerous and evil [brown] outsider snuffs out the limitless potential of the best of our [white] society. More details soon followed. Not only were Jack and Saskia among the country's academic elite, destined

FIGURE 9 Jack Merritt and Saskia Jones

for greatness, but they were dedicated to supporting the underdog, in the form of offenders and ex-offenders. They were giving their time freely to help people like Usman Khan to navigate life after prison and to avoid going back inside. Some commentators even suggested that the victims' own naivety – believing in these dangerous people – was responsible for their deaths.

In most cases of this kind, the media would have been able to close the book on this case as a clear example of good versus evil, light versus darkness, villains and heroes. Two things changed the story.

First, as the politicians grew more and more rabid in their calls for 'locking prisoners up and throwing away the key', especially for people like Khan, Jack Merritt's father, David – no doubt imploding with grief – took to Twitter. He was angry: 'My son, Jack, who was killed in this attack, would not wish his death to be used as a pretext for more draconian sentences or for detaining people unnecessarily.'

As commentators and politicians spouted more and more extreme rhetoric, with many on social media falling back on clichéd calls for the return of the death penalty for 'these scum', David Merritt wrote a short article for the *Guardian* in which his fury was palpable: 'Jack would be seething at his death, and his life, being used to perpetuate an agenda of hate that he gave his everything fighting against. We should never forget that.'

This fightback from a grieving father was not what the media or the politicians had expected. But as if the intervention of David Merritt was not enough, a second piece of news emerged to interfere with the neat stereotypes and easy categorisations of a double murder in broad daylight. As soon as the story broke, several unidentified 'heroes' were pictured, as part of a group of bystanders who tackled Khan on London Bridge immediately after the fatal stabbings of Jack and Saskia, disarming and disabling him until the armed police unit arrived.

The bravery of these men, running towards Khan when they had no idea what dangers they faced and without any way of knowing that the 'suicide vest' was a fake, was illustrated by footage from a dozen camera angles. One man walked away, holding up one of Khan's bloodstained knives, making loud and clear to all that he was not the attacker to ensure that he would not be shot by the arriving police team. Another was pictured astride Khan, who was by this stage prostrate on the pavement, punching out while holding the killer fast to the floor, reluctant to let go even when commanded to do so by an armed officer.

Just as the 'life should mean life' message had been undermined by the poignant views of Jack Merritt himself, preserved for ever in his Twitter feed, it unravelled even more when the identities of some of the 'heroes' began to emerge.

One of them was James Ford, forty-two, who was out of prison for the day. Ford was on the verge of release from a life sentence for a murder that he committed in 2003. He strangled his victim and cut her throat, leaving her body on waste ground in Ashford, Kent, close to her home. Ford called the Samaritans forty-five times after the murder and eventually told one of the volunteers on the confidential helpline that he had 'killed a girl' and was feeling suicidal. The Samaritans counsellor on other end of the line broke the organisation's rules and called the police, which quickly led to Ford's arrest for the murder.

Following Khan's attack on Saskia Jones, Ford 'rushed to the scene and tried to save [her] life' and also to help others affected. 'His actions during the attack', it was reported, 'had probably saved lives.'

John Crilly was forty-eight years old on the day of the attack. Despite being around half Crilly's age, Jack Merritt acted as a mentor to the older man. They had met at HMP Grendon in Buckinghamshire as Crilly was coming to the end of an eighteen-year sentence for the robbery and manslaughter of an elderly man, Augustine Maduemezia, in Manchester in February 2005. Crilly had originally been convicted of murder on the basis of 'joint enterprise' (he had not personally attacked the victim), but the more serious offence was later quashed and reduced to manslaughter on appeal. The Court of Appeal noted that Crilly had made 'huge progress' since the events of 2005.

FIGURE 10 John Crilly and Jack Merritt

Had the appeal been refused, Crilly could not even have applied for parole until 2025, as his 'minimum term' for murder was twenty years.

Jack Merritt was a course coordinator of an educational programme at the prison where Crilly used his years of incarceration to study for a law degree with the Open University. Jack proudly attended Crilly's graduation ceremony and the two were photographed together; the new graduate in colourful academic robes. After his death, Crilly called Jack 'the best guy I ever met'.

Crilly himself made no excuses for his past, telling a BBC reporter: 'I was lost in drugs. I had a bad life, I've changed it, but I wasn't guilty of murder. I totally accept what I did and it was wrong. That's important to me. I would have done the time, I would have done every day of that.' Thankfully, as it turned out, by November 2019 John Crilly had been released and was present at the Fishmongers Hall event.

After witnessing the attack on his friend and mentor, Crilly did not hesitate to pick up a fire extinguisher and give chase, along with several other ex-offenders from the Learning Together programme. Video footage showed Crilly confronting Khan, spraying him in the face at a time when he would have been completely unaware that Khan's suicide vest was a fake. Seconds later the police arrived on the scene, but Crilly's intervention, at the very least, helped prevent Khan from committing acts of violence against anyone else.

There are many layers of irony and coincidence in the interlinked stories of Jack Merritt, Saskia Jones, Usman Khan, John Crilly and James Ford. One of the most glaring is the fact that both Khan and Crilly had their original indeterminate sentences, which would have required them to apply for parole before release, quashed on appeal. In Khan's case, this led to him being released directly from a high-security prison onto the streets, when he was still clearly of a mind to carry out acts of deadly terror in pursuit of his distorted ideological goals. Although subject to probation supervision, the reality is that, once Khan set out to commit murder, no licence conditions were going to stop him. In Crilly's case, the Court of Appeal had directly facilitated his release in good time to place him on London Bridge, willing to risk his own life to protect others, including – unsuccessfully – that of his great friend, Jack Merritt.

Of all those caught up or tragically killed in this sequence of events, John Crilly perhaps best represents what it is that I seek to argue in this book. A damaged child, criminalised from a young age, addicted to drugs, part of a terrible crime, yet somehow – undoubtedly in some way due to people like Jack Merritt – Crilly emerged to a different life. He found redemption in education, in interacting with people who treated him with respect and who had faith in his potential, whatever he had done. It cannot be without significance that Crilly spent the latter part of his sentence at HMP Grendon, one of a handful of prisons renowned for its humane regime and its focus on rehabilitation and life after release.

Who knows whether, given the same chances, it would have been possible for nineteen-year-old Usman Khan to have taken the same route as Crilly, rather than the one that saw him emerge from the high-security prison that took away most of his twenties, to die a few months later with two police bullets in his head.

What I do know for sure – from the hundreds of defendants, complainants, family members and witnesses I have come across in my career – is that a binary worldview, based on victims and villains, is neither valid nor helpful to us. I would go further and say that the simplification of the human condition, setting the 'good people' against the 'evil monsters', is one of the most important reasons why so much crime happens in the first place. So why do we think this way?

INTO THE DARKNESS – BRITAIN'S MOST DANGEROUS MEN

We have seen how the United States largely pursues criminal justice policies that set aside pragmatism and humanity in favour of dogma and moral extremism. Richard Nixon, Ronald Reagan and now Donald Trump have all been elected on vitriolic 'tough on crime' platforms.

Boris Johnson, too, was equally keen in his 2019 campaign to trumpet his credentials as an advocate of harsh sentencing policies and greater use of prisons in the name of setting apart evil criminals from the rest of society.

These politicians appeal to a narrative of evil maniacs and the otherness of the criminal that certainly plays well in the ballot box. That, of course, is why we see these clichés return time and again in election cycles, no matter what the reality on the ground.

My journey in criminal justice has been long, but one case in particular sticks in my mind, out of the hundreds I have handled during my career. Not just for the truly incredible and shocking events that lay behind it, but also because at the end of the case I gained a unique opportunity for an insight into the minds of the most serious of criminals. The experience ended with a day spent face-to-face with the 'most dangerous men in Britain', who were not necessarily what I expected.

Twenty years ago, I was briefed as junior counsel to defend a man charged with eight counts of attempted murder. He was accused of shooting five people at point-blank range and endeavouring to kill three others. By some miracle, not one of the victims died. Bullets missed vital organs and, in one case, entered the victim's elbow, travelled up the humerus and lodged itself in his armpit.

Olatunde Adetoro, know to all as 'Tunde', was the same age as me, thirty at the time, but our lives could not have been more different. I had been to law school, qualified as a barrister, and was starting to make a career for myself at the criminal bar. Tunde was a professional armed robber.

FIGURE 11   Olatunde 'Tunde' Adetoro in 1999

Tunde grew up on the mean streets of Cheetham Hill in East Manchester. His young life followed the timeworn pattern of exclusion from school, trouble with the police from an early age, arrests, prosecutions and periods in and out of prison. None of that justifies for a moment what happened one spring day in 1999 but, after many years reflecting on the following extraordinary events and all that I have learned in the decades since then, I have no doubt that Tunde's history and his actions are inextricably linked.

In 1999, Tunde was on the run from the police, wanted for a series of armed robberies for which his brother, David had already been sentenced to twenty-six years. His other brother, Adeshegun, was also a serious criminal, and at the time their sister was the girlfriend of a notorious Manchester gangster, Anthony 'White Tony' Johnson, who was gunned down in a car park at the age of twenty-two as part of a gangland feud.

There was little doubt that, as soon as the police got hold of Tunde, he would be joining his brothers behind bars – for a very long time. So he did what professionals do when they are under pressure: he went to work. Tunde put together a gang and decided to carry on with the family business by planning a 'cash in transit' robbery. In the end, the plan failed in dramatic fashion.

PC Dave Bentley and a colleague were on a routine motorway patrol, travelling in a marked Range Rover, northwest of Manchester, one warm Friday in April. They received a radio message to intercept a Rover saloon, in convoy with a Renault Clio, heading south towards the Bolton Wanderers football stadium. One of the cars had false number plates and the other was linked to a police investigation.

When the patrol officers caught up with the two cars, they saw something strange for the time of year. All of the heavily built male occupants of the two cars were wearing gloves.

Traffic officers they may have been, but it did not take a seasoned detective to work out that something was amiss. PC Bentley switched on the blue lights and sirens and pulled ahead of the Rover saloon. The police car's lighting system flashed up arrows at the rear to indicate that the smaller car should pull over onto the hard shoulder, which it duly did.

And that is where this traffic stop turned into something that neither officer would forget for the rest of their lives.

After the two cars had pulled to a stop, with the Range Rover 30 feet ahead of the target vehicle, PC Bentley opened the passenger door of the police car and turned to look behind him. What faced the young officer was Tunde Adetoro, dressed all in black, balaclava over his face, pointing a handgun straight at him. And then the shooting began.

Without hesitation Tunde began firing a Smith & Wesson pistol at the police car, which had no form of ballistic protection. PC Bentley ducked down behind the passenger door, bullets passed over his head but, by some quirk of aim and fate, not one of them hit him. He would later say: 'I felt the bullet part my hair. If I hadn't ducked, it would have hit me straight in the chest.'

As the police officers checked themselves for bullet wounds, the gunman and his driver made their escape, pulling off at the next junction and looking for some way to cover their tracks. They jumped out of the Rover at some traffic lights, by now armed not only with the handgun, but with a loaded – and even more deadly – AK-47 assault rifle.

The two men ran to a Ford Fiesta, sitting at traffic lights, and ordered the stunned female driver out of the car at gunpoint. They drove off, leaving her behind at the side of the road. Seeing what had happened, the driver of a tipper truck rammed into the Fiesta, in an unsuccessful effort to block the small car's escape. He was faced with the sight of

FIGURE 12 The AK-47 assault rifle used in the shootings

FIGURE 13   Video taken from the police helicopter showed Olatunde Adetoro getting into the Ford Fiesta

the AK-47 being pointed right at him. Miraculously, at that exact moment, the rifle jammed and the Fiesta made off at speed, leaving the shaken driver unharmed.

Kathryn McNamara was stationary at the wheel of her silver BMW coupé on the outskirts of Bolton when she turned to find an AK-47 directed at her face, right next to her car window. The two occupants of the Fiesta had abandoned the smaller and slower car in favour of Kathryn's much faster model. She was forced out of the BMW and the getaway driver, Andrew Dennis, made off at high speed. Tunde was in the front passenger seat, still armed to the teeth, window open and ready to fire.

By this stage, there was a police helicopter overhead (call sign 'India 99') and every armed-response unit on duty in Manchester had been called to the area. The net was closing fast and things were getting desperate for Tunde, who knew that capture would mean only one thing – a life sentence. A young woman, Amanda Ryan, was taken hostage and, as she crouched in the rear seats of the BMW, she heard Tunde suggest a new escape strategy to Dennis – he would shoot someone in order to get the police off their tail. And that is exactly what he did, not once but five times.

Peter Hayles was installing cables by the road, between Bury and Rochdale, when the silver BMW pulled up next to him, and the passenger – Tunde – beckoned him over, asking for directions. As soon as Hayles got to the car, he saw the barrel of the Smith & Wesson and, seconds later, the gun went off. Hayles had been shot in the leg and fell to the ground in agony.

The BMW made off as the communications officer in the helicopter began to radio increasingly urgent messages to the police control room, which in turn kept the overall firearms commander informed of events. The police had no way of knowing whether Peter Hayles would live or die. All they knew was that members of the public were being shot at random on the streets of Greater Manchester.

The BMW sped off and, a mile further on, pulled alongside Dr Saranth Senerath-Yapa, who was driving to work near Rochdale, his elbow resting on the windowsill of his car. Tunde took aim and fired at the doctor from just a few feet away, fracturing his right arm. By some miracle, the bullet did not cause more serious injury.

Just a few hundred yards further along the road, prosecution lawyer Martin Mckay-Smith was shot in the leg as his motorbike was overtaken by the BMW. Three men were down but still the police pursuit continued, with several armed response vehicles at the scene, and the helicopter following overhead, filming all of the shootings, one after the other. Tunde took potshots at the police vehicles, but no officer was hit.

James Gallagher was the oldest man to be shot. A 75-year-old D-Day veteran, it is a terrible irony that he suffered his most serious wound not in Normandy, but as he waited for a bus near Rochdale Hospital, over fifty years after the war came to an end. Gallagher too was shot in the leg at close range and fell to the ground. Clearly a man of robust temperament, he was later to comment on the events: 'I have always thought the man was not shooting at me personally. I just happened to be there.' Of that there is no doubt.

The final victim was David Hassall, who was riding his pushbike along Manchester Road when Tunde opened fire and shot the cyclist in the hip. Dennis drove faster and faster in a desperate attempt to escape, while Tunde leaned from the passenger window and continued to fire at the pursuing armed police officers. Bullets were flying everywhere.

The firearms commander had reached the limit of what he could allow on his watch. With reports of multiple casualties and gunshot wounds, he could have been facing another massacre, just three years after the worst mass shooting in British history, at Dunblane Primary School in Scotland. The police communications recording captured his decision: 'Cease pursuit! Cease pursuit!'

They did not know it, but Tunde Adetoro and Andrew Dennis were seconds away from making a clean escape, following that command from the control room. It was not to be. At almost the exact moment of the 'Cease Pursuit' order – which would have brought the armed response vehicles to a stop and the police helicopter to a holding position – Dennis lost control of the BMW and crashed into a lamppost, close to the centre of Rochdale.

Seconds later the firearms officers arrived and moved in to arrest the two men as they alighted from the getaway car and tried to escape on foot. Amanda Ryan remained in the car, head down in the back seat, until an armed response officer came to find her and reassure her that she was finally safe. In the end she would be one of the key witnesses to events that day.

You would have thought that the case would be a simple one for the police and prosecution, but as it turned out there was a twist in the tale.

Tunde did not hesitate in his choice of defence lawyer. In the late 1990s, Chris Davis acted for many of the most serious organised criminals in Manchester and the North-West. Still only thirty himself, Chris had built a formidable reputation for his fearless defence of those accused of armed robbery, drug trafficking and fraud.

Chris was a force of nature. Utterly relentless in his pursuit of evidence to defend his clients, he applied his considerable energies and intellect to identifying weaknesses in the prosecution case and, in particular, to rooting out misconduct on the part of police investigation teams. But what possible defence could there be for Tunde Adetoro? Video evidence from the helicopter, ballistics evidence from the recovered bullets, firearms and cartridge casings, Amanda Ryan inside the car, the victims, police officers and other eyewitnesses – on the face of it the case was overwhelming.

Tunde's defence was that the shooting he did that day was to defend himself from the police, who had tried to kill him from the outset. With a healthy measure of professional scepticism, Chris explored Tunde's version of events. His client was adamant in this line of defence – the police had tried to shoot him dead, including at the point of his arrest, just after the BMW had crashed.

The case was at a relatively early stage, but one thing Chris knew for sure – no police officer had admitted firing a single shot during the whole sequence of events. Was Tunde serious about alleging a police 'shoot to kill' plot? He was. That was therefore the defence which the legal team was obliged to put forward, whatever our personal feelings may have been.

Many lawyers, used to hearing defences ranging from the merely improbable to the downright ludicrous, might have sought to persuade a client in Tunde's situation that nobody was going to believe that the police had tried to kill him. Not Chris. Tunde claimed there had been an attempt to shoot him, with a bullet narrowly missing his head at the moment of his arrest by armed police officers. Chris did something then that few lawyers would have done. He hired a ballistics expert and the two of them went to the crime scene to see what they could find.

Pulling up on Mellor Street in his Saab convertible, Chris was an incongruous sight. Well over 6 feet tall, slim, bespectacled and ramrod-straight in his bearing, he would have stood out, wandering the pavements of Rochdale, even without his tailored suit and immaculate silk tie. With him in the car was his witness, John Bloomfield, one of the leading experts on firearms and ballistics in the country. They both began walking the street, Chris taking one direction and John the other.

Working from stills taken from the grainy 1990s helicopter video footage, the two men determined the location where the BMW had smashed into the lamppost and the two putative robbers had bailed out to make their unsuccessful attempt to escape on foot.

Unsure of exactly what he was looking for, Chris assiduously scanned each paving stone for something that might be a bullet hole. A few minutes into the search,

Chris found a fresh hole in the pavement. He called John Bloomfield over and asked him what it was. 'That's a bullet crater,' the expert replied, without hesitation.

'Are you sure?' Chris asked, somewhat incredulous.

'One hundred per cent,' said Bloomfield.

They were in the exact place where Tunde Adetoro and Andrew Dennis had been brought to the ground by the armed response team, the members of which had all denied firing a single shot on the day of the incident.

The two men spent a few minutes looking at the crater, no more than an inch across the top, as traffic continued to flow on the road beside them. Some of the cars slowed a little to check out the two men in suits, kneeling on the pavement, staring most intently at something. A police car passed by, its occupants also paying careful attention before moving smoothly away.

Bloomfield explained to Chris that he would need to have the crater tested for the components of police ammunition in a laboratory in order to confirm – with scientific certainty – the theory of which he was completely confident, from appearances alone. But how do you get a paving stone from a public pavement to a laboratory for testing?

Luck played a part. A man pulled up beside them in a car and told them he worked for the council. 'What are you doing?' he asked, with moderate interest.

'I want to buy the street!' Chris announced, in his usual understated manner.

'That's a bit much,' replied the council official, deadpan.

'How about just one paving slab then?' Chris countered.

With a handshake the deal was done; a call was made and just five minutes later a crew of council workmen arrived, dug up the paving slab and loaded it into the boot of Chris's

Saab. From there it went to the garage at Chris's home in Cheshire, before onward transport to Bristol University, for forensic testing.

A week later a police officer called Chris on his mobile to ask if it was true that he had bought a paving slab in Rochdale. 'What I do or do not do as a hobby is my business,' Chris replied, giving nothing away.

Days passed and more witness evidence from the scene of the arrests began to emerge, from those close by at the time. Some of the independent witnesses gave accounts that did not quite fit with the police evidence. At least one of them clearly recalled hearing a gunshot, several seconds after the BMW came to a violent stop and the – by then unarmed – male occupants ran off down the street. Another witness saw 'a man in a white shirt' positioned over the prone arrestees and saw him 'fire a gun'.

As the evidence of a police shooting mounted, Chris Davis walked into Rochdale Police Station to file an official complaint on behalf of Tunde Adetoro. He was seen by a senior officer, who dutifully recorded the details. 'What is the nature of your client's complaint, Mr Davis?' the officer asked. 'Conspiracy to murder by members of Greater Manchester Police,' Chris informed him, 'named and unnamed.' The hostility towards Chris from the officers in the station was palpable as he left.

The defence team looked into the police system for the issue of bullets to armed response officers at the beginning of their shifts and for their return at the end. On the face of it the system seemed foolproof and secure. Each officer would turn up for work and, before he went on patrol, visit the armoury and sign out his personal firearms – an MP5 carbine and a 9mm Glock pistol – together with sufficient ammunition for both weapons. In the case of the MP5 that meant thirty 9mm x 19mm rounds.

Our team gained access to the paper slips used for the bullets signed out on the day of the Rochdale shootings. All of the armed response officers on duty had signed out the same number of rounds as they had later signed back in at the end of their shifts.

The lab results from the bullet crater came back positive for antimony, a 'lustrous grey metalloid'. This was not a substance found routinely on the pavements of Rochdale or anywhere else. Most ammunition is predominantly composed of lead, but the rounds used by Greater Manchester Police, in their Heckler & Koch MP5 carbines at that time, contained a high proportion of . . . antimony. The test was positive for one of the key components of the bullets issued to the very officers who had been involved in the arrest of Tunde Adetoro.

We now had eyewitness reports *and* scientific evidence which, on the face of it, supported the otherwise incredible allegations made by our client against the police.

The case had been going on for months when Chris Davis decided to take a family holiday. And that is when things turned very strange indeed. The day after Chris flew abroad, his office sent him a fax of the front page of the *Manchester Evening News*, which carried the story of a revelation about the events of that April day, when Tunde was arrested.

In an unprecedented move, Greater Manchester Police had held a press conference about the key evidence, right in the middle of a live case that was heading inexorably towards trial. In all my years at the Bar I have never known such a thing to happen in any other case. There are formalities to be observed for the disclosure of evidence to the defence and the court, and strict rules to prevent publicity that may prejudice the outcome of a criminal trial. Calling the press and the local television stations is not part of that process at all.

'One of my officers has come forward,' announced a sober-faced Chief Constable to the assembled journalists, 'to confirm that he *accidentally* discharged his weapon in the course of the arrest of Olatunde Adetoro and Andrew Dennis on twenty-third April 1999.' The officer's name was PC Maybe. The officer concerned was 'deeply embarrassed' about his actions and 'afraid he may have let his colleagues down. It was a very difficult situation, but it has no significance to the criminal proceedings against the defendants,' the Chief Constable explained.

There would be 'no further comment about the matter', the world was informed. As an exercise in damage limitation, it has to be said, this was a novel and impressive attempt. To this day Chris believes that the police announcement was timed precisely to coincide with his departure on a twelve-hour flight to the southern Indian Ocean.

The 'accidental discharge' explanation did leave open one important question. How did PC Maybe's ammunition records, of the bullets withdrawn and the bullets returned, come to match up? Even taking into account the version of events given in the press conference, the firearms officer should have been one short when he got back to the police station.

The answer was an odd one. Armed response officers apparently kept a 'bucket of spare bullets' of all sizes, just in case they needed them when the armoury was closed. In order to make the records match, he had taken a bullet from the communal bucket and handed that one to the armourer, along with the twenty-nine that he had not fired from his MP5. All very embarrassing, so the story went, but 'nothing else to see here' was the message. PC Maybe had indeed returned to the police station one round short. This loophole did of course undermine the whole system for keeping track of ammunition and, unsurprisingly, things were tightened up considerably after the case.

THE ROCHDALE SHOOTINGS TRIAL

The trial of Tunde Adetoro, Andrew Dennis and Francis Dixon (who was in the second car on the motorway) began on 4 May 2000 in high-security conditions.

As the defendants were High Risk Category A prisoners, they were bussed the short distance from Strangeways prison each day with the sort of security detail normally reserved for a visiting president. Police motorcycle outriders closed off the junctions, armed response vehicles were positioned ahead and behind the prison van, and the police helicopter hovered constantly above, keeping an eye out for anyone minded to try to free the prisoners by force.

Inside the court building, officers searched and scanned anyone entering or leaving Court 1. Members of the armed response unit were secreted behind the entrance and exit doors, just out of sight of the jury. The jurors themselves were identified only by a number and were picked up at an undisclosed location each morning, and dropped off there each night, to prevent jury tampering. In the courtroom, the defendants were housed in the – then relatively novel – surroundings of a transparent plexiglass cage, which formed the dock of the court, directly facing the judge's bench.

I took my seat, immediately in front of the dock and adjacent to the jury box, behind my leader, Jack Price

QC, a veteran Northern Circuit Silk, who took the whole thing very much in his stride. Alistair Webster QC, who later became – and remains – a colleague in my chambers, opened the case for the prosecution. Amanda Ryan, Kathryn McNamara and all those who had been shot went into the witness box, as did PC Maybe – giving an awkward demonstration of his 'accidental misfire' during the arrests – and so it went on . . . until six weeks later, the jury retired to consider its verdict.

The first day of deliberations turned into a second, then a third, and then it was Friday afternoon and time for the weekend break.

The prosecution and police team looked distinctly ill at ease as the jury was brought back into court at the end of the day. Had PC Maybe cost them what should have been a certain conviction? Did the jury have doubts about just who had been doing the shooting that day, and why?

'Will the foreman please stand and answer my first question either yes or no,' the clerk of the court instructed. 'Has the jury reached a verdict on *any* count against *any* defendant on which you are all agreed?'

'No,' said the foreman.

There was a wave of unvoiced surprise in court, bordering on shock among the police investigation team, with whom I had maintained friendly relations throughout the trial. Extraordinarily, after almost a week of deliberations, there were no verdicts at all, in a case where the shooting of five people in broad daylight had been captured on video from the sky above.

The jury was sent home for the weekend and the presidential convoy returned the three defendants to Strangeways prison, in jubilant spirits.

Halfway through the following week, nerves jangling on all sides, the jury returned its verdicts. Tunde Adetoro was convicted of a total of twenty-one counts, including eight of attempted murder. Francis Dixon and the getaway driver Andrew Dennis were convicted of conspiracy to commit armed robbery and of carrying firearms.

Dennis received what was considered a comparatively lenient sentence of fifteen years, from which he would be released in under a decade. Dixon and Tunde each got life. In fact, Tunde received eight concurrent life sentences and would not be eligible even to apply for parole for a minimum of fourteen and a half years, half of his – and my – then lifetime.

At the end of the trial Chris Davis, Jack Price QC and I trudged through the layers of security and down to the cell area in the basement of the court; all of our efforts, from paving-stone purchase to Jack's powerful closing speech, ultimately in vain. It is difficult to explain to those who have not chosen the life of a defence lawyer why there is such a sense of deflation and disappointment at losing a trial, regardless of the merits of the case and the strength of the evidence. This is the case no matter what we may personally think of the client's actions or the consequences for the victims.

The truth, for me at least, is that every case is made up of a body of evidence, to which the judge applies the law and from which the jury decides the verdict. My job, in the words of the Bar Code of Conduct, is to 'fearlessly defend my client'; to seek to achieve the best possible legal outcome for him or her. Every defeat, irrespective of the details of the case, feels like a failure in that mission.

After a few minutes, Tunde was brought into the conference room and freed from the wide array of handcuffs and restraints used by HM Prison Service on only the highest-security prisoners.

We sat at the table, as ever bolted to the floor.

'Did he say fourteen years?' asked Tunde.

We all nodded in sombre fashion, with Chris – ever the stickler for detail – adding, 'and a half'.

'That's not too bad,' Tunde declared with equanimity, keen to lift our mood. 'I can do that.' The whole of his thirties and most of his forties written off in prison – and that was that.

THE SPECIAL SECURE UNIT AT HER MAJESTY'S PRISON WHITEMOOR

Aside from a couple of visits to discuss the prospects of appeal, I did not see Tunde Adetoro again for many months. By that time, he had been moved from HMP Strangeways, a 'local prison' not intended for long-term prisoners, to the Special Secure Unit at HMP Whitemoor, the highest-security prison facility in the country at the time.

Chris Davis and I set off by car on a long journey from the North-West of England to the heart of the Cambridgeshire fens, where Whitemoor sits – a brooding presence, visible from miles around in every direction. This was a location from which any escapee would be readily spotted, given the flatness of the landscape and the lack of hiding places.

In 1994, six prisoners did manage to escape from the SSU at Whitemoor, including several IRA members and a leading London gangster, after they somehow smuggled a gun into the unit. They were all recaptured in short order and security levels at Whitemoor, especially in the SSU, were dialled up to the highest level ever seen in a British prison.

By the time that Chris and I visited in late 2000, it took almost an hour to get through the main prison screening, before undergoing a completely separate security process to access the SSU itself. All that, in order to sit in a conference room, separated from the client by a thick pane of Perspex. Visits to the unit were all 'closed', meaning no direct contact of any kind with the prisoner, even for lawyers, who are usually exempt from such regulations.

This was not a social visit. It was not even a visit just to see Tunde, now that all possibility of appeal had been exhausted and he had been incarcerated for almost two years, with well over a decade to go.

Chris and I had come to see all of the prisoners of the SSU in a single day. This was a most unusual form of prison 'speed dating', where each of the highest-risk prisoners in the country would be brought to the opposite side of the screen, one after the other, to tell us about life in the SSU. We were being instructed by the whole group of prisoners to try to get the place closed down.

For anyone who has not been to a maximum-security prison like Whitemoor, even if you have visited a 'normal' establishment, it is hard to convey the sheer, soulless inhumanity of the place. Once inside the walls of the main prison, through the first wave of security, there was no sign of the real world left. Forbidding cell blocks with windows heavily barred, concrete walls towering around the perimeter, blocking all signs of the real world outside, barbed-wire-topped steel fences with ubiquitous heavy metal doors, locked and secured.

And from there the journey continued, as Chris and I were led through a baffling sequence of pathways, gates and doors, subjected to a further X-ray scan and a comprehensive physical search – mercifully fully clothed – and finally into the small conference room, where we would spend the rest of the day. Two chairs were bolted to the floor, a little too far away from the writing desk in front of us; a microphone and speakers were built into the security screen, and that was it. Our metal pens had been taken away – transparent plastic ballpoints were the only writing material permitted. Just in case.

Tunde was brought in first, dressed in de rigueur tracksuit and trainers, carrying at least a fifth more muscle mass than when I had last seen him in Manchester, following the trial. He had been a fearsome sight then, but months with nothing to do but lift weights had transformed his physique into that of a professional bodybuilder. His neck was roughly the width of his head, possibly a little wider.

In a calm and measured voice, Tunde told us about life in the SSU. The prisoners were watched twenty-four hours a day and could never be alone with a single guard. This was an effort to prevent the sort of corruption of which Tunde and the other high-risk prisoners were believed capable. It was so much harder to bribe two officers at the same time, the theory went.

All movement was monitored and time out of the prisoners' cells was severely limited. The 'outdoor' exercise yard, required to comply with prison regulations, was topped by a heavy mesh screen, to prevent helicopter extraction, and barely a sliver of light found its way inside. Neither Tunde nor any of the other men in the SSU ever had a direct view of the sun. Not even a blade of grass was allowed to flourish before it was eliminated by weed killer. Birds would fly into the overhead screen, become hopelessly entangled and slowly die, only to be cleared away once every few weeks, when they started to rot.

'This is the end of the road,' Tunde told us. In every conceivable way, for him and his fellow prisoners, it most certainly was.

We next met with Kenneth Noye, a wealthy London criminal serving life for the murder of a young man whom he stabbed to death in a 'road rage' incident on the M25 in 1996. Following the murder, he went on the run in Spain for several years. Noye had previously admitted killing a police officer in the grounds of his large English home, but had been acquitted by the jury on the basis of self-defence. He had no such luck in his second murder trial.

Noye was a muscular but otherwise diminutive man, in his early fifties, who chose his words carefully. He was still in the process of seeking to appeal his conviction at the time. The main witness at his trial, a shadowy figure by the name of Alan Decabral, had been shot dead in a contract killing just days before our visit.

A tall and intelligent young man in his twenties was next; the head of a cocaine-importation operation, which supplied most of eastern England with the drug. He was serving a twenty-eight-year sentence and had decades left to go. He was taking it all in his stride.

Bekir Arif, part of a Turkish Cypriot crime syndicate from South-East London, complained about his dental health. 'I'm doing twenty-three fucking years in this fucking place and I've got a fucking toothache', he exclaimed, nursing a swollen mouth. Arif had been sentenced for conspiring to supply 100kg of heroin, with a street value of over £12 million, and was considered at high risk of escape.

One after another they came into the room, sat on the other side of the thick screen and told us their stories. Much of what they said I cannot repeat, even after all these years, but all of them spoke of the systematic destruction of the spirit that Whitemoor represented. Could Chris and I do anything about it?

I will never forget the men I met that day, designated by the state as the absolute worst of us; the sort of people for whom many would say that 'death is too good for them'. And yet. Making no excuse or justification for the acts of violence committed by some of them, the men who sat across from me were just that – men. They were human beings, with the same range of emotions, fears and even dental maladies as the rest of us.

Chris and I left at the end of a fascinating day of human intrigue that had left its mark on both of us. We prepared and issued a formal legal letter, threatening on behalf of all of the most dangerous men in Britain that our clients would bring a claim against the Home Office, under the newly minted Human Rights Act, if conditions at the SSU did not improve. Surprisingly perhaps, given the nature and reputation of the inmates, the government caved in and, at least for a time, the SSU at Whitemoor prison was closed down. All of the men we had seen were sent elsewhere, to complete their sentences in secure but less soul-destroying conditions. Perhaps even the odd blade of grass may have been permitted to flourish at the institutions to which they were transferred.

As time passed, eventually parole was granted and all of the surviving men held in the SSU in October 2000 have been released to live among us; Tunde Adetoro, like me turning fifty and no doubt reflecting from time to time on that drive through Rochdale, described in a BBC report as 'the day the bullets flew'; Kenneth Noye is in his seventies and subject to stringent monitoring by his parole officer, even now.

Bekir Arif's long years in prison did nothing to deter him from 'the life'. In March 2016, at the age of sixty-two, when many in his world would have left organised crime to younger men, Arif found himself listening once again to a judge of the Crown Court, telling him to stand to be sentenced. 'The Duke', as he is known by all in the underworld, received eleven and a half years, for yet another drugs conspiracy. He will be eligible for his free bus pass long before he gets the chance to use it.

Each of the prisoners did their hard time, in the Special Secure Unit and elsewhere. Tunde always treated me with courtesy and respect. He studied in prison and improved his mind in a way that was never available to him on the streets of Cheetham Hill, the tough East Manchester community where he and his brothers grew up. I wondered, then and now, whether the two baby boys, he and I, coming into the world within weeks of each other, were really so different after all.

Why is one bird able to soar above the clouds and land where it will, while another becomes hopelessly entrapped in the mesh, vainly thrashing away in a futile effort to escape, before dying a slow and painful death? Almost every serious criminal I have represented could have taken a different path had he not faced abuse, trauma or neglect as a child. They are not evil and intrinsically different from those of us who did not face such extreme childhood events.

Nor are they somehow fundamentally inferior to those who went through those same experiences yet managed to emerge to live a life within the law. Those who commit crimes are not bad people. For a whole variety of reasons, usually for a short period in their lives and on a handful of occasions, they do some bad things. None of us has the right to place them into a different category of humanity as a result. With different beginnings, any one of us could have ended up in the dock of a criminal court, hearing a sentence of imprisonment being passed upon us. It benefits nobody to frame criminal justice policy through a flawed binary lens of good versus evil. We need to be pragmatic, compassionate, and implement policies that actually work to reduce crime and protect our society.

Now CEO of a large corporation, Chris Davis left the practice of criminal law in 2007, at the age of thirty-eight, and has not worked on a case since.

'I HAVE NEVER REALLY THOUGHT ABOUT GOOD AND EVIL' – GRANTT CULLIVER

Grantt Culliver had killed twenty people. He was a hard man to track down.

For many years, Grantt was the Warden of Holman Correctional Facility, Alabama's maximum-security prison. The sprawling establishment is set among the endless cotton fields of the state, just off Interstate 65, a few miles from the border with northern Florida. Built in 1969 to house just 581 prisoners, Holman is now home to well over 1,000 men, held in desperate conditions. Almost 200 of them are on Death Row . . . waiting.

A 2016 report, published after Grantt Culliver had moved on, described Holman as 'the most violent prison in America'. Murder, physical attacks and rape were said to be rife amongst the inmates, and staff, frequently victims of violence themselves, were leaving much faster than replacements could be recruited.

Once every few months the atmosphere would turn sombre and Grantt Culliver would be called upon to perform one of the Warden's key responsibilities – acting as the state's executioner.

After his stint at Holman, Grantt Culliver moved to the state capital to take up a senior administrative role with the Alabama Department of Corrections. I was determined to track Grantt down to seek his views on crime and punishment, and in particular his perspective on the three occasions when he had flicked the switch to activate the electric chair at Holman, and the seventeen more when he had depressed the syringes to perform a lethal injection. Twenty of the most wretched of souls were consigned to the beyond at Grantt Culliver's hands.

The Alabama Department of Corrections itself was unwilling to speak to me. ADOC is besieged by countless lawsuits and federal investigations into prison conditions in the state. It was not surprising that Grantt's former employer was unwilling to part with his contact details.

I managed to get a lead via a contact, working in the Alabama law enforcement community, and I eventually obtained Grantt Culliver's mobile phone number. Several texts and voicemails later, he sent me a message, agreeing to a telephone interview. His precise location at that time was unclear.

I called at the appointed time, to hear what was clearly the background noise of a bar. Grantt was distracted by some companions. 'Shall we rearrange and speak tomorrow?' I asked. He agreed.

The following evening I finally managed to conduct a full interview with Grantt – he proved a thoughtful and intelligent subject. I was anxious not to appear overly inquisitive about the executions he had personally carried out and asked his views on a range of topics, based on his many years at the coalface of the criminal justice system in one of the toughest regimes in the world.

Despite being ultimately responsible for locking up over a thousand men each night during his period as Warden of Holman, Grantt was still grappling with the concept of prison and, as an African American, was clear that 'justice is not blind [to race]'.

I asked him about the concept of deterrence, including that supposedly created by the threat of a death sentence. 'Maybe there was a time when deterrence played a part, back when justice was more swift,' he told me, 'but I don't think people doing crimes nowadays think about long sentences or a possible death penalty.'

Grantt saw the same news reports as the rest of us, and his years of daily contact with the most serious offenders in America had led him to the conclusion that 'people just commit crimes. Mass shootings, the killer always commits suicide by cop. He never faces the victims or the justice system.' Deterrence, for those determined to die in the course of their crimes, was plainly ineffective, Grantt believed, and he could think of no other category of criminal for which the risk of incarceration was a reason not to commit a crime in the first place.

Prison was often a safe haven, and recidivism was so high that even the longest sentences and the worst conditions did nothing to reduce the crime rate overall, Grantt reflected, as he opened up later in our interview: 'Guys are inside for twenty years and come out in their fifties with no idea what the world is like out there. No family, parents elderly or dead, many friends killed by drugs or a gun. Neighbourhood completely different to the one they grew up in, can't get a job. They'll soon commit a crime and be back inside.'

Although he did not for a minute agree with me on everything, Grantt's experience largely confirmed the views set out in this book. He was adamant that the focus of the sentencing process, in prison and out, should be on rehabilitation and preparing offenders for the world facing them when they were released. Young people, in particular, he believed, needed support and mentoring, not least as many grew up in single-parent homes with only TV and electronic devices to raise them.

Volunteering in a youth centre for children between six and fourteen years of age, Grantt had been shocked by the complete lack of respect they showed to anyone. 'It's an eye-opener for sure,' he said. 'Most of them have at least one parent in the [criminal justice] system. These kids are soon heading the same way and crime becomes the only way for them to survive.'

Ever the diplomat, Grantt would only go so far as to say that 'the War on Drugs does not appear to work. People are arrested every day for drugs, there are drugs in prison, it never ends.'

Finally, I brought the discussion round to the topic of good and evil; a subject that surely lay behind his life's work, and especially the twenty occasions when he had personally taken another person's life, by order of the State of Alabama.

'I never thought that deep about good and evil,' Grantt told me, sounding genuinely surprised to be asked. I probed his views of the men he had put to death, all of whom he had met and spoken to, sometimes many times, before the fateful day arrived.

'There are some evil people,' he said, with a reflective tone, 'but overall I believe there is some good in everybody. Even the people who had done terrible things were, for the most part, not terrible people.' He told me of conversations with condemned men about politics, religion, their children, in which they came across just like anyone else. He would often meet their families during visits and was surprised by the relative normality of it all.

'Nobody struck me as totally hateful or evil,' Grantt concluded, 'but some of them got on your nerves.'

This fits completely with my own assessment of those who have taken lives, harmed others in unimaginable ways, even children, in a very different criminal justice system, thousands of miles across the Atlantic Ocean from Holman Correctional Facility. Even those responsible for the most awful of crimes retain a spark of goodness, a glimmer of humanity, however well hidden.

I asked Grantt the question to which I had been leading. How did he feel about the executions for which he was personally responsible?

'It was a job,' he said, matter-of-factly, 'I got promoted to Warden and I knew it was one of the duties. Executions were carried out by the state, not by me.'

Considering the men in his custody and those whose lives came to an end by his hand – guided by the State of Alabama – Grantt revealed a degree of distance, that surely must have been necessary to protect himself. 'For a very long time in my career,' he told me, 'I seldom wanted to know what crimes they had committed. Sometimes I needed to know but mostly I never even asked.'

SITTING IN JUDGEMENT

In the course of my travels in the US, I interviewed several judges, prosecutors and police chiefs. Most would only speak to me 'off the record', but at least by doing so they showed they were willing to open up about their views, even if sometimes these seemed to change in the course of our discussions.

One federal judge, sitting in her spacious modern chambers, stylishly appointed and with panoramic views of the cityscape beyond the courthouse, told me that Americans would always have an Old Testament approach to crime and punishment. She began by summarising her own position.

'I believe that some people are just *plain evil*,' she said. 'They are beyond the social norms and will kill cold-bloodedly over and over again. They have no redeeming qualities, can never be rehabilitated and should not be on the street.' She spoke of the rise of child sexual abuse on the Internet, which had featured in cases before her, ruminating that 'if the public knew the numbers, the sheer magnitude of the issue, the sado-masochism, they would not believe it.'

I challenged her on whether there was a middle ground between a purely rehabilitative approach to criminal justice and the punitive US approach, founded on categorising certain citizens as evil and morally depraved.

'We all share certain human emotions and motivations,' the judge declared. 'Hunger, anger, coveting and, of course, lust . . . We can all relate to those.' She paused for a moment and then stated, in a calm and considered – judicial – tone: 'I don't think people are inherently bad.'

I did not point out that this was not what she had appeared to tell me, on the topic of good and evil, just a few minutes before. Perhaps, even for federal judges of the United States of America, things are not always as straightforward as they appear.

Another judge told me: 'The death penalty does not affect rates of homicide at all, but in the end people want it, and it's a jury that decides whether to put the defendant to death.'

Our discussion ranged over the topics of this book, and I was surprised at the complete disconnect between the judge's personal views of what worked and what did not in criminal justice, set against the madness of laws he was required to enforce and – at election times – to enthusiastically endorse. He recognised that a large proportion of prison inmates were not dangerous or violent, that children and young men in particular would generally leave crime behind given the right support, and that often they were incarcerated with adult offenders and ended up following the same path.

Despite spending most of his legal career as a prosecutor, often arguing for harsh jail sentences or even death, before appointment to the bench, the judge's considered view was that criminals were not immoral, let alone amoral. They became inured to certain behaviours, due to their life experiences, but the picture was never a simple one. He mentioned a brutal murder in a crack house where one of the eyewitnesses, himself a frequent resident of various penal institutions, was horrified by the animal abuse perpetrated by the residents. The human violence was something he had become more used to over the years. I have frequently encountered the same selective morality among some of my most dangerous and violent clients – they often have a strong and protective relationship with their mothers and draw a line at any crime against children, especially sex offences. Possibly, for some, the existence of such targets merely provides a legitimised outlet for violence, simmering away beneath the surface all along.

As for the narrative of othering prisoners as monsters, when it came to the sentencing in particular, this judge took a sanguine and realistic view. 'It is politically expedient to be seen to listen to the victim,' he said, 'and an emotional, morally defined course is a prerequisite in the public mind.' He was clear that the US system was almost entirely focused on punishment and that the many elected officials in the justice system, especially prosecutors and judges, had no option but to mouth the platitudes of good and evil, purely to win and remain in office.

Another state court judge agreed to meet me for lunch at a stylish restaurant in downtown Montgomery, the state capital of Alabama. We ordered salads and, again unwilling to be named – 'election coming up' – he told me of the times when he had imposed the death sentence on a defendant. Like Grantt Culliver, the judge saw his role as part of the conveyor belt, processing a man from the street to the death chamber, as a necessary part of the job.

With the benefit of anonymity – 'Couldn't say this in public if I wanted to get re-elected!' – he was clear in his view. 'I was fortunate growing up and in my career,' he told me, 'but if I couldn't feed my kids and crime was the only option, things might have been different.' There were some 'really bad people', he believed, but not so many in the scheme of things. 'Compare my kids to kids the same age, whose parents are in the justice system as defendants – what are the chances those other kids will do well in life?'

Thanking the judge for lunch – he insisted on paying – I was struck by his thoughtful approach to the law, crime and punishment, but equally by how little of that thought would ever be applied to the judgements he made in court. Mandatory sentences would be upheld, death sentences imposed, the crushing wheels of justice would continue to turn.

I met with a former Alabama Parole Board official, now working in the private sector, who explained that her views on the subject of the criminal mind all derived from her Christian faith. 'I believe all human beings are basically bad,' she told me, over fried pork chops in a diner on the outskirts of Birmingham, Alabama, 'but we are all capable of redemption.' Considering the thousands of men and women sitting in prison, whose fate depends on a parole decision, but also reflecting on human behaviour more generally, she observed, 'a lot of the things we do are based on whether anyone will notice'.

She had seen no evidence that Alabama's use of the death penalty or its draconian sentencing laws had any deterrent effect. 'A man came out on parole after years in jail. He was actually at Holman when executions were carried out, and after release he went out and killed a cop – a capital crime. There's no deterrent there.' I have seen the same phenomenon time and again in my own career – clients emerging from some of the worst conditions in the prison system, only to commit another serious crime shortly after being released. One client even managed to escape from prison, towards the end of a long sentence for armed robbery, and committed a further similar crime whilst on the run from the authorities. Such examples do not provide evidence of the deterrent effect of long sentences.

Finally, I met with the Chief of Police of the city of Montgomery, Alabama; a place rife with drugs, murder and violence of every kind. A career police officer, African American and in later middle age, Chief Ernest N. Finlay took a few minutes to warm up, as we sat in his expansive conference room inside police headquarters, overlooked by the state flag. They are not used to English accents in those parts, and certainly not to being asked philosophical questions about law-and-order policy.

Before long, though, the Chief seemed to relish the chance to give voice to some of the conclusions he had reached over a long and distinguished law-enforcement career. 'People of colour,' he told me without a shadow of doubt, 'get the short end of the stick.' He explained that a vast number of African Americans, in particular, should not be in jail. Despite extremely high levels of drug-overdose deaths in Alabama, and his own view of addiction as a 'disease not a crime', Chief Finlay could see no path towards serious drug law reform in the state. 'In the South?!' he exclaimed. 'No way, the South is hardcore!'

We moved on to the question of good and evil. 'I believe in folks' goodness,' he said, 'regardless of their crimes. I believe in change; I still talk to them with respect and use kindness.' Overall, he believed, drugs represented the biggest problem of all; not the essential character of human beings.

The Chief spoke movingly of his own efforts to reach out to young people in the city as a mentor, even – especially

– when they became caught up in crime and gangs. He had seen the positive impact, particularly of black role models, from kindergarten to high school, turning out young people who were models of good behaviour. 'It's just not consistent,' he pointed out, regretfully.

As we stood at the end of our meeting, the Chief asked his assistant to find me some mementoes of our visit – a Police Academy baseball cap and T-shirt and a document folder with the seal of the department embossed on the front. He was a generous and deeply kind man, capable of seeing good in even the most violent and dangerous of men.

'You have reminded me to get in touch with a young boy I am trying to help out. He's thirteen, lives in a dysfunctional home, a decent enough kid – a good athlete – but on the verge of becoming a gang banger. I get him to help out with my yard work, talk to him – I am going to give him a call right now, arrange to meet up.' I have no doubt that the Chief was true to his word and rang the boy, perhaps in the process saving him from a different path in life, one that had the potential to take him away from goodness and into the darkness of crime, punishment and the American Way.

REFLECTIONS

For further insights, as I sat down to write the last pages of this book, I turned to a doctor of the mind. Dr David Ho is one of Britain's leading consultant forensic psychiatrists, with decades of experience in secure hospitals and locked wards, treating and analysing those responsible for some of the most awful crimes. As a young registrar at a secure hospital, he had come across the serial killer Peter Sutcliffe – 'The Yorkshire Ripper' – who brutally murdered thirteen women and will never be released.

We spoke one damp December afternoon. As with others to whom I had posed the question about the essence of good and evil, Dr Ho seemed a little surprised to be asked. 'It's an interesting question,' he said, thinking for a moment before answering. 'Evil is rarely useful from a medical point of view. It does not help to make sense of people who commit horrendous crimes.'

We spoke at length of sociopaths and psychopaths; those for whom no medicine or therapy seemed to change their fundamental behaviours. 'There are no reliable neurobiological findings that are specific to a diagnosis of psychopathy,' he explained, 'no clear physical differences between the most violent people and the rest of us'.

Sutcliffe, the American serial killer Ted Bundy and other psychopaths – they were focused entirely on their own gratuitous pleasure, regardless of the effect on others along the way. 'For them, the pursuit of gratification is not an impulse; it is a way of life and it just happens that their primary drivers are achieving sadistic pleasure and causing pain. Really they are just selfish.'

Dr Ho viewed the concept of evil as essentially a religious designation, representing the opposite of the righteous and the holy. 'Even serial killers do not have horns. They are not the devil. And ninety-nine per cent of the time, probably more, they do not behave in an evil way at all.'

There are some who will always pose a risk to others – compulsive paedophiles, murderers and – yes – psychopaths. Dr Ho spoke of a programme of therapy in Broadmoor Secure Hospital in which he had played a part, seeking to treat psychopaths with drugs and even, in some cases, with a decade of talking therapy. 'It cost over £200 million,' he explained, 'working with those with Dangerous Severe Personality Disorder.'

The results? 'It made absolutely no difference to their behaviour whatsoever. They were sent back to prison.' He continued: 'There is a very small proportion of the population who can never be rehabilitated and who need to be removed from society for ever. Not necessarily in prisons but in secure therapeutic communities, maybe villages or farms surrounded by walls, where they can live away from those they would harm.'

Over the past twenty-six years, I have met men and women who have committed the worst of deeds. They have killed, raped and maimed their fellow human beings. They have stolen, damaged and destroyed the property of others. They have lied, bullied and blackmailed their way to money, sex, power and control.

In recent times, I have travelled the United Kingdom and around the world, listening to the life experiences of those who have also spent their careers at the coalface of justice. I have sat down with those who have spent months, years, virtually a lifetime behind bars.

Through the lens of all my own experiences – and of those from whom I have heard – I see these men and women, some grey and ashen from decades 'behind the door', others fuelled with anger, drugs and resentment, and I just cannot bring myself to judge them evil. I cannot place them in a cage marked 'outsider' and draw comfort from my own superiority, just because I am not one of those designated by society as 'criminal'.

And if I cannot bring myself to judge a man evil, to set him apart from society by that mark, then what of goodness?

Are some of us incapable of committing a wicked act, no matter what life throws at us?

Dr David Ho considered the ideal of 'the good man' and was clear that 'the evidence is limited on that too. There may be some weak genetic association, of "do-gooders" running in families, of generational philanthropic behaviour, but, in the end, all behaviour is multi-factoral. It's difficult.'

It is difficult indeed, but if we are ever to break free of the cycle of crime and violence, perpetuated as much by our criminal justice system as by those behind its bars, we need to travel beyond the binary of good and evil. We need to see criminal behaviour as a series of acts that cause our society and its citizens harm and for which we are all – to some degree – responsible. It achieves nothing to place the perpetrators of those acts into some category of humanity that marks *them* out as different from the rest of *us*.

If we criminalise and brutalise a child, if we lock him up and take away his identity, if we deprive him of a sense of place in society, we should not be surprised when, time and again, he emerges from incarceration and exacts a price, in money or blood, for all that we have done to him.

The verdict

This book began with Stuart Ross, awaiting trial in HMP Belmarsh, as part of an international drug-trafficking and money-laundering conspiracy.

His case came before a jury seven months after I first visited him. By that time it was clear that the prosecution case was weaker than the defence case was strong – an odd phenomenon of the criminal trial. In essence, there were gaps enough in the prosecution evidence, links missing in the chain, to allow us – just possibly – to establish a reasonable doubt as to Stuart's guilt.

If Stuart's own explanation of events were ever to be exposed to scrutiny in court, any doubt might be extinguished in the jury's mind. And so, for week after week of the prosecution case, I cross-examined police witnesses about gaps in surveillance records, the lack of telephone and forensic evidence connecting Stuart to key events, and flaws in the voice-analysis evidence of recorded incriminating phone calls, attributed to Stuart by the police.

We spent a day discussing the wisdom of Stuart entering the witness box in his own defence. Would he be the icing on the 'cake of doubt' baked by my painstaking cross-examinations of the weeks before? Or would he be the author of his own misfortune, providing the prosecution with the ammunition needed to obtain a conviction?

In the end, Stuart signed a piece of paper, which read as follows:

> I, Stuart Ross, have decided not to give evidence in my own defence. I confirm that I make this decision of my own free will and that no pressure has been put on me not to go into the witness box. I have been fully advised by my counsel, Mr Daw, and by my solicitor. I understand that the jury may hold against me my failure to give evidence, in reaching their verdict. I accept that risk and it is my responsibility and choice alone.

I made my closing speech, along with the seven other defence barristers in the case, acting for the rest of the defendants on trial. The judge summed up and the jury retired to consider its verdict.

We waited. Verdicts began to emerge. One by one all of the co-defendants were convicted until only Stuart's case remained unresolved. Several days into retirement, the jury sent a note. 'We are deadlocked,' it read.

After a brief consultation with Stuart, I told the judge, with the jurors waiting in a room outside the court, that we wanted the jury to be declared 'hung' and for them to be discharged. Given the outcome for the other defendants, all now facing decades in prison, a 'draw' seemed the best result Stuart could expect. A hung jury would inevitably mean a retrial, but at least we would live to fight another day.

Surprisingly, given the clear language of the jury's note, the judge disagreed. 'I think I will give them a bit longer tomorrow morning,' he intoned, ominously, as if perhaps he knew something about the state of play in the jury room that we did not (I am sure he had no such knowledge, in fact, but serious trials breed paranoia of many kinds).

The next morning, before the court sat, I went down to the cells to see how Stuart was doing. Like Tunde Adetoro, although for different reasons, he was a high-security prisoner, manacled with heavy-duty handcuffs that dug deeply into the wrists. 'How are you feeling?' I asked, with little optimism in my tone.

'Brilliant!' he declared, with genuine enthusiasm. 'I'm looking forward to going home today.' It turned out that Stuart's confidence levels were so high that he had given away all of his hard-earned prison property, built up over many months on remand – radio, games console, even 'premium bedding'; privileges earned for good behaviour. This was an extraordinary level of confidence for someone who could just as easily be heading back to Belmarsh in a prison van, to begin a very long sentence indeed.

We did not have to wait long to see if Stuart's positivity was justified. Less than an hour after the jury went back into retirement, the tannoy sounded throughout the court building, for 'all parties in the case of Ross to return to Court 7'. My most optimistic thought was that the jury had sent another note, declaring its inability to reach even a majority verdict (meaning a minimum of ten jurors in agreement with either guilty or not guilty).

The usher at Court 7, a lady I had known for many years, gave me a friendly smile. 'It's a verdict, Mr Daw,' she whispered in a confidential tone. She made it sound like it might be an early Christmas present. I thanked her for the information, but I was not so sure that it was good news.

Minutes later, with the court fully assembled and the tension palpable, Stuart was brought alone into the secure glass dock and the twelve jurors took their seats in the jury box.

'Will the foreman please stand,' instructed the clerk of the court. He did.

'Has the jury reached a verdict upon which at least ten of you are agreed?'

I could not look up from my notepaper, which bore a solitary word – 'Verdict' – followed by a blank space for the insertion of the letter 'G' alone or the more pleasing combination, 'NG'.

'We have,' answered the foreman.

My stomach turned over as always, despite all my years in this job. I experienced a momentary wave of nausea, my heart rate increasing. On the outside, I maintained a poker face; an essential tool of the trade.

'Do you find the defendant, Stuart Ross, guilty or not guilty?'

I glanced up ever so briefly, braving a look at the foreman, as he looked down at a piece of notepaper to confirm what he was about to say.

'Not guilty,' he declared, without hesitation. There were audible gasps from Stuart's family in the public gallery, possibly a raised eyebrow of surprise from the judge, and I was finally able to breathe again.

I turned to look at Stuart, standing behind me in the dock, and I am sure he mouthed: 'I told you so', with a broad grin across his face.

An hour later, Stuart, various of his friends and family, the other members of the legal team and I were in a pub, a short walk from the court building where the trial had taken place. We saw the convoy of prison vans, motorcycle outriders and all, taking the other defendants back to prison to begin their sentences. The longest sentence had been twenty-eight years and the shortest, for one of the lesser conspirators ('tailenders' as we call them), eleven years.

For a man who had been a high-security prisoner for more than a year, Stuart slipped back comfortably into life on the outside. He entertained everyone with some of the moments of humour in prison and talked of the things he was looking forward to getting back to, now that the trial was over.

After a pint or two I said my goodbyes and left Stuart to continue the celebrations, well into the night. He took me aside, just before I departed, and looked me straight in the eye. 'I can never thank you enough for this, Chris,' he told me, without a hint of emotion, 'but if there is ever anything you need, and I mean *anything at all*, get in touch and it will be done, no matter what.'

We shook hands firmly and I walked the short distance back to my chambers, where I checked my pigeonhole to find that a set of papers had arrived for another case, also a major drugs conspiracy trial. A conference had been booked for me to see the client in prison at 9 a.m. the following day.

I thought back to Stuart's words – '*anything at all*' – and wondered how far that offer had been intended to go. I thought also of him standing at the bar getting another round in, just as the other defendants were arriving for processing back into prison, where they were destined to remain for almost 100 years between them.

In the end, other than to me and my career, to Stuart of course, and to those defendants for whom the verdict went a different way, did any of it really matter?

Would there be fewer drug deals on the streets of London that night? Would the circle of crimes, of violence, of death from overdose and addiction, be smaller, larger or exactly the same?

Or was it really just a show trial? A legal circus? The visible representation of all that we as a society believe a criminal justice system should be? Cracking down on criminals by locking them up and throwing away the key?

Did it make a blind bit of difference whether Stuart went home to his own bed that night, rather than back to prison, to be locked away for a very long time?

A few minutes later, I cleared my mind of Stuart's trial, which had been the most important thing in my professional life for the previous three months. I opened the new brief, wrapped in pink ribbon, to read the case against the client I would see the following morning, bright and early, in a stark prison visiting room.

EPILOGUE

The Dark Web and the Internet of Crime

In 2005, I was instructed to defend a client accused of 'Internet piracy' on a massive scale. At the time I used a Nokia mobile phone which, in addition to the – now largely obsolete – function of making calls, could also be used to send text messages of up to 160 characters, at a cost of about 15 pence each. And that was it.

The case was the first of its kind to be prosecuted in Britain and followed a three-year investigation by the Federation Against Copyright Theft (FACT), a trade body representing corporations in the entertainment industry. The operators of a file-sharing 'web forum' – which went by the catchy name of 'PIR8' – had been charged with the criminal distribution of music and video content, whose copyright was owned by FACT members.

I had spent my career – up to that point – defending the crimes that lie behind most of this book, those carried out in the 'real world': bank robbery, drug trafficking, fraud, rape and murder. The Internet piracy case presented a conceptual challenge for me and for all of the lawyers involved, including the judge.

Conventional notions of what evidence looks like – paper documents, eyewitnesses, forensic evidence and the like – were of little use in understanding the PIR8 case. We were served with all of the evidence in digital form via the – then novel – mechanism of a computer hard drive, onto which all of the witness statements, documentary exhibits and downloaded files had been copied.

Up to this point, I had been involved in a few cases with 100,000 pages or more of documents – truly massive cases of international fraud and money laundering, with warehouses full of paper files in the possession of the prosecution. But such cases were exceptional and the great majority of prosecution files, even in the most serious and complex of cases, ran to no more than a few hundred or a few thousand pages at most. Twenty lever-arch files, around 8,000 or so pages, would have been considered a very document-heavy matter indeed at that time.

The hard drive on the PIR8 case, if one were to print the contents onto paper, would have run to over 4 *million* pages. And this was in 2005, when the Internet was in its relative infancy and most of the distribution of illegal music and video content was still by means of physical media – CDs and DVDs in particular.

Chris Davis – purchaser of paving slabs – and I travelled to Scotland, where the exhibits in the PIR8 case were stored, to see for ourselves what the case involved. We were shown boxes and boxes of DVDs and CDs, with labels and inserts printed to look as genuine as possible. There were also computer servers, upon which the original content was stored and copied, using antique disc-writers, at a relative snail's pace in comparison with the ultra-high-definition streaming of the 2020s.

There were also financial records, including payments made and received, and unencrypted emails between the conspirators, all of which combined to lay bare the structure of the PIR8 operation. With the resources of the entire entertainment industry supporting the prosecution, it did not take long for the case to take shape. There appeared to be no escape for the men who had been charged, including my client.

All eight of the defendants, ranging in age from twenty-one to a positively ancient – in Internet years – thirty-seven years old, eventually pleaded guilty to the serious offence of Conspiracy to Defraud, which carries a maximum sentence of a decade in prison. The leader of the gang received a sentence of four years' imprisonment and the others somewhat less, down to 150 hours of community service work for those whose responsibility extended to little more than pressing 'play' and 'record' at the same time.

FACT published the defendants' PIR8 usernames, alongside their real names, in a press release at the end of the case – Mack, Leafy, Taz, Killalot, Monkfish, Toon, Trinity and Eda began their sentences on 8 December 2006. It was official – crime in Britain had moved online.

The sentencing judge described the case as 'ground-breaking' and made clear that he viewed the prison sentences he imposed as involving a 'strong deterrent element'. If, by that, he intended to stem the use of the Internet as a vehicle for criminal behaviour, whether copyright fraud or anything else, he might as well have given the defendants a first class ticket to Las Vegas and a million dollars each in spending money, for all the difference those prison sentences made to anything.

Looking back over fifteen years, to the Internet of 2005 and the quaint criminality of Mack, Leafy and their crew, the benefit of hindsight really does make clear just how 'innocent' it all was (save to the large corporations who own the copyright). It also shows how wrong we were to think that the very first case of Internet crime such as this was that different to the crimes we had been used to dealing with before. In the end, the defendants were caught and convicted on a mixture of physical evidence (difficult to explain all those fake CDs and copying machines), their own communications and, one of the oldest clues of all: the money trail through good old-fashioned bank accounts.

Today, things really are very different indeed.

I found a tour guide – who chooses to remain anonymous – who agreed to take me to the corners of the Internet where most of us never venture.

It is said that some 90 per cent of online content exists below the surface, unsearchable by Google and inaccessible via a conventional web browser. Much of the hidden material is entirely innocuous; held in what is known as the Deep Web, comprising secure commercial files, such as banking records, medical and academic databases and the content of our emails and social media accounts.

Beneath that layer, though, lies the ultimate tool to facilitate crime on a worldwide scale: the Dark Web. And that is where my tour took me, as daylight faded outside, one wintry afternoon in early 2020.

In the 'real world', most respectable British people would not be able to locate the most serious of criminals – those willing to do or supply the most illicit of things – without considerable effort and risk.

It took less than ten minutes to find them on my virtual tour. The first few minutes or so were spent creating a Virtual Private Network, or 'VPN', that would disguise my location and identity, allowing me to browse the Internet with total anonymity. The next step was to download a special browser, capable of accessing websites with the domain suffix '.onion', used to designate content held off the grid of Google's algorithms ('onion' refers to the many layers of secrecy involved).

The VPN software showed my location and Internet Protocol – 'IP' – address (the identifier of any device accessing the Internet) changing before my eyes. I was no longer in Britain but in Turkey and then Vietnam and South Korea before I lost track. My IP address changed too – not once but several times – and for all I knew my laptop could have been posing as a smart thermostat in Montreal or a refrigerator in Rotterdam by the end of the process.

A few keystrokes later and I was looking at the menu of 'The Hidden Wiki': in appearance a rudimentary version of Wikipedia itself. In content, it was something very different indeed. The array of options was dazzling and shocking, both in its variety and its nature.

One of the first menus contained a long list of advertisements for drug suppliers.

One layer beneath this was 'The People's Drug Store', with its comprehensive stock inventory, including 'HIGH PURITY COCAINE'.

Firearms of every kind could be purchased and shipped worldwide, with a promise of packaging 'which will clear customs anywhere'. All of the guns included at least a magazine or two of ammunition, to get the purchaser started.

Drugs

- Drug Market⬚ - Anonymous marketplace for all kinds of drugs.
- Greenroad⬚ - Biggest marketplace with full working escrow.
- Weed&Co⬚ - Weed / Cigarettes ... Prix Bas / Low Price ... weed / cigarette
- EuCanna⬚ - 'First Class Cannabis Healthcare' - Medical Grade Cannabis Buds, Rick Simpson Oil, Ointments and
- Peoples Drug Store⬚ - The Darkweb's Best Online Drug Supplier
- Smokeables⬚ - Finest Organic Cannabis shipped from the USA
- CannabisUK⬚ - UK Wholesale Cannabis Supplier
- DeDope⬚ - German Weed and Hash shop (Bitcoin)
- BitPharma⬚ - EU vendor for cocaine, speed, mdma, psychedelics and subscriptions
- Brainmagic⬚ - Best psychedelics on the darknet
- NLGrowers⬚ - Coffee Shop grade Cannabis from the netherlands
- The Pot Shop⬚ - Weed and Pot Shop Trading for longer than a year now! (Bitcoin) -UPGRADED DOMAIN-
- Steroid King⬚ - All the steroids you need. (Bitcoin)
- Wacky Weed⬚ - Hi Quality Green at Wacky Prices

FIGURE 14   Websites for drug supplies, advertised on 'The Hidden Wiki'

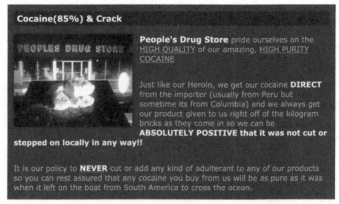

FIGURE 15   A website offering heroin and 'high purity' cocaine

The Dark Web stores on display accepted – in fact insisted upon – payment in cryptocurrency, with Bitcoin the most popular, allowing funds to be transferred instantly and anonymously anywhere in the world.

This is what a criminal marketplace looks like when it is placed beyond national boundaries, outside regulation and law, subject only to the basest of human wants and guided entirely by the quest for profit.

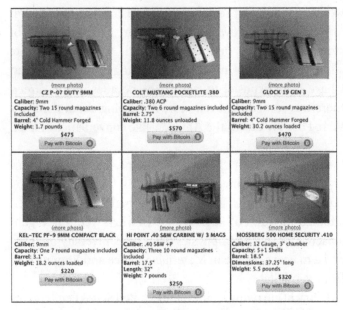

FIGURE 16 Firearms of every kind are on sale, packaged to 'clear customs anywhere'

Commercial (E)

■ Darkscandals⚐ Real rape, humiliation, forced videos and much more extreme videos! (Pack 8 is out! More than 1800 video files in the packs).

■ TeenPorn⚐ The best selection of amateur teen porn videos from the deep web

FIGURE 17 Horrifying descriptions of video products on sale

Vendors proudly advertised fake identity documents for any country, stolen and compromised credit cards, 'pre-shredded' and counterfeit currency, discounted 'carded' goods (purchased by fraud), surveillance services, 'black hat' hacking and on and on. Item 20 on the menu was entitled, with nasty irony, 'erotica', as if it might offer no more than a virtual burlesque show. The menu descriptions offered something far darker and more frightening.

Just seeing these menu options was enough. I shut down the browser, the VPN and returned to the more familiar world of Google. It really did feel like arriving home from a journey into a dystopian nightmare. I felt a sense of stomach-churning doom about it all. Somehow, despite all of the videos of murder and photographs of the dead I have been exposed to, across the decades of my career, there was something even more disturbing about the Dark Web. Possibly due to the Amazon-like convenience of it all.

Ross William Ulbricht is a handsome, highly intelligent and personable American, now in his thirties, who grew up in Austin, Texas, graduated from high school and even attained the rank of Eagle Scout. Ulbricht went on to gain a bachelor's degree in physics from the University of Texas and a master's degree in Materials Science and Engineering from Penn State.

Ulbricht currently resides at the United States Penitentiary in Tucson, Arizona, where he is serving a 'double life sentence' and an additional forty years 'without the possibility of parole'. He is one of the 50,000 Americans serving LWOP in the City of Incarceration. Ulbricht's crimes included money laundering, computer hacking and conspiracy to traffic narcotics. A further indictment for incitement to murder, alleging that Ulbricht had hired a hitman to carry out a contract killing, was eventually dismissed.

Ulbricht has made many attempts to appeal his conviction, relying on allegations of illegal conduct by the federal agents behind the case. All of those appeals have failed, up to and including a final unsuccessful effort at the United States Supreme Court. Ulbricht will die in prison.

Before his arrest Ulbricht was said to have used the online pseudonym 'Dread Pirate Roberts' ('DPR'), named after a character from William Goldman's 1973 novel, *The Princess*

Bride, which also became a blockbuster film. In Goldman's novel Dread Pirate Roberts was an alias used by several men to disguise their real identities and provoke fear in the minds of their victims. Ulbricht claimed, too, that there was no single man – certainly not him – to whom the sobriquet belonged.

What then lay behind Ulbricht's crimes? He was one of the men behind a Dark Web site by the name of Silk Road, which was launched in 2011 as an 'online marketplace' for precisely the same products as I found on my more recent tour. Hundreds of millions of dollars in sales were made; of drugs, guns, extreme pornography and the rest.

A jury of twelve at the Federal Courthouse in Manhattan decided that it did not matter how many pirates there were – the defendant was one of them. They convicted Ulbricht after deliberating for less than a day. His fate was sealed.

The US authorities were very proud of the arrest and prosecution of Ross Ulbricht and happy indeed at the sentence imposed and upheld by the courts.

And yet, just as with every other example of law enforcement I have come across, leading to prosecution and sentences of extreme length or even death, I question what really changed as a result of the Ulbricht case. Is the world a better place because a young man, however misguided the application of his talents, is due to spend the next fifty years or more growing old in a prison cell? Will fewer teenagers be stabbed or fatally shot on the streets as a result? Will fewer drug users succumb to addiction, self-destruction and overdose? Will any of us sleep more safely in our beds?

Dread Pirate Roberts
@DreadPirateSR

Follow ⌄

20 minutes to go. You can never kill the idea
of #silkroad.

8:01 am - 6 Nov 2013

FIGURE 18 The relaunch of the Silk Road website was announced
on Twitter

The answer can, perhaps, be found on Twitter, in a post
from the Dread Pirate Roberts 'official account', just a
month after Ulbricht's arrest in October 2013.

Right on time, Silk Road 2.0 went live and – within a
few hours – over 500 product listings had appeared. Dread
Pirate Roberts was back in business.

AFTERWORD

PLUS ÇA CHANGE...

November 2020. The nation is in lockdown for a second time. A silent killer stalks the land. All efforts to contain it have seemingly failed.

I find myself, as so many times before, waiting for a client to be brought into a prison visiting room. But this time I have not made a long journey to some far-flung location. I have not been subjected to the rigmarole of booking in, locking my belongings away, producing my identification and submitting to scans and searches, in order to gain admission.

For the first time in my career, for a prison 'visit', I am sitting at home, casually dressed, with a mug of tea and a laptop in front of me. I open up Skype and enter the contact information for the prison visiting room, over 200 miles away. A few seconds later, my client appears on the screen, wearing a bright orange uniform, indistinguishable in shade from the jumpsuits sported at Guantanamo Bay and many high-security establishments in the United States. In this case, orange is simply the colour of outfit issued to those inmates who are assigned to cleaning duty in the prison; nothing more sinister than that.

This is our initial meeting and 'Nathan' is nervous in the extreme. He is experiencing his first taste of the criminal

251

justice system. The youngest son of a respectable and successful family, Nathan had never before been arrested – let alone charged and convicted – for any crime, up until a few days earlier, when his home was raided by a team of police officers. They turned the place upside down and recovered computers, paperwork and – of course – his mobile phone. (Mobile phones have been the source of the most incriminating evidence in many serious criminal cases for at least the past twenty years).

Nathan was taken to a police station, interviewed and, on the advice of the rushed and overworked duty solicitor, said nothing at all. The next day he was charged with conspiring to import millions of pounds' worth of Class A drugs, allegedly using his family's logistics and shipping business as a front for an organised criminal gang. After a brief appearance before the magistrates' court, again by video link, Nathan's case – given the potential for a twenty-five-year sentence – was sent straight to the Crown Court. He was remanded in custody, pending trial, which would not take place until well into the following year.

'I am not guilty!' he insists. Thus, the eternal cycle of drugs and crime and law enforcement and courts and prison begins again. I listen patiently, wait calmly, and then – once he stops talking – I tell Nathan how the system works, what will happen next and how I am going to help him ...

JUSTICE IN THE AGE OF COVID

The first edition of *Justice on Trial* went to press in the spring of 2020, right in the middle of a national lockdown in Britain. The criminal courts were at a virtual standstill, with jury trials suspended, unprecedented backlogs developing at every stage of the process, prisons full to bursting and no end in sight.

Writing now, almost a year later, as a third and – possibly – final period of lockdown nears its conclusion, I hoped to report a new dawn for our criminal justice system. Surely, with the nation on its knees, whole sections of the economy wiped out, government debt at record levels and the nation's finances in tatters, now must be the time for a radical overhaul of the system, which was already broken before all this began?

My optimism, however, has not been matched by the reality of what has happened in the past year. During this period of unprecedented crisis, second only to times of war in the disruption of our daily lives, all of the strands of this book have played out in a predictable but damaging way. This afterword offers a welcome chance for me to set down how the pandemic has affected the whole criminal justice system, beginning with our prisons.

SOLITARY CONFINEMENT

In the early stages of the first lockdown, we saw the prison population remain relatively stable, as remand times for those already awaiting trial went up but fewer people were charged and imprisoned for new crimes. With the courts sitting mostly empty, before too long some of those on remand were released on bail, while others reached the end of their sentences and emerged into a different form of imprisonment in the outside world (locked down like the rest of the population). There was talk amongst some British politicians of a radical approach to releasing low risk inmates, a response adopted by a number of states on the other side of the Atlantic; sadly, this largely came to nothing.

In the spring of 2021, as I write this, the overall prison population is down by around 7 per cent (6,000 prisoners), from 84,000 immediately before the first lockdown to around 78,000 towards the end of the third. Surely, given my bold agenda to close all prisons, I should see this as a small step in the right direction? If only.

Having spent much of 2020 advocating an immediate programme of release for low-risk prisoners, not least to reduce overcrowding and the spread of COVID, I was saddened to see a very different approach adopted by the government and prison authorities. Far from introducing special measures to reduce the prison population, most inmates were simply placed into solitary confinement (using the euphemistic and now ubiquitous term 'self-isolation' to disguise the reality of the experience). Family visits and education programmes were suspended, exercise limited to a few solitary minutes a day at best, and still the virus ravaged the prison population, killing inmates and staff alike.

The reason for the significant fall in the overall prison population was a very simple one. It had nothing to do with a courageous government plan to finally empty out the prisons of those who really do not belong there at all: the mentally ill, the addicted, the abused, the homeless and the vulnerable. It was simply that the police made fewer arrests, prosecutors were presented with a smaller number of CPS advice files and the courts were not operating at capacity to try offenders and to sentence them.

In other words, fewer offenders were being caught, prosecuted and sent to prison for new crimes. Over the months and years to come, this backlog, greatly increased by the pandemic, will work its way through the early stages of the criminal justice process and, before too long, the prison population will once again head upwards, eventually breaking the previous record of 88,000, set almost a decade ago.

I make this prediction with a sense of exasperation, albeit one born of realism given the direction of travel of recent government announcements on sentencing policy. As I sit at my desk, the Ministry of Justice trumpets yet another round of increases in prison sentences for a range of crimes. The press release for the Police, Crime, Sentencing and Courts Bill falls back on the same tired rhetoric found in the speeches and manifestoes of politicians for as long as I can remember.

There are promises to 'keep offenders behind bars for longer', to 'crack down on knife crime', to introduce 'tougher penalties', including Whole Life Orders for teenagers (the British version of America's Life Without Parole, which I discussed in chapter 2), and 'life sentences for killer drivers', and on and on it goes. There is even room in the bill to ensure that children convicted of serious crimes will find it harder than ever to have their sentences reviewed once they turn eighteen and enter the adult prison system.

The Justice Secretary, Robert Buckland QC, an otherwise decent and thoughtful man, could not help himself. He jumped on the bandwagon, stating that 'this government has pledged to crack down on crime'. Following her habit of doubling down on the rhetoric, the Home Secretary, Priti Patel, went even further, bragging that the new laws will put 'thugs ... behind bars for longer'.

It is clear that neither of these senior government ministers could see the irony of the mismatch between the stated aim of the bill ('cutting crime and making communities safer') and the inevitable result in the real world of simply sending more and more people to prison for longer than ever before.

In terms of sentencing and imprisonment, one thing is obvious: nobody in the government has been influenced to act on the reform agenda of *Justice on Trial*. Except, perhaps, one junior minister. The very next day, after the new laws were announced, Chris Philp, the justice minister directly responsible for sentencing policy, went on the record with a striking comment: 'harsher sentencing tends to be associated with limited or no general deterrent effect.' As the headline in *The Times* put it, with admirable clarity and concision, 'Longer jail terms don't stop crime ... admits minister'.

It is difficult to think of a more telling and dispiriting state of affairs, or indeed of a better example of all that is wrong with the politics of crime and punishment, than the fact that the very man responsible for sentencing policy *knows* that the laws, which he is forced to support to keep his job, categorically *will not work*.

DRUGS, DRUGS AND – YES! – MORE DRUGS

Chapter 3 charted the history of drug use by human beings over millions of years. We explored the complex worldwide supply chains which deliver prohibited substances – in their infinite variety – from their points of origin to the streets of Britain, Europe and the United States.

How then did the drug trade cope with a global pandemic, lockdowns, travel restrictions and a host of other measures to restrict movement and trade? Surely, you might think, there must have been an impact on traffickers' ability to produce, transport and supply drugs?

In Britain, drug trafficking was the one form of crime which went up during periods of lockdown. And not just a little bit, as this Home Office chart shows.

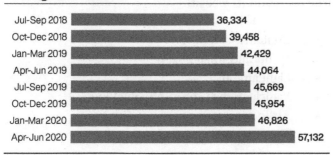

Drug offences recorded by police in England & Wales

Jul-Sep 2018	36,334
Oct-Dec 2018	39,458
Jan-Mar 2019	42,429
Apr-Jun 2019	44,064
Jul-Sep 2019	45,669
Oct-Dec 2019	45,954
Jan-Mar 2020	46,826
Apr-Jun 2020	57,132

FIGURE 19

During the first UK lockdown, in the second quarter of 2020, drug offending – already on the rise for several years – increased by a whopping 22 per cent.

Just think about that for a minute. Many parts of the UK were at a standstill, roads and streets largely empty, police numbers and operations down due to COVID infections amongst officers, and yet drug arrests and seizures went through the roof. Demand was up, as people stayed at home and looked for distractions as the days and weeks blended together, but how on earth did the traffickers manage to keep supplies moving?

Where there is consistent demand for a product, from which large profits can be made, supply chains will be established and, in times of disturbance, those routes will adapt in a multitude of ways. The steps drug traffickers took to fuel the demand during lockdown became a reflection of the restrictions in place. It helps to understand what the principal methods of importation of drugs are, in order to see how readily the market could adapt. Britain's National Crime Agency publishes a helpful guide to the subject, setting out all of the main drug routes on its website:

- Container shipping
- Yachts and small boats
- Light aircraft
- Vehicle traffic from continental Europe
- Airline passengers
- The post and fast parcels.

It will be immediately obvious that some of these methods of importation would have been difficult to maintain during lockdown. The use of yachts, small boats, light aircraft, vehicles from Europe and airline travel all shrank to a fraction of their usual level. So, drug traffickers did what they always do. They adapted and moved supplies to the other routes.

Container shipping, postal and parcel routes all saw big increases in drug seizures during the pandemic, in many cases involving very large quantities in single shipments. Importers were prepared to risk losing a higher than usual percentage of the product in order to ensure that enough drugs made it through to satisfy the insatiable demand. The NCA published regular updates of its 'successes' in 'disrupting organised crime gangs' throughout 2020 and into 2021. This example, from February 2021, is typical of the news releases from the agency:

> Ten people have been arrested in North London in relation to the seizure of approximately 2.3 tonnes of cocaine imported to the UK in a consignment of bananas … The drugs – potentially worth £184 million had it been sold on the UK streets – had already been removed by Border Force officers at Portsmouth International Port … The container had arrived on a cargo ship from Colombia the day before.

One of the senior police officers leading the operation went on the record with a typically bullish assessment of its success. It is worth considering his comments in a little detail:

> This significant seizure means that these dangerous drugs cannot reach the streets of London and beyond, where they have the potential to cause great harm to people and communities … Whilst these operations are complex and resource intensive, they are vital to disrupt organised criminal networks and to ensure we keep our communities safe … We know there is an inextricable link between drugs and violence – that is why tackling the importation and supply of drugs is a crucial part of our work to reduce violent crime in London.

Despite all of this hyperbole, cocaine and other drugs continued to flow, violence and turf wars were played out as ever on the streets of Britain and all of the many harms associated with the prohibited market carried on as if

COVID did not even exist. None of the things this officer said, no doubt with the best of intentions, actually matched up with the real world. It turned out that even 2.3 tonnes of pure cocaine, worth an astronomical £184 million on the streets, was no more than a drop in the ocean. There was more chance of disrupting the banana market, by using the fruit to hide the drugs, than of making a serious dent in the drug trade.

SUFFER THE CHILDREN

We have seen that the government lost no time in looking to introduce ever harsher penalties for young people, including life without parole for teenagers in some cases. All of the harms identified in chapter 4 continued unabated under lockdown. And in one area things got much worse.

For some time in Britain, children have been exploited by drug gangs in so called 'County Lines' operations, where young people are used as couriers to move drugs from city hubs to outlying suburban and rural communities. There has been a big increase in such activity over the past year and it has become harder and harder to detect.

The Children's Society, a charity supporting young people, explained what was going on: 'organised crime gangs have changed their tactics to ensure they're not detected, like putting children in taxis instead of trains when transporting drugs.'

They went on to say, 'it is also worrying that many children are missing out on contact they were previously having with teachers and social workers during lockdown.' In other words, a perfect storm had developed of children out of school, with time on their hands and little contact with caring professionals, ripe to be exploited by drug gangs eager to ensure continuity of supply to the valuable 'County Lines' routes, established over the past decade.

One mother, 'Jenny', summed up the problem, after her teenage son disappeared: 'it wasn't until a good few days of him being missing that I found out from friends talking on social media that he had "gone up country". I realised he was being exploited. I had no idea that people out there prey on children, gain their trust and use them to sell drugs in other parts of England.'

Sadly, for Jenny and so many other mothers and children, lockdown has done nothing to prevent children from being victimised, treated as criminals and – in too many tragic cases – killed as part of the cycle of drug prohibition and child criminalisation that does so much harm to our society. Will we ever learn?

REDEMPTION AND FORGIVENESS

I have not been in contact with Tunde Adetoro for almost twenty years, since my last visit to him at Whitemoor Prison, towards the beginning of his eight life sentences. But I spoke recently to someone who met Adetoro face to face, just a few months before he was released from an open prison, after spending fifteen years inside.

Martin Mckay-Smith was one of those, as he put it, 'so unwise as to be shot' by Adetoro, during that extraordinary armed rampage through the streets of Greater Manchester in 1999, described in chapter 5. Spotting that her boss had made a cameo appearance in *Justice on Trial*, a young lawyer contacted me to ask for a signed copy of the book as a retirement present for Mr Mckay-Smith, who had spent many years as a prosecution lawyer. I was happy to oblige.

Some months later, I was surprised and humbled to receive a delightful message from Mckay-Smith, containing kind words about the book, as well as a light-hearted factual correction to my description of events: 'I was not overtaking the perpetrators in the BMW before they took aim but they overtook me as I was riding at a restrained 40 mph – the limit!' He went on to explain that he had taken the chance to meet Adetoro in prison as part of a restorative justice programme. Intrigued as to how the encounter had gone, and its impact on both men, I asked Mckay-Smith if he would speak to me.

We finally managed to arrange to speak on Zoom, and I immediately noted his warmth and kindness. He spoke of his lifelong passion for motorcycles, which had led to him riding through Rochdale on a classic Yamaha RD 350LC on that fateful day, almost twenty-two years earlier. He told me of the surgical operations, treatment and physiotherapy he had to endure after being shot by Adetoro at almost point-blank range, resulting in a shattered tibia and the need for a fixator to support the leg. I was particularly struck by Mckay-Smith's palpable sadness at the impact of his injuries on his freedom to spend time with his family.

Despite the immeasurable suffering of the experience of being shot, and all that followed, Mckay-Smith's Christian faith – of which he spoke with passion – led him to accept the invitation of the Probation Service to meet with Adetoro in a prison on the Wirral, south of Liverpool. He had reflected many times over the years on forgiveness, an act so out of fashion in our 'throw away the key' culture. Could meeting Adetoro play even a small part in bringing about rehabilitation and change? A date was set and, surprised that Adetoro was willing to meet at all, Mckay-Smith went along to the prison with the pastor of his Baptist Church.

The full detail of what passes between victim and offender in such meetings is confidential and Mckay-Smith is an honourable man, who respects such understandings with deep integrity. However, he did tell me that he believed that Adetoro was sincere in his remorse. He made no excuses and fully acknowledged that his life was 'out of control' in the months leading up to his arrest for the shootings in 1999. Having had little formal education to speak of before receiving his sentence, in prison Adetoro was studying for a degree. He was a very different man, as he looked ahead to fifty, from the one he had been in his late twenties.

As Adetoro sat and listened intently to his victim's story, and the impact of the crime, Mckay-Smith observed his attacker's huge physical build, the result of thousands of hours in prison gyms up and down the land. Hearing Adetoro speak, Mckay-Smith asked himself the same question I did all those years ago: 'what would he have been if he had not spent all this time in prison?'

The meeting ended with a powerful moment for both men, an emotional connection from two perspectives on a shared experience. 'I believe only God can forgive you', Mckay-Smith told Adetoro, 'but insofar as I *can* forgive you, I do.' Reflecting on the encounter during our Zoom conversation several years later, the retired lawyer was driven to the same conclusion as me. 'We are all capable of terrible things,' he told me, 'but I believe in the truth of the adage "There but for the grace of God go I".'

OUT OF THE DARKNESS

On my prison video conference, I watch the clock on the Skype call count down towards the end of our allotted hour, at which point a prison officer knocks on the door, in time-honoured fashion, to tell us that 'time's up!'

Before we finish there is an important topic to discuss. The prosecution case against my client is founded on a novel and interesting piece of evidence. The police have had a rare victory against the sort of encrypted technology I described in the epilogue. As organised criminals had been moving away from conventional mobile phones and messaging services, a pan-European police sting had managed to crack a heavily encrypted communication system by the name of Encrochat.

Believing they were immune from police monitoring, drug traffickers had been sending each other unguarded messages using the service, setting out the full details of their trade. Many of these messages had been recovered by the police from the Encrochat server, laying bare the movements of drugs all over Europe. It turned out that my client was one of 1,000 people consequently arrested on the basis of evidence from Encrochat. One of the special handsets, ordinarily completely impossible to break into, had been recovered from under his bed.

'We have got some work to do on this one,' I told him, just as the clock reached the hour and the screen went blank.

ACKNOWLEDGEMENTS

On 8 May 2019 I received an email from a man I had never heard of, who had read a piece I had written for *The Spectator* on the legalisation of drugs. 'I wondered if you would be interested in developing some of your ideas into a book proposal?' he wrote. I had not thought of doing so but I agreed to meet him, and a few weeks after that, Bloomsbury commissioned me to write this book.

Without Jamie Birkett's email, you would not be reading these words. He is a quite brilliant young editor at Bloomsbury and for his vision in reaching out to me in the first place, and his skill in gently refining the manuscript from its original bloated state, I am grateful beyond words.

Given my busy diary in the courts, I would not have been able to complete the monumental research that lies behind this book without the efforts of three people in particular. My assistant, Hilary Jauncey, who has been tireless in her efforts to coordinate interviews, transport arrangements and the recruitment of researchers, was also the first to read the manuscript. Her comments and proofreading were essential to the final product, and I cannot thank her enough.

From a pool of well over 100 applicants for two research positions on the book, Hilary whittled it down to a shortlist of five. Adam Keenaghan and Lauren Smith were head and shoulders above the rest. They each took their separate chapters and produced research notes of extraordinary quality and detail, which were essential to the drafting process and to meeting Bloomsbury's deadline for delivery of the manuscript. Once again, without Adam and Lauren the book could not have been finished on time.

Naturally, any errors remaining on these pages are my responsibility alone.

The whole team at Bloomsbury has been incredibly supportive, and the professionalism of Rachel Nicholson, Jude Drake and Lizzy Ewer in supporting the publication has been something to behold. My publicist, Karon Maskill, introduced by cheese expert Alice Dyson, has also offered invaluable support since joining Team Justice.

So many people gave their time to speak to me about the subjects covered in these pages. Some of them did not want their names to be mentioned and I respect their wishes. They know who they are and I thank them for taking a risk in talking to me at all.

In purely alphabetical order, the following interview subjects deserve special mention, both for their insights and for their kindness in sitting down with me, sometimes for many hours: Dr Aline Bervini, Dr Barbara Broers, Judge Bill Burgess, Chef de Section Jean-François Cintas, Ann-Marie Cockburn, Carla Crowder, Grantt Culliver, Shay M. Farley, Chief Ernest Finlay, Dr Martin Glynn, Marc Guéniat, Jennifer Hasselgard-Rowe, Lyn Head, Dr David Ho, Robert 'Sam' Houston, Charles 'Denny' Hughes (a friend for life), Dr Timothy E. Hughes, Gethin Jones, Attorney-General Olivier Jornot, Professor Dr Ton Liefaard, Serge Longère, Aylia McKee, N. Price 'Trey' Oliver, Caitlin J. 'CJ' Sandley, Governor Brenda Stewart, Khalid Tinasti, Sir Thomas Winsor.

I would not have been involved in any of the cases whose details are set out in this book without instructions from solicitors, so many of whom have supported my career over the past twenty-six years. Some of them will recognise their own cases in the text and others, I hope, will remember working with me over the years, helping me to develop my skills and to gain insights into so many aspects of our criminal justice system. I am sure that I will miss some names (sorry!), but my thanks go to all of those who have ever sent me a brief, large or small, including Barry Cuttle (a legal legend and still going in his eighties!), Ian Lewis, Mike Rainford, Dan Morrison (who deserves a book to himself), Daniel Astaire, Kristina Harrison, Margaret McCormack, Steven Teasdale, Kerry Morgan, Fida Hussain, Shahid Choudhry, Richard Derby, Phil Youdan, Paul Schofield, Shaun Draycott and many more.

Chris Davis deserves special mention, not only for providing such excellent material for the book, but for the faith he showed in a very young junior barrister by instructing him in the biggest criminal case of the year in 2000. I would not be where I am today without Chris, and I love him, his daughter (my god-daughter) Lizzie, Donna, Sam and the whole family to bits.

I spotted Adam Rasul as a young paralegal, and he has gone on to become one of my closest friends but also a lawyer of enormous talent and commitment to his eclectic mix of clients. He has supported my legal career, my TV projects and this book with unstinting enthusiasm. I cannot thank him enough. Adam has a massive future ahead of him and I look forward to sharing his journey.

I have had some great clerks over the years but Louise Cuttle (my first!), David Wright, John Hammond, James

Hotchin, Guy Williams, Emma Makepeace and Lee Johnson have all greatly helped my legal career over the years.

Several close friends played an important part in the genesis of the book. David Misan (stalwart of the Anglesea Sessions and unofficial King of Soho) introduced me to Adrian Chiles (once the most successful broadcaster in Britain!), who has become a close friend. Adrian invited me onto his BBC 5 Live radio programme to talk justice and it was he who suggested I should write for *The Spectator*. Adrian was another key link in the chain to the publication of this book. My good friend Nick Gargan was always on hand to give his careful and considered thoughts.

Lara Prendergast of *The Spectator* happily commissioned pieces from me with the minimum of fuss and I thank her, Fraser Nelson and the team there for their support with my writing.

I would also like to add my profound gratitude to Martin Mckay-Smith and Professor Nicola Padfield for their considerable assistance with the Afterword.

On a personal level I thank my parents, Alan and Sandy Daw, for their unfailing support throughout my life. My dad worked so hard on building sites, at the expense of his knees, to support our family and I wanted for nothing as a child. My mum taught me to read at a very young age and I have no doubt that her efforts contributed to such literary skill as I may possess. I thank them both from the bottom of my heart for everything.

My wife Ruth has been there for most of my legal career. She has made it possible for me to have the time to write at all. She is a truly incredible person and I have no idea how she does everything each day. Not the least of Ruth's achievements are her tireless efforts in bringing up our four wonderful children, each of whom has played a part in the writing process, mostly by getting in the way of it!

Florence would want me to point out that, despite a frequent lack of concentration on her own studies in class, she did spot a typo on page 1 of the first draft, which none of the professionals had noticed. Arthur was the least distracting of the bunch, save for the occasional sound of his basketball hitting the ground beneath my office window. Elsie is – I am sure – right when she tells everyone that she is 'going to be a better lawyer' than her dad. And five-year-old Stanley? It is a good day when he agrees to wear any clothes at all – we all need a Stanley in our lives.

If I have left anyone out, you have my sincere apologies and thank you so much.

Chris Daw QC
April 2021

BIBLIOGRAPHY

CHAPTER 1

Bartlett, R. (1986), *Trial by Fire and Water: The Medieval Judicial Ordeal* (2nd edn, 2014), Oxford: Oxford University Press.

Duhaime, L. (2009), 'Law and Justice in the Mayan and Aztec Empires (2,600 bc–1,500 ad)', in *Duhaime's Encyclopaedia of Law,* Duhaime.Org. http://www.duhaime.org/LawMuseum/LawArticle-642/Law-and-Justice-in-the-Mayan-and-Aztec-Empires-2600-BC-1500-AD.aspx

Gramlich, J. (2019), 'Only 2% of federal criminal defendants go to trial, and most who do are found guilty', Pew Research Center. PewResearch.Org. https://www.pewresearch.org/fact-tank/2019/06/11/only-2-of-federal-criminal-defendants-go-to-trial-and-most-who-do-are-found-guilty/

Harris, T. (2010), 'Trial by jury: has the lamp lost its glow?', *Diffusion: The UCLan Journal of Undergraduate Research*, 3(2): 1–14. bcur.org/journals/index.php/Diffusion/article/download/151/132

Hastie, R., Penrod, S. D., and Pennington, N. (1983), *Inside the Jury* (reprinted 2002, 2013 Lawbook Exchange Ltd), Cambridge: Harvard University Press.

Holland, T. (2005), 'Justice, roman style', History Extra, https://www.historyextra.com/period/roman/justice-roman-style/

Hume, D. (1778), *The History of England from the Invasion of Julius Caesar to the Revolution in 1688* (vol. 3, reprinted 1983), Indianapolis: Liberty Fund. https://oll.libertyfund.org/titles/hume-the-history-of-england-vol-3

King, N. J. (2000), 'The American Criminal Jury', in N. Vidmar (ed.), *World Jury Systems*, Oxford: Oxford University Press.

Potter, H. (2015), *Law, Liberty and the Constitution: A Brief History of the Common Law*, Woodbridge: The Boydell Press.

Tumanova, D. Y., Sakhapova, R. R., Faizrahmanova, D. I., and Safina, R. R. (2016), 'The origin of a jury in ancient Greece and England', *International Journal of Environmental & Science Education*, 11(11): 4154.

Habeas Corpus Act 1640.
Bushel's Case (1670) 124 E.R. 1006.

CHAPTER 2

BBC News (6 July 2019), 'How Norway turns criminals into good neighbours'. https://www.bbc.co.uk/news/stories-48885846

BBC News (6 July 2019), 'Prisoner release checks "put public at risk" – chief inspector', https://www.bbc.co.uk/news/uk-48923455

Davis, A. Y., and Rodriquez, D. (2000), 'The challenge of prison abolition: a conversation', *Social Justice*, 27(3): 212–18.

Daw, C. (6 July 2019), 'China's surveillance technology is terrifying – and on show in London', *Spectator*. https://www.spectator.co.uk/2019/07/chinas-surveillance-technology-is-terrifying-and-on-show-in-london/

Departmental Committee on Prisons (1895), *The Gladstone Report*, PP. (C.7702) LV 1.

Dickens, C. (1836), 'A Visit to Newgate', in *Sketches by 'Boz', Illustrative of Every-day Life and Every-day People*, London: John Macrone, St James's Square.

Elliott, D. (2019), 'Alabama faces deadline to address dangerous and deadly prison conditions', NPR. https://www.npr.org/2019/05/21/725066218/alabama-faces-deadline-to-address-dangerous-and-deadly-prison-conditions?t=1563261190969&t=1564850710019

Equal Justice Initiative (12 March 2018), 'Alabama's prisons are deadliest in the nation', EJI.org. https://eji.org/news/alabamas-prisons-are-deadliest-in-nation

Equal Justice Initiative (2 June 2017), 'Mass incarceration costs $182 billion every year, without adding much to public safety', EJI.org. https://eji.org/news/mass-incarceration-costs-182-billion-annually/

Haubursin, C., and Barton, G. (12 April 2019), 'How Norway designed a more humane prison: does prison architecture have to be cruel?', Vox, https://www.vox.com/videos/2019/4/12/18301911/norway-humane-prison

Henley, W. E. (1893), 'Invictus', in *Book of Verses* (4th edn), New York: Charles Scribner's Sons.

HM Chief Inspector of Prisons for England and Wales (2019), *Annual Report 2018–19*, London: HM Inspectorate of Prisons.

Home Office (1981), *Home Office 1782–1983: To Commemorate the Bicentenary of the Home Office*, London: The Home Office.

Howard, J. (1777), *The State of Prisons in England and Wales*, Warrington: Printed by William Eyres.

Howard League for Penal Reform, 'History of the penal system', Howardleague.org.

Independent (7 October 1993), 'Howard seeks to placate "angry majority": Home Secretary tells party that balance in criminal justice system will be tilted towards public. Colin Brown reports', https://www.independent.co.uk/news/uk/howard-seeks-to-placate-angry-majority-home-secretary-tells-party-that-balance-in-criminal-justice-1509088.html

Life in Norway (2018), 'Prisons in Norway: inside a Norwegian jail', Lifeinnorway.net. https://www.lifeinnorway.net/prisons/

Mcleod, A. M. (2015), 'Prison Abolition and Grounded Justice', *UCLA L. Rev.*, 62: 1156–1239.

Ministry of Justice (2016), *Story of the Prison Population: 1993–2016 England and Wales*, London: Ministry of Justice.

New York Times (29 April 2019), '"No one feels safe here": life in Alabama's prisons', https://www.nytimes.com/2019/04/29/us/alabama-prison-inmates.html

Pakes, F., and Gunnlaughsson, H. (2018), 'A more Nordic Norway? examining prisons in 21st century Iceland', *The Howard Journal*, 57(2): 137–151.

Plato (2004), *The Laws* (reprinted with revisions), London: Penguin Books.

Priestley, P. (1989), *Jail Journeys: The English Prison Experience Since 1918*, London: Routledge.

Prison Reform Trust (2019), *Prison: the facts - Bromley Briefings Summer 2019*, Prisonreformtrust.org.uk.

Prison Reform Trust (2019), *Bromley Briefings Prison Fact File Winter 2019*, Prisonreformtrust.org.uk.

Rothman, D., and Morris, N. (eds) (1995), *Oxford History of the Prison: The Practice of Punishment in Western Society*, Oxford: Oxford University Press.

Scott, D., and Gosling, H. (2016), 'Before prison, instead of prison, better than prison: therapeutic communities as an abolitionist real utopia?', *IJCJ&SD*, 5(1): 52–66

Southern Poverty Law Center (2019), 'Federal judge orders reforms to prevent suicides in alabama prisons', Splcenter.org. https://www.splcenter.org/news/2019/05/06/federal-judge-orders-reforms-prevent-suicides-alabama-prisons

United States Department of Justice: Civil Rights Division (2019), *Investigation of Alabama's State Prisons for Men*, https://www.justice.gov/opa/press-release/file/1150276/download

Transportation Act 1717.

Prison Act of 1898.

Firearms Act 1968.

Crime (Sentences) Act 1997.

CHAPTER 3

Aaron, P., and Musto, D. (1981), 'Temperance and prohibition in America: an historical overview', in Moore, M., and Gerstein, D. (eds), *Alcohol and Public Policy: Beyond the Shadow of Prohibition*, Washington DC: National Academic Press.

Barry, E. (2019), 'Chloroform in childbirth? yes, please, the Queen said', *New York Times*, https://www.nytimes.com/2019/05/06/world/europe/uk-royal-births-labor.html

Borman, T., 'Did this beloved Queen of Britain use drugs?', Smithsonian Channel, https://www.smithsonianmag.com/videos/category/history/did-this-beloved-queen-of-britain-use-drugs/

Carrigan, M., Uryasev, O., Frye, C., et al., (2015), 'Hominids Adapted to Metabolize Ethanol Long Before Human-Directed Fermentation', *Proc. Nat'l. Acad. Sci. USA*, 112(2): 458–63, https://www.ncbi.nlm.nih.gov/pmc/articles/PMC4299227/

Guerra-Doce, E. (2015), 'Psychoactive substances in prehistoric times: examining the archaeological evidence', *Time and Mind*, 8(1): 91–112. https://www.tandfonline.com/doi/abs/10.1080/1751696X.2014.993244

Human Rights Watch (2018), 'Philippines' Duterte confesses to "drug war" slaughter' (2018), Hrw.org. https://www.hrw.org/news/2018/09/28/philippines-duterte-confesses-drug-war-slaughter

Lawler, A. (2019), 'Oldest evidence of marijuana use discovered in 2500-year-old cemetery peaks of western China', Science, https://www.sciencemag.org/news/2019/06/oldest-evidence-marijuana-use-discovered-2500-year-old-cemetery-peaks-western-china

Mars, S. (2003), 'Heroin addiction care and control: the British system 1916 to 1984', *J. R. Soc. Med.* 96(2): 99–100, https://www.ncbi.nlm.nih.gov/pmc/articles/PMC539406/

Meyer, K. E. (1997), 'The opium war's secret history', *New York Times*, https://www.nytimes.com/1997/06/28/opinion/the-opium-war-s-secret-history.html

Nixon, R. (1971), 'Remarks about an intensified program for drug abuse prevention and control', Washington DC: The White House.

Perkin, H. (1969), *The Origins of Modern English Society* (2nd edn, 2002), London: Routledge.

Reagan, R. (15 October 1982), 'Speech on drive against crime', Washington DC: Department of Justice.

Reynolds, J. R. (1890), 'On the therapeutic uses and toxic effects of Cannabis Indica', *Lancet* 1(3473): 637–8.

Saah, T. (2005), 'The evolutionary origins and significance of drug addiction', *Harm Reduct. J.* 2(8), https://www.ncbi.nlm.nih.gov/pmc/articles/PMC1174878/

Vorobyov, N. (2018), 'Russia's harm reductionists are once again under attack', Filtermag, https://filtermag.org/russias-harm-reductionists-are-once-again-under-attack/

Welsh, I. (1993), *Trainspotting*, London: Secker & Warburg Ltd.

Anti-Drug Abuse Act 1986.

Controlled Substances Act 1970.

Dangerous Drugs Act 1967.

Harrison Act 1914.

Misuse of Drugs Act 1971.

International Convention relating to Dangerous Drugs 1938.

International Opium Convention 1912.

United Nations Single Convention on Narcotic Drugs 1961.

Volstead Act 1919.

Webb et al. v United States 249 US 96 (1919).

CHAPTER 4

Anonymous (1814), *The Philanthropist, Or, Repository for Hints and Suggestions Calculated to Promote the Comfort and Happiness of Man,* [vol IV], London: Richard and Arthur Taylor.

Barber, P. (2017), 'Young people in children's homes 15 times more likely to be criminalised, says Howard League', The Justice Gap, https://www.thejusticegap.com/young-people-childrens-homes-15-times-likely-criminalised-says-howard-league/

BBC London (2016), 'Youth offending – can the UK learn from Spain?', https://www.youtube.com/watch?v=MEXfFjjoDyE

British Youth Council (2019), 'Written evidence submitted by the National Youth Agency', BYC018. https://www.byc.org.uk/wp-content/uploads/2019/06/BYC018-National-Youth-Agency.pdf

Burke, R. H. (2008), *Young People, Crime and Justice,* Cullompton, Devon: Willan Publishing.

Gentleman, A. (2011), 'Life in a young offenders' institution', *Guardian,* https://www.theguardian.com/society/2011/nov/21/young-offenders-institution-ashfield

House of Commons (2006), *Report of the Zahid Mubarek Inquiry,* HC1082-I, London: The Stationery Office, https://assets.publishing.service.gov.uk/government/uploads/system/uploads/attachment_data/file/231789/1082.pdf

James, E., and MacDougall, I. (2010), 'The Norway town that forgave and forgot its child killers', *Guardian,*

https://www.theguardian.com/theguardian/2010/mar/20/
norway-town-forgave-child-killers

Ministry of Justice (2019), *Youth Justice Statistics 2017 to 2018: Statistics Bulletin*, London: Ministry of Justice, https://assets.publishing.
service.gov.uk/government/uploads/system/uploads/attachment_
data/file/774866/youth_justice_statistics_bulletin_2017_2018.pdf

Pook, S. (26 June 2006), 'Family of teenager in racist cell murder demand change', *Telegraph*, https://www.telegraph.co.uk/news/
uknews/1522319/Family-of-teenager-in-racist-cell-murder-
demand-change.html

Prison Reform Trust (2019), *Prison: the facts – Bromley Briefings Summer 2019*, Prisonreformtrust.org.uk.

Vize, R. (2019), 'Hardliner Priti Patel is the wrong person to tackle knife crime', *Guardian*, https://www.theguardian.com/
society/2019/aug/02/priti-patel-tackle-knife-crime

YouTube (2018), 'Inside the UK's toughest youth prison', https://
www.youtube.com/watch?v=-B9fXC5ggOw

Grand Duchy's Memorial A70 of 1992, the 'Law on the Protection of Youth'.

United Nations Convention on the Rights of the Child 1989.

V v. UK; T v. UK 24888/94, (1999) 30 EHRR 121.

CHAPTER 5

BBC News (10 July 2000), 'The Day the Bullets Flew', http://news.
bbc.co.uk/1/hi/uk/827536.stm

BBC News (13 December 2019),'London Bridge: Staffordshire Police Probed Over Contact with Usman Khan', https://www.
bbc.co.uk/news/uk-england-stoke-staffordshire-50762638

Carter, H. (6 December 2019), '"I had a Bad Life, I've Changed": Killer John Crilly Made a Vow After Being Released . . . 12 Months Later He Defended People Against a Terrorist on London Bridge', *Manchester Evening News*, https://www.manchestereveningnews.
co.uk/news/uk-news/how-london-bridge-killer-freed-17373720

Giordano, C. (2019), 'London Bridge Attack: Isis Claims Responsibility as Footage Emerges of Usman Khan, "I Ain't No

Terrorist'", *Independent*, https://www.independent.co.uk/news/
uk/home-news/london-bridge-attack-latest-isis-terrorism-
usman-khan-interview-a9228026.html

Luther, M. (1883), *Werke,* Weimar: Hermann Böhlau.

Merritt, D. (2 December 2019), "'Jack Would be Livid his Death
Has Been Used to Further an Agenda of Hate'", *Guardian*,
https://www.theguardian.com/uk-news/2019/dec/02/jack-
merritt-london-bridge-attack-dave-merritt

Sawer, P. (30 November 2019), 'London Bridge Attack: Prisoner
Who Confronted Terrorist is not A Hero, Say Family of the
Woman he Murdered', *Telegraph.* https://www.telegraph.co.uk/
news/2019/11/30/london-bridge-attack-prisoner-confronted-
terrorist-not-hero/

Swinford, S. (3 December 2019), 'Criminals Like Usman Khan are
Just Too Tough to Crack, says Boris Johnson', *Times*, https://
www.thetimes.co.uk/article/criminals-like-usman-khan-are-
just-too-tough-to-crack-says-boris-johnson-c9s0pq7cw

Teague, M. (21 October 2016), "'It's a Bloodbath": Staff Describe
Life Inside America's Most Violent Prison', *Guardian.* https://
www.theguardian.com/us-news/2016/oct/21/holman-prison-
alabama-guard-speaks-out

Tracey, C. (24 April 2018), 'Man Released After Joint Enterprise
Conviction Quashed', BBC News, https://www.bbc.co.uk/news/
uk-43840635

AFTERWORD

National Crime Agency website, https://www.nationalcrimeagency.
gov.uk/what-we-do

National Crime Agency website, https://www.nationalcrimeagency.
gov.uk/news/2-3-tonnes-of-cocaine-seized-before-reaching-uk-
streets

UK Government Press Release: 'Justice overhaul to better
protect the public and back our police', https://www.gov.uk/
government/news/justice-overhaul-to-better-protect-the-
public-and-back-our-police

PERMISSIONS

The following are reproduced by kind permission of the copyright holders.

TEXTS

Quotations on page 22 and pages 38–39 from N. Morris and D. Rothman (eds), *The Oxford History of the Prison: The Practice of Punishment in Western Society* (Oxford: Oxford University Press, 1995). Reproduced by permission of Oxford Publishing Limited through PLSclear.

Quotation on page 46, The Howard League for Penal Reform.

Quotation on pages 75–76 from D. Scott and H. Gosling, 'Before Prison, Instead of Prison, Better than Prison: Therapeutic Communities as an Abolitionist Real Utopia?' (2016) 5(1) *IJCJ&SD*, pp. 52-66, reproduced by permission of *The International Journal for Crime, Justice and Social Democracy*.

Quotation on page 103 from H. Perkin, *The Origins of Modern English Society* (London: Routledge, 1969), p. 280, by permission of Taylor & Francis, Informa UK Limited.

Quotation on page 109 from P. Aaron and D. Musto, 'Temperance and Prohibition in America: An Historical Overview' (Washington DC: National Academies Press, 1981), with permission of National Academies Press.

Statistical information in chapter four reproduced by permission of The Prison Reform Trust.

IMAGES

Figures 1–4: The Prison Reform Trust

Figure 5: The National Archives

Figure 6: The Birmingham News/AL.com

Figure 7: Keystone-SDA

Figures 11–13: Press Association

Figure 19: Press Association/Home Office

All other images are in the public domain.

INDEX

NOTE ON THE AUTHOR

One of Britain's top defence barristers, Chris Daw QC writes on criminal justice issues for *The Spectator* and several national newspapers. He appears as an expert source on radio and television, is a prominent legal commentator on social media and the co-presenter of the BBC One documentary series *Crime: Are We Tough Enough?*

Chris tweets at: @crimlawuk and posts topical legal content on his YouTube channel – Chris Daw QC – and on LinkedIn.

NOTE ON THE TYPE

The text of this book is set in Minion, a digital typeface designed by Robert Slimbach in 1990 for Adobe Systems. The name comes from the traditional naming system for type sizes, in which minion is between nonpareil and brevier. It is inspired by late Renaissance-era type.

CW00456233

POWER
POSITIVITY

I AM
BOLD

quadrille

FORTUNE FAVOURS THE BOLD.

Latin proverb

IN ORDER TO BE AN ICON, YOU NEED TO BE BOLD. HOW DO I DEFINE BOLDNESS? STEPPING OUTSIDE OF YOUR COMFORT ZONE.

Saweetie

COURAGE IS RESISTANCE TO FEAR, MASTERY OF FEAR – NOT ABSENCE OF FEAR.

Mark Twain

EITHER LIFE ENTAILS COURAGE, OR IT CEASES TO BE LIFE.

E.M. Forster

FEAR MADE THE GODS; AUDACITY HAS MADE KINGS.

Claude Prosper Jolyot de Crébillon

DON'T BE SO NERVOUS ABOUT EVERYTHING.

Maggie Smith

THE COURAGE OF LIFE IS OFTEN
A LESS DRAMATIC SPECTACLE
THAN THE COURAGE OF A FINAL
MOMENT; BUT IT IS NO LESS
A MAGNIFICENT MIXTURE OF
TRIUMPH AND TRAGEDY. A MAN
DOES WHAT HE MUST – IN SPITE
OF PERSONAL CONSEQUENCES,
IN SPITE OF OBSTACLES AND
DANGERS, AND PRESSURES –
AND THAT IS THE BASIS OF
ALL HUMAN MORALITY.

John F. Kennedy

YOU GAIN STRENGTH, COURAGE AND CONFIDENCE BY EVERY EXPERIENCE IN WHICH YOU REALLY STOP TO LOOK FEAR IN THE FACE. YOU ARE ABLE TO SAY TO YOURSELF, 'I LIVED THROUGH THIS HORROR. I CAN TAKE THE NEXT THING THAT COMES ALONG.' YOU MUST DO THE THING YOU THINK YOU CANNOT DO.

Eleanor Roosevelt

I LOVE TO SEE
A YOUNG GIRL
GO OUT AND
GRAB THE
WORLD BY
THE LAPELS ...

LIFE'S A BITCH. YOU'VE GOT TO GO OUT AND KICK ASS.

Maya Angelou

I'M TOUGH, AMBITIOUS, AND I KNOW EXACTLY WHAT I WANT. IF THAT MAKES ME A BITCH, OKAY.

Madonna

**BY AUDACITY,
GREAT FEARS
ARE CONCEALED.**

Marcus Annaeus Lucanus

GO TO THE EDGE OF THE CLIFF AND JUMP OFF.

BUILD YOUR WINGS ON THE WAY DOWN.

Ray Bradbury

I DO LIKE A BIT OF DANGER. GUNS, CARS, RUNNING, BULLETS. I'M UP FOR IT.

Florence Pugh

WE CAN NEVER BE CERTAIN OF OUR COURAGE UNTIL WE HAVE FACED DANGER.

François de La Rochefoucauld

COURAGE IS RIGHTLY ESTEEMED THE FIRST OF HUMAN QUALITIES, BECAUSE, AS HAS BEEN SAID, IT IS THE QUALITY WHICH GUARANTEES ALL OTHERS.

Winston Churchill

DO ONE THING EVERY DAY THAT SCARES YOU.

Mary Schmich

I'M REALLY CONFRONTING
ALL THE THINGS THAT I'VE
EVER BEEN SCARED OF AND
I'M JUST FINDING THIS REALLY
EXUBERANT FREEDOM IN
LIFE. YOU CAN'T BE HAPPY
IF YOU'RE SCARED.

Will Smith

SO WHATEVER YOU WANT TO DO, JUST DO IT. DON'T WORRY ABOUT MAKING A DAMN FOOL OF YOURSELF. MAKING A DAMN FOOL OF YOURSELF IS ABSOLUTELY ESSENTIAL. AND YOU WILL HAVE A GREAT TIME.

Gloria Steinem

BRAVERY NEVER GOES OUT OF FASHION.

William Makepeace Thackeray

COURAGE IS VERY IMPORTANT. LIKE A MUSCLE, IT IS STRENGTHENED BY USE.

Ruth Gordon

ACTION IS THE ANTIDOTE TO DESPAIR.

Joan Baez

THE BRAVE AND
BOLD PERSIST EVEN
AGAINST FORTUNE;
THE TIMID AND
COWARDLY RUSH TO
DESPAIR THROUGH
FEAR ALONE.

Tacitus

IF YOU REALLY WANT TO LIVE EMPOWERED, YOU'VE GOT TO FACE THOSE FEARS.

Bear Grylls

WHEN PEOPLE TRY TO TELL YOU TO STAY IN YOUR LANE, DON'T LISTEN. DO NOT LISTEN.

Reese Witherspoon

COURAGE IN DANGER IS HALF THE BATTLE.

Plautus

TALK WITHOUT EFFORT IS NOTHING.

Maria W Stewart

I HAVE PAID MY DUES
AND FOLLOWED EVERY
RULE FOR DECADES,
SO NOW I CAN BREAK
THE RULES THAT NEED
TO BE BROKEN.

Beyoncé

WE MUST WALK CONSCIOUSLY ONLY PART WAY TOWARD OUR GOAL, AND THEN LEAP IN THE DARK TO OUR SUCCESS.

Henry David Thoreau

TWENTY YEARS FROM NOW,
YOU WILL BE MORE DISAPPOINTED
BY THE THINGS YOU DIDN'T
DO THAN BY THE ONES YOU DID DO.
SO THROW OFF THE BOWLINES.
SAIL AWAY FROM THE SAFE
HARBOUR. CATCH THE TRADE
WINDS IN YOUR SAILS.
EXPLORE. DREAM. DISCOVER.

H. Jackson Brown

IF IT'S GOING TO BE DONE,
LET'S DO IT. LET'S NOT PUT
IT IN THE HANDS OF FATE.
LET'S NOT PUT IT IN THE HANDS
OF SOMEONE WHO DOESN'T
KNOW ME. I KNOW ME BEST.
THEN TAKE A BREATH AND
GO AHEAD.

Anita Baker

HE WHO IS NOT COURAGEOUS ENOUGH TO TAKE RISKS WILL ACCOMPLISH NOTHING IN LIFE.

Muhammad Ali

**FORTUNE CAN
TAKE AWAY RICHES,
BUT NOT COURAGE.**

Seneca the Younger

THE BEST HEARTS ARE EVER THE BRAVEST.

Laurence Sterne

**A VAST DEAL
MAY BE DONE
BY THOSE WHO
DARE TO ACT.**

Jane Austen

YET YIELD NOT THOU, BUT GO MORE BOLDLY ON, WHERE FORTUNE LEADS, TILL VICTORY BE WON.

Virgil

IT'S BETTER TO BE BOLDLY DECISIVE AND RISK BEING WRONG THAN TO AGONISE AT LENGTH AND BE RIGHT TOO LATE.

Marilyn Moats Kennedy

'SING LOUD!'
MY FATHER ALWAYS
TOLD ME. 'JUST IN
CASE SOMEONE
IS LISTENING.'

Patti LaBelle

YOU HAVE TO DO OR DIE!

Fridtjof Nansen

I HATE TO SEE A THING DONE BY HALVES; IF IT BE RIGHT, DO IT BOLDLY; IF IT BE WRONG, LEAVE IT UNDONE.

Bernard Gilpin

IF I WASN'T MAKING MISTAKES, I WASN'T MAKING DECISIONS.

Robert W. Johnson

SEIZE
THE DAY.

Latin proverb

SUCCESS FOR THE MOST PART ATTENDS THOSE WHO ACT BOLDLY, NOT THOSE WHO WEIGH EVERYTHING, AND ARE SLOW TO VENTURE.

Xerxes I

WOMEN ARE LEADERS EVERYWHERE YOU LOOK – FROM THE CEO WHO RUNS A FORTUNE 500 COMPANY TO THE HOUSEWIFE WHO RAISES HER CHILDREN AND HEADS HER HOUSEHOLD. OUR COUNTRY WAS BUILT BY STRONG WOMEN, AND WE WILL CONTINUE TO BREAK DOWN WALLS AND DEFY STEREOTYPES.

Nancy Pelosi

THERE'S SOMETHING SO
SPECIAL ABOUT A WOMAN WHO
DOMINATES IN A MAN'S WORLD.
IT TAKES A CERTAIN GRACE,
STRENGTH, INTELLIGENCE,
FEARLESSNESS, AND THE
NERVE TO NEVER TAKE NO
FOR AN ANSWER.

Rihanna

**COME, LET US BE BRAVE –
LET US WALK INTO THE
DARK WITHOUT FEAR,
AND STEP INTO THE
UNKNOWN WITH SMILES
ON OUR FACES, EVEN
IF WE'RE FAKING THEM.**

Neil Gaiman

TO BE PASSIVE IS TO LET OTHERS DECIDE FOR YOU. TO BE AGGRESSIVE IS TO DECIDE FOR OTHERS. TO BE ASSERTIVE IS TO DECIDE FOR YOURSELF.

Edith Eva Eger

FREEDOM LIES IN BEING BOLD.

Robert Frost

**A WOMAN WITH
A VOICE IS,
BY DEFINITION,
A STRONG WOMAN.**

Melinda Gates

NOTHING VENTURED, NOTHING GAINED.

Anon

PEOPLE WILL STARE. MAKE IT WORTH THEIR WHILE.

Harry Winston

I THINK WE ALL KNOW BOLDNESS WHEN WE SEE IT. NOTHING MAKES ME SMILE MORE THAN WHEN I SEE SOMEONE BEING FULLY THEMSELVES, WITH THEIR OWN INDIVIDUAL STYLE AND CHARACTER, WHATEVER THAT IS.

Angelina Jolie

I KNOW PEOPLE ARE NOT USED TO SEEING CONFIDENT, EDUCATED, HAPPY, CHUNKY AFRICAN AMERICAN GIRLS, AND I DON'T CARE. THEY'RE JUST GOING TO HAVE TO GET USED TO IT.

Precious Lee

SHE WAS NOT IMPOLITE; SHE WAS DIRECT.

SHE WASN'T COLD; SHE WAS BOLD.

James Marsden (on Ilaria Urbinati)

THEY'LL TELL YOU YOU'RE TOO LOUD, THAT YOU NEED TO WAIT YOUR TURN AND ASK THE RIGHT PEOPLE FOR PERMISSION. DO IT ANYWAY.

Alexandria Ocasio Cortez

WHATEVER YOU CAN DO OR DREAM YOU CAN, BEGIN IT. BOLDNESS HAS GENIUS, POWER, AND MAGIC IN IT.

Johann Wolfgang von Goethe

OF COURSE I AM NOT WORRIED ABOUT INTIMIDATING MEN. THE TYPE OF MAN WHO WILL BE INTIMIDATED BY ME IS EXACTLY THE TYPE OF MAN I HAVE NO INTEREST IN.

Chimamanda Ngozi Adichie

**BE BOLD,
TAKE COURAGE ...
AND BE STRONG
OF SOUL.**

Ovid

YOU FAIL, AND THEN WHAT?
LIFE GOES ON. IT'S ONLY WHEN
YOU RISK FAILURE THAT YOU
DISCOVER THINGS. WHEN YOU
PLAY IT SAFE, YOU'RE NOT
EXPRESSING THE UTMOST
OF YOUR HUMAN EXPERIENCE.

Lupita Nyong'o

THIS CONFIDENCE IS NOT
SOMETHING THAT HAPPENS
OVERNIGHT. I HAVE BEEN
WORKING ON IT FOR A LONG
TIME. I LOOK IN THE MIRROR
AND DO AFFIRMATIONS: 'YOU
ARE BOLD. YOU ARE BRILLIANT.
YOU ARE BEAUTIFUL.'

Ashley Graham

**TIMIDITY
DOES NOT INSPIRE
BOLD ACTS.**

Mae Jemison

IT'S IMPORTANT TO TEACH OUR FEMALE YOUTH THAT IT'S OK TO SAY, 'YES, I AM GOOD AT THIS', AND YOU DON'T HOLD BACK.

Simone Biles

BEGIN, BE BOLD, AND VENTURE TO BE WISE.

Horace

**VIRTUE IS BOLD,
AND GOODNESS
NEVER FEARFUL.**

William Shakespeare

THE WAY OF THE
SUPERIOR PERSON IS
THREEFOLD; VIRTUOUS,
THEY ARE FREE FROM
ANXIETIES; WISE
THEY ARE FREE FROM
PERPLEXITIES; AND
BOLD, THEY ARE FREE
FROM FEAR.

Confucius

I WANT TO PRESENT
A VERY STRONG AND
BOLD IMAGE, BUT WITH
FEMININITY. I LOVE
BEING SWEET AND
SALTY ALL TOGETHER.

Keke Palmer

HE WAS A BOLD MAN THAT FIRST ATE AN OYSTER.

Jonathan Swift

NOTHING WILL EVER BE ATTEMPTED, IF ALL POSSIBLE OBJECTIONS MUST FIRST BE OVERCOME.

Samuel Johnson

WHETHER YOU COME FROM A COUNCIL ESTATE OR A COUNTRY ESTATE, YOUR SUCCESS WILL BE DETERMINED BY YOUR OWN CONFIDENCE AND FORTITUDE.

Michelle Obama

RESULTS ARE OFTEN GAINED BY IMPETUOSITY AND DARING WHICH COULD NEVER HAVE BEEN OBTAINED BY ORDINARY METHODS.

Niccolo Machiavelli

**DON'T BE AFRAID
TO GO OUT ON A LIMB.
THAT'S WHERE
THE FRUIT IS.**

Arthur F. Lenehan

IF YOU THINK YOU CAN, YOU CAN.

Mary Kay Ash

THE BITTEREST TEARS SHED OVER GRAVES ARE FOR WORDS LEFT UNSAID AND DEEDS LEFT UNDONE.

Harriet Beecher Stowe

WHEN YOU REACH FOR
THE STARS, YOU MAY
NOT QUITE GET THEM,
BUT YOU WON'T COME
UP WITH A HANDFUL
OF MUD EITHER.

Leo Burnett

ONLY THOSE WHO DARE TO FAIL ...

CAN EVER ACHIEVE GREATLY.

Robert F. Kennedy

HE WHO HAS CONFIDENCE IN HIMSELF WILL LEAD THE REST.

Horace

IF YOU ARE GOING TO SURVIVE IN BUSINESS, SHOWBUSINESS OR ANY BUSINESS, THEN YOU HAVE TO BE BOLD.

Rebecca Ferguson (singer)

PATIENCE CAN BE A GOOD THING – BUT NOT NECESSARILY. SOMETIMES IT'S NOT SO BAD TO BE IMPATIENT.

Helen Mirren

YOU MAY BE DISAPPOINTED IF YOU FAIL, BUT YOU ARE DOOMED IF YOU DON'T TRY.

Beverley Sills

IF I'M TOO STRONG FOR SOME PEOPLE, THAT'S THEIR PROBLEM.

Glenda Jackson

SCREW AGREEABILITY, SCREW FEELING LIKE YOU'RE NOT WORTHY OF DEMANDING WHAT IS RIGHT.

Lily James

WE ARE THE HERO OF OUR OWN STORY.

Mary McCarthy

DON'T COMPROMISE YOURSELF. YOU ARE ALL YOU'VE GOT.

Janis Joplin

HOW MANY CARES ONE LOSES WHEN ONE DECIDES NOT TO BE SOMETHING, BUT TO BE SOMEONE.

Coco Chanel

NO GUTS, NO GLORY.

Anon

DO NOT WAIT TO WAIT TO STRIKE TILL THE IRON IS HOT ...

BUT MAKE IT HOT BY STRIKING.

William Buell Sprague

**NOT TO DARE
IS TO DWINDLE.**

John Updike

I'VE LEARNED THAT
I'M ALLOWED TO BE
HAPPY, GLITTERY,
BOLD, SASSY, AND TO
NEVER APOLOGISE
FOR THAT SIDE
OF MYSELF.

Kelsea Ballerini

POWER'S NOT GIVEN TO YOU. YOU HAVE TO TAKE IT.

Beyoncé

LIFE IS EITHER A DARING ADVENTURE OR NOTHING AT ALL.

Helen Keller

Quadrille, Penguin Random House UK,
One Embassy Gardens, 8 Viaduct
Gardens, London SW11 7BW

Quadrille Publishing Limited
is part of the Penguin Random House
group of companies whose
addresses can be found at
global.penguinrandomhouse.com

Published by Quadrille in 2024

www.penguin.co.uk

A CIP catalogue record for this book
is available from the British Library

ISBN 9781784887247
10 9 8 7 6 5 4 3 2 1

Publishing Director: Kajal Mistry
Editorial Director: Judith Hannam
Senior Commissioning Editor:
Kate Burkett
Text curated by: Satu Fox
Editorial Assistant: Harriet Thornley
Design: Claire Warner Studio
Senior Production Controller:
Sabeena Atchia

Colour reproduction by p2d

Printed in China by RR Donnelley Asia
Printing Solution Limited

The authorised representative in
the EEA is Penguin Random House
Ireland, Morrison Chambers,
32 Nassau Street, Dublin D02 YH68.

MIX
Paper | Supporting
responsible forestry
FSC® C018179

Penguin Random House is committed
to a sustainable future for our
business, our readers and our planet.
This book is made from Forest
Stewardship Council® certified paper.